P

Restructuring Britain

The Economy in Question
edited by John Allen and Doreen Massey

The Changing Social Structure
edited by Chris Hamnett, Linda McDowell and Philip Sarre

Politics in Transition
edited by Allan Cochrane and James Anderson

The following are associated Readers published by Hodder and Stoughton in association with The Open University

Uneven Re-Development: Cities and Regions in Transition
edited by Doreen Massey and John Allen

Divided Nation: Social and Cultural Change in Britain
edited by Linda McDowell, Philip Sarre and Chris Hamnett

A State of Crisis: The Changing Face of British Politics
edited by James Anderson and Allan Cochrane

Open University Course D314 Restructuring Britain
(Details of this course are available from the Student Enquiries Office,
The Open University, PO Box 71, Milton Keynes MK7 6AG)

Restructuring Britain

POLITICS IN TRANSITION

edited by

Allan Cochrane and James Anderson

SAGE Publications
in association with

The Open
University

First Published 1989, Reprinted 1994

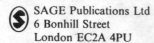 SAGE Publications Ltd
6 Bonhill Street
London EC2A 4PU

SAGE Publications Inc
2455 Teller Road
Thousand Oaks, California 91320

SAGE Publications India Pvt Ltd
32, M-Block Market
Greater Kailash – I
New Delhi 110 048

British Library Cataloguing in Publication data

Politics in transition. – (Restructuring Britain).
   1. Great Britain. Politics
   I. Cochrane, Allan, *1948*–   II. Anderson, James, *1941*–
   III. Open University   IV. Series
   320.941

   ISBN 0–8039–8201–1
   ISBN 0–8039–8202–X Pbk

Library of Congress catalog card number 88–84134

Typeset in Linotron 202 Times by
Fakenham Photosetting Ltd, Fakenham, Norfolk

Printed in Great Britain by J. W. Arrowsmith Ltd, Bristol

Contents

Course team

John Allen, Lecturer in Economic Geography
James Anderson, Lecturer in Geography
Chris Brook, Lecturer in Applied Regional Studies
Allan Cochrane, Senior Lecturer in Urban Studies
Chris Hamnett, Senior Lecturer in Geography (Course Team Chair)
Pat Jess, Staff Tutor, Northern Ireland
Linda McDowell, Senior Lecturer in Geography
Doreen Massey, Professor of Geography
Philip Sarre, Senior Lecturer in Geography

Consultants

Joe Doherty, Lecturer in Geography, University of St Andrews
Patrick Dunleavy, Reader in Government, London School of Economics and Political
    Science
Mark Goodwin, Lecturer in Geography, Goldsmiths College, University of London
Laurence Harris, Professor of Economics, The Open University
Richard Meegan, Senior Research Member, CES Ltd, London
Simon Mohun, Lecturer in Economics, Queen Mary College, University of London
Chris Pond, Director, Low Pay Unit
Mike Savage, Lecturer in Sociology, University of Surrey
Peter Taylor, Reader in Political Geography, University of Newcastle upon Tyne
Nigel Thrift, Reader in Geography, University of Bristol

External assessors

John Urry, Professor of Sociology, University of Lancaster (Course Assessor)
Huw Beynon, Professor of Sociology, University of Manchester
Paul Lawless, Principal Lecturer in Urban and Regional Studies, Sheffield
Andrew Sayer, Lecturer in Urban Studies, University of Sussex

Tutor testers

Cliff Hague, Senior Lecturer, Town and Country Planning, Heriot-Watt University,
    Edinburgh
Mark Hart, Lecturer in Environmental Studies, University of Ulster at Jordanstown
Jill Vincent, Research Fellow, Centre for Research in Social Policy, Loughborough
    University of Technology

Course support

Melanie Bayley, Editor
Ann Boomer, Secretary
Sarah Gauthier, Secretary
Rob Lyon, Graphic Designer
Ray Munns, Cartographer/Graphic Artist
Carol Oddy, Secretary
Varrie Scott, Course Manager
Jane Tyrell, Secretary
David Wilson, Editor

Restructuring Britain: introduction

Politics in Transition is part of a series on the changes which have reshaped the economic, social, political and geographical structure of the UK since the end of the 1950s. Each book is free-standing and can be read on its own, or it can be studied as part of the Open University course *Restructuring Britain*. One of the books deals with questions about the structure of the economy, production and work; another deals with changes in social structure and culture, including class, gender, race, income, wealth and consumption; this book is concerned with the reshaping of politics and the role of the state. Together with three associated Readers, the three textbooks form an integrated theoretical and empirical analysis of the changing structure of contemporary Britain.

There have probably been few periods in recent history when change of some sort has not been on the agenda; it is one of the defining characteristics of modern society. Yet the last two or more decades do seem to have been marked by transformations of a very different order, and moreover transformations which in different ways and with different timings have affected a wide range of aspects of society. The place of the UK in the international world has changed: its role in the international economic order has shifted quite dramatically and its political position between Europe and the USA has been renegotiated. Within the economy the shift from manufacturing to services has been reinforced, and with it the whole economic geography of the country. The future of cities and of some regions is at stake; and at national level the question must be whether the economy can survive by exporting services. Such shifts, together with wider changes in the labour process, have transformed the occupational structure of the workforce. While unemployment has risen, the most rapidly growing segment of the population in paid work is that of professionals, managers and administrators. But in the less well-paid parts of the economy, many of the new jobs have been in part-time and increasingly in casualized employment. All these changes in the economy have gone along with changes in the social structure too. There has been talk of 'the end of the working class' – certainly of the old image of the male-dominated kind, working in manufacturing – and of the burgeoning of white-collar middle strata: processes that are mirrored geographically in the counterposition of the recent fortunes of different regions of the country. Has women's lot been improved by all this, or are women now caught in an even more contradictory position? And how important have changes in consumption patterns been in moulding the shifting social structure? There have also been changes at the political level, and attempts, some more successful than others, to break the mould of the old party politics and to end the comfortable old consensus. It has, indeed, been the period when the very term 'restructuring', if not newly invented, has been rehabilitated and put to frequent use.

This series is built around an examination of these changes. Perhaps most fundamentally we wanted to explore the questions: what is the nature of all this change; does it amount to a structural change; are we at some kind of historical turning-point?

In order to get to grips with these issues, a number of different threads have been chosen, which run throughout this series. There are three, and they are necessarily intertwined with each other as their investigation develops.

The *first* is simply the empirical changes themselves. *Restructuring Britain* covers a wide range of empirical material, and our aim is to investigate it bearing in mind always the questions: what kinds of change have these been; has there been structural change? One point to make from the start is that we want to consider the material geographically, that is, to take the spatial dimension as integral to our whole concern. Thus, while our key question concerns periodization, an underlying hypothesis is that different eras of history are bound up with distinct forms of uneven development. The argument is not that they merely happen together, but that they are integrally related to each other.

But one cannot examine empirical data for structural change, either social or spatial, without some notion of what structural change might be. So this, too, is an enquiry which runs through the series. How can one characterize distinct historical eras, or spatial formations; how does one assess what are the key relations; or what features can be said to be dominant? Indeed what does 'dominant' mean in this context? This in turn raises questions of the conceptualization of systems, and of structures themselves.

The *second* concern is to investigate the debates which have taken place within the social sciences about the nature of these empirical changes and about their explanation. Some theories and debates span all three books in this series, since their scope itself ranges from economic to political; the nature of the structural change they postulate or debate involves all aspects of society. Other theoretical debates tend to be more confined in their scope relating to perhaps only one or a bundle of the empirical changes we are considering here. Many of them, too, do not have an explicitly geographical element, and in some of these we have tried to inject our own spatial perspective, drawing out from them what are in some cases already implicit geographical implications. This is not appropriate in all cases, of course; but what we are after in the end is to analyse the nature of the reorganization of economic-social-political relations over space, and the impact of that.

Thirdly, we stand back even further from the empirical changes and explore how those debates within the social sciences can themselves be assessed. Here we examine the different questions which distinct approaches may address, even when they appear to be examining 'the same phenomena' and to be engaged in the same debate. The different modes of 'self-evaluation' implied by various theoretical approaches are pointed to, and the varying ways in which they relate to 'evidence' are contrasted. Much of this links back quite directly to, and intertwines with, the issues explored under the first heading – different theories, indeed, have quite distinct notions even about what is structural change.

The structure of the series

The Economy in Question introduces some of the theoretical debates over economic aspects of these issues: the definition and importance of deindustrialization, the nature of the international economic order, the characteristics of post-industrial society, the definition of service employment and its links to manufacturing, the changing organization of the labour process, and the concepts of work and economy. *The Changing Social Structure* introduces the debates over gender relations, race and class structure and changing patterns of consumption. Are we witnessing the end of the working class and the emergence of a predominantly middle-class society, dominated by private home and car ownership and a privatized and individualized social ethos? *Politics in Transition* examines the debates over the changing political role of the UK internationally, and the changing structure of politics and state intervention within the country. It looks at, amongst other things, the changing relationship between central and local government, the arguments regarding class dealignment and consumption in voting behaviour and the UK's position vis-à-vis the USA, the European Community and the Commonwealth.

There are, of course, links between all these issues. The division into three groups of issues, and indeed below that into individual chapters within each book, is made for analytical purposes. Although everything may well be connected to everything else, it is nonetheless necessary to hold things apart at certain stages of work in order to be able to explore in more depth the most salient social processes. But the links and interdependencies are still important. Indeed, one of the recent developments in the social sciences generally has been an increasing recognition of their interdependence. When considering questions of sectoral shifts within the economy, for instance, or questions of the location of industry, it is necessary also to be aware of prerequisite changes in the structure and nature of the potential labour force. And the labour force is not constructed by economic processes alone but also through cultural, political and ideological ones. To take another obvious example, neither the economic nor social changes of recent years, nor the changes in gender relations or consumption patterns can be fully considered outside the context of quite marked shifts in the political climate. Where it is appropriate we have tried to build some of the more important of these interlinkages into the texts.

One issue which does emerge from a consideration of the whole series together, and which raises again the question of the nature of the connections between the processes discussed in each of them, is the distinct timings of those different social processes. Interesting issues are raised by what seem to be the contrasting periodizations of the transformations of different aspects of British society. This raises yet again the question of what is meant by structural change.

Finally, this is very much a course about questions. By no means all the questions are simply answered. This series of Open Texts, and the associated Readers, are meant to be more guides to an exploration and a stimulus to thought, than a treatise which settles the debate. This is true, too, about questions for the future. There are clearly a number of directions in which British economy and society could go. To explore them would take a parallel series on policy. But we hope that enough light is thrown on possible options to provoke further debate about the possibilities.

Introduction

It is widely believed that substantial changes in the British political system and the structures of the British state have taken place since the 1960s. One (dominant) view is that the twenty-five years since the mid-1960s have marked the demise of the social-democratic welfare state constructed after the war and undermined the electoral basis of the political programme which was reflected in it. The arguments developed in this book start from debates about the extent and nature of the changes which have taken place in this period. Two related questions underlie the particular issues raised in the individual chapters of the book, namely: 'How is it possible to judge whether **structural change** has occurred in this area?' and, following from this, 'Has there been a restructuring of politics and the state in Britain in this period?'

These are difficult questions to address, not least because the political sphere is highly volatile. A substantial degree of (often unpredictable) change is taken for granted, as policies are reshaped, voting patterns shift and the fortunes of political parties rise and fall in the opinion polls and election results. And this change is the focus of a great deal of analysis as academics and political journalists pore over manifestos, speeches and electoral statistics. Hall comments that, 'Political time, the time of regimes and elections is short: "a week is a long time in politics". Economic time, sociological time, so to speak, has a longer dureé. Cultural time is even slower, more glacial' (1988, p. 28). In some ways the very volatility of politics makes it difficult accurately to identify underlying trends.

Instead there are conflicting temptations which it is difficult to resist. On the one hand, for example, it is tempting to extrapolate a process of dramatic and longer-term change on the basis of what may turn out to be ephemeral shifts in political behaviour. But on the other, convinced sceptics are equally likely to dismiss accumulating evidence of change on the principle that whatever seems to be happening on the surface, it is always possible to find alternative evidence to suggest that little of fundamental importance has actually taken place.

The structures of the state are somehow disconnected from the surface expressions of political conflict and this means that change is often still more difficult to identify for rather different reasons. Precisely because of the constantly changing balance of day-to-day politics, it is easy to take the stability and continuity of the UK state rather too much for granted. The state seems to provide the stable framework within which political conflict takes place. The modern UK state can be traced back to the seventeenth and eighteenth centuries, having been modified incrementally to deal with immediate tasks but retaining at least some recognizable features.

Yet for some authors this very historical continuity has left a legacy which stands in the way of pressures for social and economic modernization in the 1980s. They argue that it is this 'archaic' 'Anglo-British' state which is now in need of restructuring because it makes Britain unable to meet the demands of modernization. Others would focus their attention more narrowly on relatively recent state forms, such as the post war social-democratic or Keynesian welfare state (see Chapter 2). Whatever the emphasis, it must be clear that any analysis of change within the state has to move beyond the experience of daily politics. Changes within the state may not be as 'glacially slow' as those in culture, or even as slow as those in economy or society, but they are some way away from the fever of party and pressure group politics.

Our central concerns are not merely to reflect on the events of the quarter of a century since the mid-1960s. We also want to consider the *ways* in which such events are best analysed and the value of the theoretical debates which surround them. In other words, the aim is not merely to explain what has been happening, but to provide opportunities to judge between and assess different theoretical approaches. The intention is not to expound theories independently of the process of analysis, but to consider their usefulness in the context of historical development. This focus makes it easier to see the relationship of different theories to each other, and so to explore the extent to which each learns from the other through a process of debate as well as the experience of confrontation, which too often seems to be the dominant model for theoretical discussion.

It should be apparent from the nature of this book that it matters where and when development is taking place. At one level that may seem obvious for a book which is concerned with developments in Britain in the recent past. But its implications go beyond this common-sense interpretation, because the decision to adopt this focus itself follows from an important theoretical decision. We believe that the central issues of politics and the state which are raised here cannot be effectively discussed without locating them in a particular place at a particular time. General features of political crisis can be identified, but without allowing some expression for **uneven development** on a world scale and within individual countries they will remain bland and featureless. The experience of Britain since the 1960s highlights the importance of such an approach – the process of crisis and restructuring which we consider is British and not just the working out in Britain of a world-wide phenomenon, even if it can only be understood in the context of shifts at the global level (discussed in Chapter 1). So while Britain is an important object of study in its own right, our focus on Britain means we can consider wide theoretical issues with the help of the British case.

Just as this book focuses on Britain within a wider context, there is also a recognition that 'Britain' itself is not unproblematic. Ironically, perhaps, this can be illustrated by the very title of the series – *Restructuring Britain* – of which it is part. The 'Britain' of the title is actually the United Kingdom of Great Britain and Northern Ireland. And its restructuring has different implications for the different parts of that whole, which also influence the nature of that restructuring (and the crisis which fed into it) in different ways at different times. In Northern Ireland, for example, restructuring brought the end of existing regional government; while in Wales and Scotland it seems to have brought the possibility of regional government rather closer.

But uneven development is not only of importance at regional level. One aspect of the discussion in the chapters which follow is concerned with local government and the politics of locality which have clearly influenced and been influenced by wider processes of change. Another considers Britain's own changing position within a global system, which has itself been transformed since 1945. The process of political restructuring, then, can only be understood in the context of the changing relationships between the international, national, regional and local levels.

The overall emphasis of the book is intended to make it possible to approach the question of structural change in a way which avoids the problems of exaggerating the significance of the ephemeral whilst retaining an openness to the possibility of such change. A range of theoretical approaches is considered which helps to indicate what sort of evidence might be relevant to deciding whether structural changes have taken place. And a range of evidence is presented in ways which help to make such a judgement possible. In other words, it allows us to come closer to defining the meaning and implications of structural change.

The **periodization** of change is particularly important, because the key periods are likely to vary according to the theories adopted, even if there is often more complementarity than the supporters of competing theories themselves allow. It may, for example, in the case of Britain, be useful to note the importance of legacies from the seventeenth and eighteenth centuries, and the origins of a 'long decline' at the end of the nineteenth century, as well as a more recent reaction to the post-war boom and the political arrangements which accompanied it. Yet different theories emphasize different historical periods as 'origins' of crisis, and as a result tend to suggest alternative explanations, as well as directions for change and restructuring.

The periodization of political change is also important because it may have little in common with those adopted for economic and social change. Even if political change takes place roughly in parallel with changes in the other spheres, the fit is unlikely to be perfect. Key parts of the political and state systems may appear to survive relatively unchanged while in effect being reinterpreted to play different roles in a changed social and economic context. The changing role of the monarch is only one example. Equally, apparently substantial changes may simply be readjustments which in effect allow political institutions to play much the same role in changed circumstances. The reorganization of local government in the early 1970s may be one example of this.

Although this book is concerned with political processes, one underlying strand which runs through it, being given slightly different emphasis in the various chapters, is the extent to which and the ways in which politics relates to and builds on changes in economy and society. The unstated implication of the structure of the series of which this book is a part could be interpreted to suggest that the shapes of politics and the state are more or less consequent on underlying economic and social processes: Allen and Massey (1988) deals with the economy; Hamnett, McDowell and Sarre (1989) with social structures; and this book with politics and the state. And many of the arguments in the chapters which follow accept this implicit structure (and make it rather more explicit). They relate political change back to economic and social changes.

But, it is more important to understand – as the other books in the series also stress – that this is not seen as the only option. Many of the arguments developed here suggest a rather different – more autonomous – role for politics. Indeed, some would emphasize the ways in which political action helps to shape the development of change in economy and society, while others simply stress the dangers of trying to read off political change from social change, without identifying and explaining the links. One aim of this book is to explore the direction of political change and to identify its scale, but another, equally important, is to consider the ways in which political factors underlie and help to explain change in other areas.

This is important because very often the analysis of social and economic change is undertaken to explain the direction of political change – such as the decline of the Labour vote, the size of the Conservative vote in the South East of England and the growth of support for third parties. A political trend having been noted, it is then made inexorable by reference to 'glacially slow' and apparently irreversible social and economic trends. There is frequently no reference to the role of politics in encouraging (and discouraging) particular trends and the links between such changes and political shifts are often left unexplored. Problems of political change provide the starting-point; social and economic change is identified; and then political change is provided as evidence for the significance of the other changes (this is a point developed further in Chapter 6).

The book is organized around a series of central questions. It starts at the international level. There the main issue is the extent to which change in Britain can be explained in terms of global restructuring. This may be important in two principal ways: first, in terms of Britain as a site for changes taking place more generally (including, for example, moves towards 'post-Fordism', 'disorganized capitalism' or away from global Keynesianism); and, secondly, in terms of Britain's changing position within the global system (including, for example, the decline of empire, the rise of US hegemony and, more recently, its erosion and the development of a European dimension). In Chapter 1 the development of Britain in the post-war period is surveyed in terms of endogenous, exogenous and 'interrelational' approaches. The first seeks to explain political development through the particular experience of British politics; the second stresses the importance of external factors, over which the British state can be expected to have little control, although its behaviour may be adjusted to take account of the changes which are taking place; and the third stresses the relationship between endogenous and exogenous factors, as each influences the development of the other.

The importance of the international context is clear not only in Joe Doherty's chapter, but in Allan Cochrane's which follows, and which concentrates on the development of political crisis in Britain at the end of the 1960s and into the 1970s. In this chapter various interpretations of that crisis are considered, both as a means of illustrating the ways in which political crises may be explained and of indicating how they may be resolved. Here, too, there is a major tension between exogenous and endogenous explanations, political and economic processes. The structures of the UK state are highlighted as potentially major sources of concern, with pressures towards 'modernization' generating problems for the 'full employment' welfare state, the unity of the 'United' Kingdom and the development of corporate 'bias', without the solutions yet becoming clear.

Chapter 3 begins our consideration of potential solutions in terms of state restructuring, by looking at the changing nature of state–economy relations, and competing interpretations of this. Simon Mohun's analysis is that of an economist and his assessment of the changes is expressed through the language of different economic theories. He stresses the extent of dialogue between market-based theories (particularly contrasting the views of market pessimists and market optimists) but also indicates its absence with regard to Marxist economics, which start from a distinctly different theoretical base. The chapter presents substantial evidence from the patterns of state expenditure since the late 1970s and suggests ways of explaining it in terms of the different theories. Although it is acknowledged that significant change has taken place, Mohun is rather more sceptical about whether it represents any fundamental (or structural) change.

Chapters 4 and 5 both focus on the local levels of politics and the state, but they start from quite different directions. Like Mohun the first is principally concerned with changes in the structures of the state and their wider implications. Local government is a case developed to clarify these issues, and the focus is on local–central relations and restructuring from above. For this purpose the 'reform' of local government provides a more complete set of changes for study than had been achieved in other areas of the state, such as the National Health Service or the Department of Social Security, by the end of the 1980s. Cochrane follows through a series of debates from the early 1970s to the late 1980s, suggesting ways in which different theoretical approaches connect with each other in their analysis of change. He stresses the need to look at and bring together institutional relations within the state and changes in the wider political economy, to understand the extent to which structural change has taken place over the longer period.

One implication of the arguments in Chapter 4 is that a focus on local politics is not always a helpful starting-point for the analysis of local government or the local state. In Chapter 5 that implication is challenged very emphatically by Mark Goodwin. He stresses the importance of differentiation between local areas and emphasizes the importance of uneven economic and social development as a basis for local government and local politics. Following from the identification of difference, he explains it in terms of local social relations, and indicates some of the ways in which the implications of these have fed into differing political strategies at local level, particularly in the field of local economic strategies. His stress on the importance of local politics is a vital counterpoint to the stress on shifting state structures in the preceding chapter.

Finally, in Chapter 6, Patrick Dunleavy ties together a number of the major debates about the changing bases of political action since the mid-1960s. He looks at various explanations for the apparent decline in class as an important factor in electoral behaviour, and points to some alternative possibilities of political organization and change. He is sceptical about approaches which identify changes in the social structure and conclude that these will – of necessity – lead to changes in political behaviour. On the contrary, he suggests there may be high degree of political autonomy around a series of key issues, which are largely determined by social changes. He argues strongly, for example, that consumption cleavages and public/private divisions are increasingly good guides to voting behaviour (better than class). But he does not believe that the same cleavages will always be of the same importance: that depends on political behaviour. Thus he suggests that housing provided the key division of the late 1970s and early 1980s, but for the late 1980s and 1990s he predicts health and education will be of greater significance.

Like the other authors Dunleavy brings together a series of interpretations and explanations of what has happened in Britain since the mid-1960s. He uses that experience to reflect on the different theoretical approaches involved. Whatever the real or imagined differences between them, all the authors seek to do the same for their own subject areas, making it possible for the reader to judge between and build on the various approaches. By the end of the book, we hope that the value of this structuring principle will be clear, particularly in helping to develop an understanding and analysis of the process of change in Britain over this period and in assessing the extent to which and the ways in which restructuring has taken place.

Allan Cochrane

1 Britain in a changing international system

Joe Doherty

Contents

1.1   Introduction

This chapter has a twofold aim: first, to provide a historical narrative which charts Britain's changing position in the international system since 1945 and, second, to outline and assess the respective merits of the different theoretical frameworks and explanatory perspectives which have been proposed to account for these changes.

Britain's international standing in 1945 was to all appearances high. Victorious from the Second World War, Britain represented Europe at the Yalta and Potsdam conferences and was aligned as a superpower alongside the USA and the USSR. But exhausted from six years of continuous military conflict, depleted of resources, in debt and with exports down to a third of those of 1938, the basis for that position was fragile. In the shifting global geopolitical environment of the post-war years, Britain has experienced a process of economic and political change which, though not following an uninterrupted path, has been cumulatively downwards. Indeed 1945 can be seen as a momentary high spot in a spiral of decline which has its origins in the late nineteenth and early twentieth centuries when British hegemony on the world stage was being successfully challenged by both Germany and the United States.

The weakening influence of Britain as a political actor on the global stage in the years following 1945 is not in dispute. All commentators agree that Britain has experienced a decline in the international hierarchy of states, though the extent of that decline and whether the mid-1980s, with the economic restructuring and the revivified international political interventions of that period, saw a partial retrenchment of Britain's position in the global arena have engendered some discussion. However, there are fundamental disagreements over the reasons for this decline. We will return to consider the theoretical positions which inform these disagreements in more detail in section 1.3, but we shall outline the different perspectives here in order to provide a framework for consideration of the historical events narrated in section 1.2.

There are a variety of conflicting explanations which purport to explain the 'collapse of British power', to use Corelli Barnett's (1984) phrase. Initially we can identify two broad sets of explanations: first, those that look to **endogenous** issues such as national economic policies and political decisions, to factors which are internal to the country's economic, social and political structures; and, second, those that stress **exogenous** issues, focusing on factors which are external to Britain, particularly the changing global geopolitical scene as reflected in the increased internationalization of capital (for example, the growth of multinational corporations) and the emergence of global decision-making institutions (such as the IMF, the World Bank and various agencies of the United Nations).

This excerpt from Moran nicely summarizes the main arguments:

> The collapse of British power ... is one of the unsolved mysteries of modern history ... many accounts have been offered, none of which commands

common acceptance. For some, both the era of British power and the era of British decline are episodes in the continuing development of a world capitalist economy. To understand Britain's moment of greatness and her subsequent fall we must therefore look to the changing characteristics of the world economy and the world political system. Others have also linked decline to international events, though of a more historically particular kind. The two world wars are often seen as important culprits, dissipating Britain's wealth and destroying the international economic and political arrangements on which her power rested . . . [others are convinced] . . . that Britain's misfortune was not military involvement alone, but victorious involvement which pre-served old industries and old values ill-adapted to survival in the post-war world.

   This last argument connects to the most popular explanations for British decline, those that stress the role of domestic institutions and values . . . [These explanations] . . . share a common assumption that Britain's pioneering role as the first industrial nation was the source of her modern difficulties . . . the fatal legacy of early economic development was an industrial structure incapable of responding to modern demands . . . other observers have stressed the role of particular institutions . . . [such as] . . . an excessively powerful trade-union movement which obstructed the efficient use of manpower and machines. By contrast, some observers . . . have argued that decline was due to fatal mis-judgements by those responsible for economic policy, especially in the trea-sury . . . [which has been linked] . . . to the way that interests of financiers have shaped policy at the expense of manufacturing industry. (1985, pp. 184–5)

Moran goes on to cite two additional 'explanations', one of which focuses on the apparent disdain in Britain's culture for business and the consequent drain of talent away from industry into 'unproductive' activities. The other explanation attributes Britain's decline to the absence of a 'strong state' tradition: the inability of the British state to intervene effectively to direct industry and labour and to develop state-sponsored capitalism as in France and Japan.

   Central to this dichotomy of explanations is the question of the degree of autonomy exercised by individual nation-states in the context of a world economy and world polity. Whether endogenous or exogenous processes are favoured as the explanation for Britain's decline depends very much on the position adopted with regard to this issue. The discussion on state autonomy in the geopolitical literature parallels to some extent that some-times identified in discussions of the UK economy. In Harris (1988), for example, a division is established between, on the one hand, **world-system** approaches such as those of Wallerstein (1974) and *Taylor** (1989), which view the capitalist world-system as all-embracing and relegates the internal structure of a nation's economy to a secondary position, and, on the other hand, regulationist approaches which assign primacy to the economy of individual nation-states (see Aglietta, 1979).

   There is, however, a third perspective on Britain's political decline which in some ways bridges the gap between what may be regarded as the 'false

*An author's name in italics indicates that this article has been reprinted in the Reader associated with this book (Anderson, J. and Cochrane, A. (eds) (1989)).

dichotomy' of the endogenous/exogenous divide. Such a position is illustrated by the work of *E. A. Brett* (1986). For Brett the degree of economic
and political interdependence that has existed between the countries of the
world, especially since 1945, means that we can no longer talk of 'closed
economies' or 'sovereign state systems'. Brett here associates himself with
those that favour exogenous explanations for Britain's post-war decline and
when he further observes that the 'capacity of national governments to plan
policies is a function of their ability to control overwhelming external forces
which are decisively mediated by the activities of official and private international agencies like the IMF and commercial banks' (Brett, 1986, p. 6), he
appears to align himself with aspects of the world-system approach. But
while Brett certainly stresses the importance of external factors his analysis
is more subtle. Rather than claiming supremacy for these factors he focuses
on the interrelationship between the endogenous and the exogenous; in
particular, Brett argues that the economic weaknesses of Britain in 1945
undermined the country's ability to control external forces. It was the
reluctance of Britain's political leaders and commercial interests to let go of
the illusion that such control could be exercised, which drained scarce
resources and energies away from domestic tasks, further weakening the
national economy, exacerbating the uneven development of domestic social
and economic structures both regionally and sectorally (Massey, 1986) and
thereby compounded the difficulties of exercising external control.

The three explanatory perspectives – endogenous, exogenous and Brett's
position, which we can label **interrelational** – are distinguished from each
other not only in terms of the importance they attribute to internal and
external factors and in the manner in which they view the question of state
autonomy. They also differ from each other in terms of how they see the
relationship between politics and economics. Some researchers argue that
there are two independent realms of activity here; others view the two as
closely interrelated. Some, in a deterministic way, see politics as dependent
upon economics; others would argue (and Brett fits in here) that there is a
two-way relationship. Political power certainly reflects, and is largely dependent upon, economic (and military) power, but it does not follow from this
that economics is determinate of politics; political activity cannot be read off
from an economic basis. Rather the causal arrows have to be seen as flying in
both directions: political activity has clear economic consequences. This
position is central to the argument that external political commitments have
undermined the UK economy during the course of the post-war period and
that this weakened economy has in its turn further reduced Britain's ability
to act effectively on an international stage.

Summary of section 1.1

• Britain has experienced a decline since 1945 in its international political
position and the reasons for this decline are disputed.

- The explanations offered to explain Britain's decline are:

  – those that attribute the decline to *endogenous* factors looking to indigenous processes, internal to Britain's economy and society

  – those that attribute the decline to *exogenous* factors, seeking an explanation of decline in processes external to Britain, in the international economy and political system

  – and, thirdly, *interrelational* explanations which look to a combination of internal and external factors and in particular to their interrelationship.

1.2   Britain's changing position in the post-war world

> Great Britain has lost an Empire and has not yet found a role. The attempt to play a separate power role, that is a role apart from Europe, a role based on a 'special relationship' with the United States, a role based on being head of a 'commonwealth' which has no political structure, or unity of strength, and enjoys a fragile and precarious reality by means of the Sterling Area and preferences in the British market – this is a role about played out. (Dean Acheson, West Point, 5 December, 1962; quoted in Boyd, 1976)

Britain's post-war international position has been characterized by three often conflicting and overlapping roles: that of a country surrendering its imperial inheritance, at first reluctantly and finally with great speed in the decolonizations of the 1950s and early 1960s; that, as Brett has expressed it, of 'junior partner of the United States in the stabilization of the world economy and the strengthening of the anti-communist military alliance'; and a latter-day role as a progressively integrated member of the European Community. These roles overlap in time, but there is a cumulative chronology here with the retreat from Empire characteristic of the immediate post-war years and the assumption of the trappings of a European power becoming more prominent as the hegemonic position of the United States begins to falter in the 1970s and 1980s. This twofold division of the post-war years, from 1945 to *c.* 1973 (when Britain joined the European Economic Community) and from 1973 onwards, is used to structure the following account of Britain's changing international position.

Notwithstanding their many differences, the three theoretical positions identified in section 1.1 – endogenous, exogenous and interrelational – share at least one common perspective: they all agree that Britain has indeed experienced a decline in its international political standing and influence since 1945 which conforms, in broad outline, to the changing roles identified above. Additionally, these theoretical positions share the view that this decline pre-dates the Second World War.

To prepare the ground for a more detailed coverage of post-1945 events, we shall first briefly sketch elements of Britain's political history through the latter part of the nineteenth and first half of the twentieth centuries. This period covers the important structural changes in Britain's economy of the 1880s/'90s and the 1930s/'40s, changes which are discussed in more detail in Harris (1988).

1.2.1   Historical background

At its height the British Empire covered a quarter of the globe. Sustained by an all-powerful navy, British manufactured goods dominated the world trade routes, British garrisons controlled the strategic positions and British finance controlled the markets. Britain at this time held an unrivalled **hegemonic position**: a leadership position of such pervasive dominance that it enabled Britain to determine the international, and in some cases the domestic, frameworks within which other states conducted their political activity (see *Taylor*, 1989). This position had been built up from the time of the Napoleonic Wars and was to last until the final quarter of the nineteenth century. British **hegemony** was based on a strong domestic industrial structure (centred first on textiles, especially cotton, and later on coal and iron and engineering products) and on access to and control over a formal and informal empire of unprecedented proportions which provided raw materials for the domestic economy and a market for exported manufactured goods. India was the 'jewel' of the Empire. Here were located crucial raw materials (such as cotton), a massive market for manufactured goods (textiles, railways etc.) and a very profitable location for capital investment. Elsewhere colonized territories did not always prove as profitable, though the destructive effect on indigenous enterprise and social development was just as marked (Rodney, 1972). Parts of the informal empire – those areas not under direct political control but nevertheless dependent on British commerce and investment – were as profitable as many of the formal colonial territories. In Latin America, for instance, British finance and business was central to the operation of shipping, railways, public utilities such as ports and water supply, and to banking and insurance. On the eve of the First World War, 30 per cent of all British capital invested overseas was located in Latin America (*c.* £1000 million) and much of that was in the Argentine railways.

It was not until the last quarter of the nineteenth century that Britain's hegemonic position on the world stage was effectively challenged. In this respect the 1873 recession is a benchmark. From that time those countries with fledgling industries began considering and subsequently implementing protective tariff barriers in direct opposition to the free-trade system which it had been Britain's imperial preference and, after the repeal of the Corn Laws in 1846, its privilege to selectively operate. By the 1890s both the United States and Germany were challenging Britain in manufacturing output. In 1880 Britain produced half the world's crude steel and was responsible for 80 per cent of the world's iron exports. In 1890, however, Germany became the world's largest producer of steel, and between 1908 and 1913 produced twice as much as Britain. The United States was also increasing its productive capacity at this time and in the 1890s moved up amongst the world leaders: by 1900 the United States was the leading exporter and in 1913 produced 40 per cent of the world's steel – more than Britain, Germany and France combined.

From the 1880s to 1914 other European countries were seeking to extend their formal empires to rival that of Britain. In this context, and symptomatic of the changed position of Britain in the international arena, the Congress of Berlin in 1884–5 drew up the parameters for the partition of Africa among the European powers. For the first time in more than fifty years Britain had been obliged to enter into negotiation with other imperial nations over the delineation of spheres of influence. Britain's free hand on the world stage was further constrained by the signing of defence agreements between 1902 and 1907 first with Japan and then with France and Russia.

The First World War marked the peak of inter-imperialist rivalries arising out of changes in the latter part of the nineteenth century. It also marked the defeat of Germany (for the time-being) in the battle with the United States for succession to Britain's hegemonic role. The establishment of the League of Nations was recognition that a new world order was needed and one that could not be set up under the dominance of one country. Britain's abandonment of its former hegemonic position was vividly demonstrated in 1932 when free trade was given up in favour of a system of trade preferences with the 'white' dominion territories of Canada, Australia, New Zealand and the Union of South Africa which had become independent in 1931. Britain was on the victorious side in the First World War, as it was to be twenty-five years later, but military victory, on both occasions, masked a process of decline, which continued in the post-1945 years, in geopolitical fortunes and economic status.

While the above account of Britain's changing international position in the century preceding 1945 would, in broad outline, be accepted by most researchers, there are, among these same researchers, considerable differences over why these changes took place. It is instructive to look briefly at some of these arguments and controversies since they illustrate many of the distinctions between endogenous and exogenous explanations and highlight variations within these two broad theoretical positions; they also foreshadow similar disputes which characterize rival explanations for change in the post-1945 period. By way of illustration we can focus on the interpretations of the period of initial challenge to Britain's world domination and hegemony.

Within the endogenous perspective on the relative political and economic decline of Britain in the latter part of the nineteenth century, two rather distinct positions can be identified (Warwick, 1985). First, there is the economic explanation. The essence of the argument here is that Britain suffered from its early entry to and success in industrial development. The very investments which facilitated the rise of Britain to world domination in the early and middle part of the nineteenth century inhibited development in the latter part. At a time when Germany and the United States were innovating and investing in the new growth industries associated with chemicals, electronics and transport, Britain, lumbered with an outmoded technology inherited from the past, was unable to maintain productive efficiency and allowed these rival and rapidly industrializing countries to catch up and eventually overtake. Compounding this problem of outdated infrastructure was the decision by some British capitalists to invest overseas in financial services and capital export rather than in domestic infrastructural renewal and replacement. These decisions, it seems, could be interpreted as perfectly rational at the time and served for a while to maintain Britain's position in shipping and as financial controller of international trade; but in the long term they proved to be detrimental to Britain's hegemonic position.

A second, and rather different, explanation for Britain's late nineteenth-century decline, but one which is also associated with the endogenous perspective, focuses on the cultural characteristics and social behaviour of Britain's political and economic elite. This argument suggests that the prevailing ethos among the important decision-makers was fundamentally anti-business, anti-industrial and anti-urban; in terminology redolent of more modern times, it was anti-entrepreneurial. Industry and technology were regarded as the province of the 'practical man', to be shunned by intellectuals whose profoundly anti-utilitarian outlook pervaded the educational establishments of the day. A fear of novelty and innovation typified an essentially conservative elite at a time when innovation and the application of science to industry was required to sustain Britain's hegemonic position and see off the challenge of the emerging industrial countries (Warwick, 1985).

In contrast to these endogenous explanations of Britain's decline stand those explanations which focus on the changing international arena in which Britain was operating at this time. *Taylor* (1989) illustrates the nature of this position. In his approach, which marries the world-system approach with the theory of long waves (also discussed in Harris, 1988), he argues that capitalism goes through a series of cyclical developments, called **Kondratiev cycles** after the Russian economist who first identified them, in which a given power rises to a hegemonic position in the world economy, a position which is sustained through a period of some fifty years until effectively challenged by some rival power. Taylor argues that at the end of the nineteenth century, a period which coincided with the 'B' or downturn phase of a Kondratiev cycle, the productive capacities of the world system associated with British hegemony were exhausted and a new cycle of development with the US as the world power was emerging.

We can now turn to specific consideration of the post-1945 changes. Using the two-part division identified earlier, we look first (in section 1.2.2) at the period 1945 to the early 1970s during which Britain retained, albeit a changing, attachment to Empire and developed a special relationship with the United States, shunning for the time-being integration with Europe and, secondly (in section 1.2.3), at the post-1973 period when Britain joined Europe. We finish this account (section 1.2.4) with an overview and consideration of some more recent developments. In covering this material the emphasis will be on presenting a historical narrative; we leave explicit consideration of explanations for these events until section 1.3. However, as you go through this narrative it will be useful to keep in mind the endogenous/exogenous division and occasional reference will be made to these conflicting perspectives at key points in the text.

1.2.2   The imperial connection and the special relationship

Britain's changing international position during and after the Second World War up to the early 1970s can be illustrated by reference to three events: the Anglo-American war agreement embodied in the Lend-Lease programme and the Atlantic Charter; the process of decolonization and the Commonwealth legacy; and, finally, the Suez crisis and its aftermath. The 'special relationship' is given particular consideration in the concluding section.

The Anglo-American war alliance

The details of this alliance involved a practical concession and a concession of principle on the issue of British imperial rule. The practical concession was embodied in the terms of the Lend-Lease agreement drawn up by Churchill and Roosevelt in May 1940. The United States proposed that they would agree to the release of fifty surplus destroyers for the British war effort if Britain conceded military bases in colonial territories in the Caribbean and in Newfoundland in Canada – an unprecedented incursion into the British sphere of influence. The very basis of US involvement in the war was self-interest, offering help to the weaker European power in order to sustain European rivalry and further weakening all the contending parties, thus reducing their international orbit of operation and leaving the way clear for the penetration of US interests. To this end, under the terms of the lease Britain was obliged to agree not to send any article abroad which contained Lend-Lease materials, nor any goods, even if made in Britain, similar to those obtained under Lend-Lease (Barnett, 1984, p. 592). Having lost 40 per cent of its overseas markets, having an accumulated debt of £21 million (three times that of 1938) and having raised standard income tax to 10 shillings (50p) in the pound, Britain was in no position to refuse these conditions.

The concession of principle was embodied in the Atlantic Charter. Originally drawn up between Britain and the USA in 1941 to consolidate their war alliance it was eventually signed by twenty-six allied countries. The signatories agreed to respect the 'right of all peoples to choose the form of government under which they would live' (quoted in Barnett, 1982, p. 32). Though Churchill was later to deny that this expression of support for the concept of self-determination applied to the British colonies, it was an important concession and, as Barnett (1982, p. 40) observes, in order to save the Empire Churchill had to concede in principle to its potential dissolution.

Decolonization

Though in retreat for the best part of the twentieth century, Britain's hegemonic position, based on Empire, has left a legacy which continues to influence Britain's role and position in the international arena. The most tangible of these legacies are the formal trappings of Empire. In 1945 apart from the 'white' dominion territories of Canada, Australia, New Zealand and the Union of South Africa, Britain's colonial Empire remained intact, although under threat. In the 1920s Gandhi had started his campaign for Indian freedom and in 1947 the former imperial 'jewel' achieved its independence. Thereafter, beginning with Sudan and Ghana in the later 1950s, the bulk of remaining colonial territories in Africa, Asia and the West Indies – with some notable and important exceptions such as Hong Kong and the Falklands – obtained political independence. Today membership of the Commonwealth gives expression to the continuing ties between these former imperial possessions and reflects the maintenance of political, cultural and economic ties with the former 'mother' country (see Northedge, 1974). Though a far cry from the federation or economic bloc of the early dreamers, the Commonwealth stands not only as a reminder of Britain's imperial past but, in that it meets regularly and attempts to influence world affairs, remains as a tangible legacy of Empire. These Commonwealth links, however, have themselves been subject to intermittent strain both politically – over, for example, the Suez crisis, the Indian/Pakistan War, Rhodesian UDI and, in the late 1980s, sanctions on trade with South Africa – and economically as the former colonies have diversified their trading links and as Britain has retreated from preferential Commonwealth trading agreements and developed closer links with the European Community.

The very process of decolonization itself reflected a declining international presence for Britain. The concession of independence by Britain has to be seen in the context of a world increasingly dominated by the two superpowers of the USA and the USSR and their, albeit selective, commitment to self-determination. This was an important influence on the British decision to let the colonies go. Additionally, of course, it was the demands of the former colonies themselves that provided the most direct and immediate pressure for liberation. These nationalist sentiments were often based on a real and fundamental resentment of British rule and not infrequently took a bloody and violent form as, for example, in the Mau-Mau rebellion in Kenya. In the face of such demands and in the international climate of the post-war years, Britain conceded independence to most of its colonies through the late 1950s and early 1960s. The continued cumulative decline in

Britain's influence over her former colonies was most vividly demonstrated by the US invasion of the Commonwealth country of Grenada in 1983, an invasion that proceeded without prior notification being given to the British government. The Falklands conflict of 1982 might suggest a revival of interest in the imperial way, but, as suggested in a later section, this conflict was more an expression of an illusion of power than an expression of real power and, indeed, may have had other motivations.

The Suez crisis and its aftermath

In the decade following 1945 the Middle East was the focus for several competing claims and rivalries. Here the domination of West European powers, dating from colonial times, faced nationalist hostility, especially in Egypt, and after 1948 had to deal with the tensions and conflict between Arab and Jews over the existence of the state of Israel. Here also the cold-war rivalry between the two superpowers was given expression in competing attempts to woo the loyalty of the Arab nations. Running through all this was the inter-imperialist rivalry between the waning power of Britain and France, each trying to preserve their own sphere of influence, and the growing power of the United States, eager to take over the imperialist mantle. Interest in the Middle East was centred then, as now, on its strategic position between East and West, on its oil resources and on the vital trade link of the Suez canal.

Britain's decision along with France and Israel to invade Egypt was justified by these three powers on the grounds that Colonel Nasser, who had come to power in 1954 following the nationalist revolution of 1952, was intent on strangling Europe's oil life-line, the Suez canal, and intent on attacking Israel. The war with Egypt can be seen in retrospect as one of the last gasps of Empire: a final attempt by Britain, in particular, to exercise independent judgement and action – independent, that is, of the United States who had not been informed of the plot. The attack was to turn into a humiliating defeat. The Israelis moved first, invading the Sinai peninsular on 29 October 1956. The British and French troops were then sent in on the pretext of restoring order; their real objective was to secure the canal and destroy Egypt's capacity to threaten Israel. The combined British–French force succeeded only in so severely damaging the waterway that it was closed to navigation for several years.

The attack, an assertion of European independence, played into the hands of the ambitions of the USA to open up the globe economically and politically. Fearful of Soviet retaliation (and indeed the USSR did threaten armed intervention) and the further fuelling of Arab nationalism, the US obtained from the United Nations support for the end of hostilities and the withdrawal of foreign forces. The USA threatened to undermine both the pound and the franc through the manipulation of the world's oil market, now that Middle East supplies were cut off from Europe, through its control over Venezuelan supplies. The combination of this and universal condemnation of the invasion compelled Britain and France to retreat. A cease-fire was agreed on 6 November and the European troops withdrew before the end of the year. Vadney concludes his account of the Suez crisis:

> Thus the European campaign, while demonstrating once again Israel's military prowess, definitely ended European claims to supremacy in the region. Their armed forces proved incapable of taking charge, leaving the US as the uncontested representative of Western interests in the Middle East. (1987, p. 224)

The successful campaign against communist insurgents in Malaya and Britain's participation in the Korean War in the early 1950s had marked the high points of Britain's post-war military involvements. The Suez debacle, however, demonstrated the waning of British military power and was a major contribution to the cumulative contraction of Britain's international military role in the post-war years. In 1968, following the devaluation of sterling, Britain announced that it was unable to maintain a military present east of Suez and withdrew to the European theatre of operations. In the process it conceded to the US the role of world policing. The decision was also a landmark in the changing post-war relationship between the United States and Britain, an issue which is now taken up.

The special relationship

The goals of the United States after the end of the war were clear: first, to bring about the globalization of the world's economy and open the world's markets to the penetration of US capital, then being consolidated in the burgeoning multinational corporations; and, second, for related reasons, to curb any expansionist tendencies of the Soviet Union and contain the spread of the alternative world vision embodied in its communist ideology.

As the strongest economic and military power to emerge from the war, the United States was in a good position in 1945 to achieve these goals and for the next twenty years or so was successful in pursuing them. Through a series of military alliances and direct military interventions, complemented by huge armament expenditures and the creation of a nuclear umbrella, a worldwide network was established to monitor and check anti-American activity especially if it was communist-inspired. These military activities were accompanied by overseas loan and aid programmes, especially in Western Europe, which imposed on the recipients terms and conditions designed to break apart the trading blocs and systems of preferential agreements which had grown up during the inter-war period. These measures were built upon the Bretton Woods agreement of 1944 where a system of fixed exchange rates based on the dollar tied to the gold standard was instituted. The Bretton Woods conference also established the International Monetary Fund and the World Bank whose objectives were to 'assist in reconstruction and development', 'to promote private foreign investment' and to 'encourage the balanced growth of international trade' (Vadney,

1987, p. 66). The United States provided nearly one-third of the funds for these institutions and controlled a proportional share of the voting rights.

Britain's role in this post-war American strategy was, in 1945, potentially that of a junior partner. Despite huge debts and depleted resources, Britain with its Empire intact and imperial trade preference in place could look to a major and influential role in world affairs, albeit as a supporting cast to the leading role played by the United States. Indeed some of Britain's post-war activities might be interpreted in this manner. Britain played a central role in co-ordinating the European response to the offer in 1947/8 of the US Secretary of State George Marshall to provide the required aid for European reconstruction (the Marshall Plan for European Recovery); Britain was also a willing military ally of the United States in its fight with communism, taking up arms in Malaya (Britain's own colony) and Greece. Additionally, in 1949 Britain played a leading part in the formation of the North Atlantic Treaty Organization (conceived by Ernest Bevin); it was a participant with other European powers in the Korean War in an area of the world outside its traditional imperial sphere of operation; and the then Prime Minister, Harold Macmillan, organized in 1960 the summit of world leaders (Vadney, 1987).

However, these events have to be seen against a background of the slow erosion of Britain's global economic and political position. We have already seen how the terms of Lend-Lease and the Atlantic Charter drawn up during the war threatened Britain's economic and political strengths. The terms of the post-war loan agreement secured by Keynes from the Americans in 1945 (see *Brett*, 1986) contributed further to this process in that Britain was forced not only to accept much less than anticipated but also to abandon the imperial preferences set up in 1932 and to agree to the full convertibility of sterling, thereby opening up its imperial territories to US competition. This process was pushed even further with the signing of the General Agreement on Tariffs and Trade (GATT) in 1948, whereby signatories agreed on the redirection of world trade away from quota and preferential barriers. The Suez debacle, the abandonment of an independent nuclear arsenal and the acceptance of US missile technology, as well as the various sterling crises of the 1960s leading to the IMF agreement and the devaluation of the pound in 1967, provide further illustrations of the erosion of Britain's capacity for independent action.

The Anglo-American special relationship was founded on Britain's capacity to perform a world role, albeit under US guidance and direction. Through the 1960s Britain's ability to perform this role was placed under severe strain as domestic economic crisis placed constraints on overseas activity. The 1967 devaluation marked the culmination of these trends, the 'end of Empire' according to Brett, with the abandonment of the 'east of Suez' policy and retreat to the European and North Atlantic spheres of operation; Britain thus effectively abrogated its global military role bringing to an end the special relationship.

A reorientation towards European connections, initiated with an application to Common Market membership earlier in the 1960s, was now in full swing and with entry into the European Community (EC) agreed in 1973 it looked as though Britain was about to find the role which Dean Acheson had been so disparaging about a decade before. In earlier times such an orient-ation on the part of Britain may have been welcomed by the United States as forming the basis of an extension of the 'special relationship'. When distri-buting Marshall Aid in the late 1940s and early 1950s, the US had urged the European powers to move quickly towards integrating the continent's econ-omy in order to facilitate further the US object of the removal or at least reduction of tariff and quota barriers. The 1952 European Coal and Steel Community went some way towards this, but Britain was not a signatory, nor of course was it a member of the Common Market which began operation in 1958. By the end of the 1960s, however, the United States itself was undergoing severe strain, suffering from the same malaise that had afflicted Britain through its post-hegemonic era, namely increasing difficulty in maintaining its overseas commitments and a crisis in its domestic economy (Agnew, 1987). The special relationship ended as it had begun, under the direction of the United States which was faltering in its post-war hegemonic role.

Summary of section 1.2.2

Section 1.2.2 has illustrated the changing international position of Britain in the period between 1945 and the early part of the 1970s through a detailed examination of the country's retreat from Empire (decolonization) and from a global military presence (the Suez debacle and the withdrawal of troops from east of Suez) and, beginning with the Anglo-American war alliance, the rise and fall of a close association with the United States (the special relationship), whereby Britain for a while maintained some of the trappings of a global power as a junior partner to the ascendant USA.

Activity 1.1

While there may be some debate over the detail of the foregoing account, the broad outlines of the story of Britain's international decline would be adhered to by most researchers, no matter that they adopt an endogenous or an exogenous theoretical position with regard to the explanations for this decline. While the 'facts' may not be disputed, these same facts are not entirely neutral in their presentation; covertly and sometimes overtly, ele-ments of an explanation can be detected which suggest support for one or other of the theoretical positions.

   Look over section 1.2.2 again and note where you detect support for either an endogenous or an exogenous perspective. In each case consider what the arguments of the alternative perspective might be. For example, in dealing with the decolonization issue the manner of presentation might suggest support for an exogenous position in that Britain is here seen to comply with external pressure for independence from the colonies themselves. From an endogenous position, however, the vital question would be why did Britain concede independence at this particular time, when rebellion and demands for liberation were, after all, endemic features of colonial rule? One answer to this question might reflect on the profitability of the 'informal empire', in for example Latin America, a point which was noted in the historical introduction (section 1.2.1). You could usefully conduct a similar exercise with regard to the following section (section 1.2.3) which examines the evolution of Britain's European connections.

1.2.3 The European connection

In 1973 when Britain joined the Common Market it seemed that a decade of uncertainty had come to an end. Britain's first application to join the EC had been vetoed by de Gaulle in 1963 and a second application was similarly dismissed in 1967. De Gaulle's reasons for exercising France's veto was that in his opinion Britain was insufficiently European, too wedded to the US relationship on the one hand and the Commonwealth on the other. Given Britain's stance and attitudes towards Europe in the preceding decades, such an assessment was understandable. What de Gaulle did not take into account, or chose to disregard, was Britain's changing position (which has been documented above) with regard to these other spheres of operation.

Following the end of the war, Britain was the leading power in Europe and, as we have seen, from this position co-ordinated the European response to Marshall Aid and initiated the establishment of NATO. In addition, Britain joined the Council for Europe when it was established in 1948 (a purely advisory and discursive body with no formal powers), and in March 1948, having already concluded a defence treaty with France, signed the Brussels Treaty with Belgium, Luxembourg and the Netherlands, pledging military assistance if any of these countries were threatened or invaded.

Britain's initial predisposition to deal with Europe and be involved in the continent's affairs came to an abrupt end when Britain's system of imperial preference was threatened by talk of a European customs union and federation. The Schuman Plan of 1949 for the integration of European coal, iron and steel industries (which accounted for over a quarter of intra-European trade) proved to be the turning-point. Britain did not participate in the European Coal and Steel Commission of 1950 which eliminated internal quotas and import duties between the participating countries of France, Germany, Benelux and Italy. By distancing itself from this agreement, Britain cut itself off from effective participation in the economic recovery of Europe for the next twenty years. Clinging to a self-image as a world-power, too committed to Empire and sustained by the 'special relationship', Britain played no part in the proceedings which led up to the establishment of the

European Economic Community in 1958. However, in part as retaliation, and in an attempt to pre-empt the expansion of the EC, in the same year Britain set up the European Free Trade Area with the Scandinavian countries and Ireland.

Yet even in these last years of the 1950s the writing was on the wall with regard to Britain's world-power role, with the 1956 Suez crisis and the 1957 economic downturn. Further events in the 1960s – the Blue Streak–Polaris deal, which effectively ended any illusion about an 'independent' nuclear deterrent; the stop–go experience of the economy; the 1966 IMF intervention; the 1967 devaluation and the Basle agreement of 1968 which removed sterling as a world reserve currency – all served to emphasize the growing precariousness of Britain on the world stage. The realization in 1960 that all the European countries, bar those of the southern periphery, in the fifteen years since the war had overtaken Britain in per capita GNP, provided the catalyst for all political parties and interest groups to consider and eventually support application for EC membership.

Yet if Britain in 1973 hoped to catch the tide of EC growth, it was to be disappointed. Already that growth had ebbed from the boom years of the 1950s. In the early 1970s it was to be catastrophically hit by the increases in world oil prices and those of other raw materials and by the inflationary effects of the dollar deficit (*Brett*, 1986). Britain was particularly badly hurt by these developments in the world economy, partly because of its relative lack of strength compared to other EC members' economies. The desperate nature of Britain's predicament was vividly illustrated by the need for an IMF loan in 1976 and the relative ease with which the conditions of that loan – draconian public expenditure cuts, imposition of high interest rates, wage restraint and privatization of public assets (£500 million of BP shares sold) – were accepted by the then Labour government, preparing the way for the 'monetarist' policies of the 1979 Conservative government.

Through the 1970s and 1980s Britain's membership of the EC was fraught with controversy: over the terms of entry, negotiated by the Conservative government of Heath, renegotiated by Wilson's Labour government in 1975 and put to a national referendum for approval; over Britain's contribution to the Community's budget; over the Common Agricultural Policy and other matters. Britain at times has seemed like a reluctant partner, as with the refusal to join the European Monetary System, a state of affairs still not rectified at the time of writing (1988).

1.2.4   The 1980s and legacies from the past

We have argued above that between 1945 and the early 1970s Britain surrendered its imperial role, developed and lost a special relationship with the United States and latterly, through the 1970s, became a participating, albeit truculent, member of the European Community. Such a division is useful in identifying the major trends; it does, however, considerably simplify the complexity of Britain's international position and behaviour. Thus, while the European connection was maintained and expanded, the 1980s also saw the emergence of political tendencies associated with legacies from the past.

One of the most pervasive of these legacies has been that of Empire. This remains most tangible in the 'British' Commonwealth and in a remnant of small, mostly island, colonies and also in the continuing commitment of Britain to an admittedly considerably reduced global military role as one of the world's leading arms suppliers, as a member of NATO and as a country with vast military expenditures on nuclear and conventional armed forces. As McGrew informs us,

> In comparison with other advanced industrial states, Britain spends more on defence, both in absolute terms and as a proportion of GNP, and maintains larger professional military forces . . . It is the third largest spender on defence in the international arena and this, combined with its military capabilities, places it fourth or fifth (depending on the criteria used) in the military power hierarchy. (1988, p. 103)

In 1979, for example, Britain spent 4.7 per cent of GDP on military expenditures, second only to the USA among developed capitalist countries.

Less tangible, but pervading all of the above, we can argue that the legacy of Empire lives on in the country's political culture, or at least in the manner in which that culture is given expression by sections of the country's ruling class – in particular in their ideological commitment to maintaining Britain's role in international politics and economy and in their tenacity in holding on to the illusion that such a role is a practical reality.

This ideology was given clear expression in the triumphalist statements of Prime Minister Thatcher on the conclusion of the Falklands/Malvinas conflict in 1982:

> When we started out, there were the waverers and the fainthearts. The people who thought that Britain could no longer seize the initiative for herself. The people who thought we could no longer do the great things which we once did. Those who believed that our decline was irreversible – that we could never again be what we were. There were those who would not admit it – even perhaps some here today – people who would have strenuously denied the suggestion but – in their heart of hearts – they too had their secret fears that it was true: that Britain was no longer the nation that had build an Empire and ruled a quarter of the world. Well they were wrong. The lesson of the Falklands is that Britain has not changed and that this nation still has those sterling qualities which shine through our history. (Margaret Thatcher, Cheltenham, 3 July, 1982; quoted in Barnett, 1982)

The political culture of Britain is shot through with the trappings of Empire – from institutional and individual racism to the vision of Britain as 'Great' in more than name and the illusion that the imperial role is not yet dead. 'Atavistic imperialism', as Anthony Barnett (1982) termed it in his account of the political proceedings surrounding the Falklands conflict, has its equivalent in 'modern militarism'. The continued military investment of

Britain is a tangible outcome of such a perspective and it is one that has been adhered to by politicians of various political persuasions. The illusion that Britain is still a formidable power on the world stage and the desire to exercise this power is frighteningly real, as the South Atlantic battles only too vividly demonstrated. There were other motivations for the Falklands War, not least that an election was looming, but it was Thatcher's ability, aided by most of the news media and indeed supported by many in the opposition parties, to cash in on the imperial vision which most starkly stands out from these events.

The 1980s also saw what *Taylor* (1989) refers to as a 'reassembly of the special relationship' with the commitment of 'Reaganomics' and 'Thatcher-ism' to free-market economics and a belligerent foreign policy. This was displayed in a variety of ways: in the support of Britain for the US nuclear role; the willing deployment of cruise missiles; the purchase of Trident as the replacement for Polaris; in the Westland affair and perhaps most dramati-cally in Britain's support, alone among the European powers, for the United States' bombing raid on Libya in 1987. The reliance of Britain on the US for intelligence information during the Falklands/Malvinas War and conversely the non-consultation of Britain before the US invasion of Grenada were par for the course.

Summary of sections 1.2.3 and 1.2.4

In sections 1.2.3 and 1.2.4 we have indicated that:

• As Britain withdrew from its global military and political commitments and in the 1960s found the US umbrella a less secure shelter, it began to develop European connections, achieving membership of the European Community in 1973.

• Since 1973 these European connections have been strengthened and in this sense Britain has experienced a transformation of its global role, finally, it seems, accepting its position as a secondary, regional power.

• However, traditions die hard. The Falklands War, plus the strategic and ideological preoccupations of the Thatcher-Reagan era in particular, suggest, when added to the caution of all British administrations towards the acceptance of full European integration, that this transformation was not complete.

1.3   Theoretical perspectives

The period from 1956, the date of the Suez debacle, to 1968, when Britain contracted its military sphere of operation with the withdrawal of troops from east of Suez, can be seen as a time of crucial transformation for the United Kingdom. The first event clearly demonstrated both militarily, in the inability to defeat a former colonial power, and politically, in the humiliating withdrawal under pressure from the United States, the end of any pretensions to the role of a first-rank global power. The latter event, when combined with the several attempts to join the EC (an organization previously shunned by Britain), was a clear and tangible expression of the country's acceptance of a role as a secondary, regional power. Politically the **structural** shifts which characterized Britain's changing post-war international position can thus be identified as running: first, from 1945 to the mid-1950s when the maintenance of Empire and the special relationship with the USA allowed Britain to perform a global political role reflecting past hegemonic influence; second, from the mid-1950s to the late 1960s, a painful period of transformation when Britain cast off most of the paraphernalia of its imperial past and accepted a much contracted position of power and influence on the world stage; and, third, the period from the early 1970s through to the present day when as a secondary world power Britain has sought, albeit hesitantly, an increasing role within the European Community. This latter role has yet to be fully worked out and, as we have seen, some of the trappings of past traditions and faded glories remain to cloud the issue.

How do we explain this transformation, this decline from a global to a regional power? In this section we look more closely at the three theoretical positions identified in the introduction to this chapter which offer contrasting answers to this question. It is important to reinforce the point that these three positions are broad categorizations and a number of versions of each exist. It is our purpose here not to present an exhaustive coverage of all of these versions (a nigh impossible task), but rather to highlight the crucial differences between the three frameworks. In the following, the work of three particular authors will be emphasized to illustrate respectively the exogenous (*Taylor*, 1989), the endogenous (*Johnson*, 1977b) and the inter-relational (*Brett*, 1986) perspectives.

1.3.1 Exogenous perspectives

In the search for an explanation of the transformation of Britain's international role and position in the post-1945 period, the **exogenous perspective**, as Moran (1985) points out, ranges from those who look to specific effects of external events (such as colonial wars and demands for liberation, or the debilitating effects of world wars) to those who emphasize the embracing effects of the operation of the capitalist world system. The second of these will be the focus of attention here since the first, which emphasizes particular historical events, lacks a strong theoretical input and frequently in terms of its presentation is insufficiently distinguished from other perspectives.

Peter *Taylor* (1989), whose work has already been mentioned in the coverage of the historical background earlier in this chapter (section 1.2.1), seeks an explanation of Britain's international decline in a combination of the **world-system perspective** of Wallerstein and the **long-wave theory** of **Kondratiev**. Wallerstein argues, among other things, that the economies of individual countries are part of a structured world economy and that we cannot understand what is happening in individual countries without understanding their part in this world-system. The main concept of the long-wave theory is that developed capitalist countries go through regular fifty-year cycles of boom conditions, generated by industrial innovation, followed by slump conditions (see Harris (1988) for an extended coverage of these approaches). The essence of Taylor's argument is that Britain's post-1945 decline must be seen in the context of the development of the world economic and political system over the past two hundred years. He argues that the changes in the capitalist world-system over that period and Britain's position within it, is adequately summarized by four Kondratiev cycles which chart the rise and fall of Britain and then the United States to and from hegemony. From the end of the eighteenth century to the middle of the nineteenth, Britain established a **hegemonic position**; through the next twenty-five or so years Britain experienced 'hegemonic maturity', a time during which it exercised world domination with little or no limitation or constraint; from 1870, however, the first signs of decline with the emergence of Germany and then the United States were evident. From the end of the nineteenth through to the late 1960s, the US established its superiority over Britain and the rest of the world, first in productive efficiency (1890 to 1920), then in commerce (1910–40) and finally in finance (1940–70). Since 1970 the United States has experienced challenges to its hegemonic control (from Japan and Europe), just as the United States itself challenged Britain in the last quarter of the nineteenth century. The reasons for these shifts in global position are, from Taylor's perspective, not so much to do with the innovation theories associated with Kondratiev long waves (though innovation may be involved), but are more occasioned by the exhaustion of the productive potential associated with the dominance of a given hegemonic state, leading to the breakdown of the 'commodity chains' which link peripheral and semi-peripheral countries into a dependency link with the core.

It has been suggested by Harris (1988) that the world-system perspective, of which Taylor's is one version, is 'limited by its own generality'; that while charting the general course of world events it is unable to account for the detail of the fortunes of individual states or indeed to attribute anything but a secondary significance to individual state behaviour. Taylor's account attempts to deal with this issue by looking explicitly at the role of states within this global framework. He argues that in contrast to other perspectives which see states as *actors*, world-system perspectives view states as *instruments*, instruments of national fractions of a world bourgeois class. In the intra-class rivalry between national fractions of the bourgeoisie, individual states are used to establish economic, military and political dominance on the world stage. This dominance, however, is used in the context of the accumulation of capital on a world scale and once potential for such accumulation is exhausted a new period of intra-class rivalry emerges giving rise to a new global configuration of states.

While Taylor's account is firmly lodged in the world-system perspective, his is not as dismissive of the contribution of individual states as are some versions. Indeed Taylor goes on to suggest other ways in which states demonstrate their political significance, particularly in their role as the locus for proletarian and ethnic struggle; the implication being that these struggles, in that they are focused on the national bourgeoisie, can affect the outcome of international rivalry between fractions of the bourgeoisie. Taylor here seems to be making some gestures, though he does not develop these in relation to the case of Britain, to the importance of endogenous issues in explaining the rise and fall of states in the international order.

1.3.2 Endogenous perspectives

In the earlier consideration of **endogenous perspectives** on the decline of Britain at the end of the nineteenth century (section 1.2.1), a distinction was drawn between those positions which favoured a rather deterministic economic explanation and those which looked more to a failure of values, particularly with regard to business ethos, as the root cause of Britain's problems. This same distinction pervades the endogenous perspective on Britain's post-1945 decline.

The endogenous position which argues that Britain's international decline after 1945 was the direct result of poor economic performance both in the inter-war years and in the 1940s and 1950s is, however, difficult to sustain, at least in its cruder deterministic versions. As Warwick (1985) indicates, several commentators have shown that while the inter-war period was marked by recession, the decline of staple industries, high unemployment and large visible trade deficits, it was also a period of growth in new consumer industries, growth which compared favourably with many other industrialized countries. A similar conclusion, Warwick suggests, can be drawn for the early post-Second War decades:

> If one adds the general impression that the 1950s were years of affluence, when Britons 'never had it so good', when total industrial output and productivity in industry were growing at rates twice those of the decades before 1914, when gross fixed investment as a proportion of gross national product was more than double the pre-war levels, the overall impression gained is one of substantial economic development throughout the post 1914 period up to at least 1970. (1985, p. 108)

However, while it is clear that there was growth in Britain's economy during these post-war decades it differed from the pre-war period in that the rate of growth on several indicators – especially productivity rates and per capita GNP – lagged behind that of many other advanced industrial countries

(Warwick, 1985, p. 108). Explanations within the endogenous school for this relatively poor performance range from an emphasis on the role of the labour force (excessive wage demands, restrictive practices, trade union power, strikes) to those which look to broader issues focusing on poor industrial organization and poor management. A rather more sophisticated version of these types of argument hypothesizes that Britain has suffered from 'pluralistic stagnation' which 'holds that economic growth is retarded by the demands for protection and government favour by all manner of producer groups whose potential for blackmail governments find difficult to ignore' (Warwick, 1985, p. 109). The suggestion here is that high wages, restrictive practices and support for 'lame-duck' industries have been connived in by successive governments to the detriment of the overall growth and health of the national economy. Unable to sustain high levels of profitability and productivity after the war, Britain fell even further behind the United States in the international economic league, being overtaken by France, Germany and then Italy and thereby surrendering its world-power status and role.

At this point the cruder economic arguments of the endogenous school merge with those that stress a 'failure of values' as the root cause of Britain's post-war economic and political decline. *Johnson*'s (1977) argument is illustrative: he suggests that in post-war Britain 'the prejudice in favour of state-provided welfare services – a public monopoly in the welfare business, justified by pleas on behalf of the "poor" – has worked against the achievement of a better understanding of social needs and economic possibilities'. His basic argument, which reflected much of the thinking of the **'new right'** philosophy of the late 1970s and 1980s, is that deflection of effort from the goals of growth and profit maximization towards 'egalitarianism', towards the equitable distribution of resources, fundamentally constrained the UK economy, preventing the realization of its growth potential. In essence the political and social objectives championed by all post-war governments during the period to the late 1970s has inhibited the growth of a healthy national economy, an essential prerequisite for sustaining a strong international presence.

Endogenous explanations for Britain's post-war decline, whether of the 'economic' or 'values' type, suffer from the reverse of the problem identified for exogenous perspectives: they pay too little attention to the global political and economic context in which Britain has had to operate. The internationalization of political and economic processes has been particularly marked since the 1950s (Harris, 1988). These international processes need to be considered (if only to be dismissed as of little or no relevance) in any explanation of Britain's post-war economic and political performance; this the endogenous school noticeably fails to do. That too much autonomy is attributed to the domestic policies of individual states by the endogenous school is further suggested by transnational comparisons. As one illustration only, all core countries with which Britain is unfavourably compared established welfare systems of some form during this period (*Taylor*, 1989).

1.3.3 Interrelational perspectives

We have seen that the exogenous and endogenous schools identified above make few concessions to the views of the other (though Taylor's version of the world-system perspective is more conciliatory in this respect). A third school of thought, adopting an interrelational perspective, attempts to move beyond this impasse and take account of both internal and external processes in seeking an explanation for Britain's post-war decline. As with the other schools, the **interrelational perspective** has a variety of versions which differ from each other in terms of how the exogenous and endogenous issues are reconciled. Following on the work of Strange (1971), Blank (1977) and Pollard (1982), *Brett* (1986) has explicitly developed a perspective which sees a strong causal relationship between Britain's attempts to maintain a centre country status and the declining fortunes of the domestic economy: that is, its international role has drained energies and resources to the detriment of domestic reconstruction and growth, and concomitantly weaknesses in the domestic economy have inhibited international performance. In his analysis Brett suggests that the balance of payments deficits of 1966, the devaluation of the pound in 1967, the reduction in the defence budget at that time from £2.5 billion to £2 billion (leading to the contraction of troop deployment in 1968) and Britain's decision in the Basle Agreement of 1968 no longer to be solely responsible for the management of sterling as a reserve currency, marked a major transformation of the country's international commitments, but too late for a decisive reshaping of the domestic economy.

As a way of illustrating the nature of the relationships between the domestic and the external, between the endogenous and exogenous as seen by the interrelational school, we can briefly examine two features of Britain's post-war experience, namely the structure of the country's internal social and economic geography and the highly internationalized nature of its capital.

Uneven development and the internationalization of capital

The great manufacturing belts of Britain in the north, south Wales, Scotland and Northern Ireland were created on the back of Empire and British international dominance in the nineteenth century. Supported by a free-trade system with intermittent tariff and trade barriers, the coal, iron and textile industries of these areas were promoted at the cost of other, sometimes flourishing, industries elsewhere in the world. And just as it was the growth of Empire and British global economic dominance that shaped the domestic space-economy of a century ago, so the retreat from Empire and the decline in that dominance lies at the heart of the regional problem today as it did at the time of its first appearance during the inter-war years. Anderson captures the sequence well:

> As the historic first-comer, British industrialisation arrived without deliberate design, and triumphed without comparable competitors ... it won world

> hegemony ... from the spontaneous force of its own chronological lead ...
> The easy dominance that British industry achieved in the first half of the
> nineteenth century laid down certain durable lines of development. The first
> country to mechanise textiles and build railways, Britain generated 'develop-
> ment blocs' of interrelated capitalist development around them, embodied in
> physical technologies and spatial regions which then took on massive historical
> interia. Its enterprises started out small in size, and provincial in location; and
> the family firm persisted as a typical ownership pattern long afterwards. Its
> labour force achieved forms of collective organisation long before any other,
> reflecting the decentralised company landscape and embodied in the early bloc
> of technologies. Once set these structures became progressively greater handi-
> caps in competition with later industrial economies – which started with newer
> fixed capital, embodied in more modern technology, larger entrepreneurial
> units, and less unionised workforces. (1982, p. 72)

Massive historical inertia prevailed because it was the decision of successive
British capitalists to persist in traditional industries, in which considerable
investment had already been made, and, rather than reinvest in the domestic
economy, to move capital overseas where profits were sometimes greater
and frequently more secure. The international orientation of British capital
has a long history and in that the tradition prevails it can be regarded as
another 'legacy of Empire'. The attractiveness of Indian and Latin America
as foci of such investment in the nineteenth century has already been noted;
through the earlier part of the twentieth century the sterling area and
especially the 'white' dominion territories emerged as the most common
destination, while today Europe and increasingly the United States are the
most favoured. Lack of reinvestment has contributed to the creeping loss of
competitiveness of British manufacturing and this has further encouraged
capital export. Table 1.1 illustrates the declining productivity of British
industry during the crucial period of the 1960s.

Both the USA and the Common Market countries recorded better output
and this lack of competitive edge in Britain compounded by the growth in
manufacturing production and exports in such countries as Japan and
Sweden established the context for an acceleration in the export of British
manufacturing capital. As Hudson and Williams (1986, p. 5) have observed
in 1950 only twenty-three UK manufacturing firms had six or more subsi-
diaries overseas; by 1960 there were thirty. Industrial capital was here
merely following a post-war trend already well established by finance capital: between 1946 and 1951, Brett tells us, £910 million of private investment
went to the sterling area while an additional £380 million was exported to the
rest of the world; this was reinforced by the overseas investment of £345
million of public money. Through the 1970s the export of capital became
characteristic not only of industrial and finance capital, but also of
institutional capital such as pension funds and unit trusts. The removal of all
capital export controls by the Conservative government on coming to power
in 1979 exacerbated the trend: the net overseas holdings of British capital
rose from £8000 million in 1979 to £28 000 million in 1981 and had reached
£80 000 million by 1986.

Table 1.1 Indices of industrial production

	The Six*	UK	USA
1958	100	100	100
1959	106	105	114
1960	119	113	117
1961	127	113	118
1962	135	114	128
1963	145	119	135
1964	152	128	144
1965	158	132	157
1966	167	133	172
1967	170	132	173

* France, West Germany, Italy, Belgium,
Netherlands, Luxembourg

Sources: OECD General Statistics; EEC General
Statistical Bulletin (after Boyd, 1975, p. 20)

While it is certainly the case that the continuing commitment of British
capital to overseas investment in preference to domestic investment has
been central to the post-war economic and social malaise of the country,
especially in the older manufacturing regions and inner-city areas, it is also
the case that this same commitment lies at the heart of the strength and
vigour of the British stock market and the influential international role that
the City of London plays on the world financial stage. Anderson (1982) sees
the years between 1963 and 1967 as crucial in this context. In the earlier year
when the US blocked foreign borrowers from the New York bond market,
the result was the creation of an offshore Eurodollar market into which the
British merchant banks moved quickly, a move which was encouraged by
the effective ending of the sterling area as a coherent economic zone
following the devaluation of the pound in 1967: 'London as a world financial
centre entered a new phase – of transformation and expansion – while
Britain as a manufacturing nation slid into stagnation' (Anderson, 1982, p.
61). Deregulation further encouraged this expansion and London has
emerged as a focus for considerable financial investment by foreign banks
and financial services. Here a booming economy – despite the hiccup of the
crash of 1987 – based on control of the world's financial markets and
associated with a burgeoning of professional services such as accountancy
and various legal activities, stands in stark contrast to the decaying industrial
landscapes of the traditional, empire-based regional economies. As Massey
argues:

> . . . a century of history of the British state shows it to be transfixed by a
> political and economic role once briefly held in the nineteenth century and no
> longer tenable . . . and the contradiction continues. In the twenty years since
> manufacturing employment began to fall in absolute terms, each dominant

political and economic strategy has in the end and under one pressure or another, sacrificed the interests of the home-based economy to those of banking capital and the internationalised sections of manufacturing industry. (1986, p. 50)

Summary of section 1.3

In this section we have looked in detail at three contrasting explanations of Britian's post-war decline.

● *Exogenous perspectives* look for explanations of this decline in the operation of the world economy of which Britain is part. The boom/slump cycle of that economy and the rise to world leadership of a new hegemonic power, the United States, are seen as the crucial processes.

● *Endogenous explanations* of Britain's post-war decline range from those that are based on a crude form of economic determinism whereby erroneous domestic economic priorities wasted resources and prevented Britain from fulfilling its economic potential, that is a weakened national economy led to international decline, to other versions which build on this domestic/international relationship but suggest that the root cause was a failure of 'values', such as the prioritizing of non-economic, egalitarian objectives which subverted economic growth and undermined the country's global position.

● In reconciling aspects of the endogenous and exogenous perspectives on the international decline of Britain, the *interrela.ional school* accepts the world-system categorization of the hegemonic rise and fall of Britain and the United States. Within the context of global economic and political trends, the interrelational perspective sees Britain as caught up in the traditions of its imperial past: imprisoned by this historical legacy Britain is unable to recognize its limited room for manoeuvre in the changed economic and political circumstances of the post-war period and in a vain attempt to preserve its status as a world power, it squanders whatever advantages it had over other industrialized countries to the detriment of its domestic economy. Britain today, as the next chapter will demonstrate, still suffers from that legacy.

1.4   Conclusion

A recurring theme of domestic politics since the early 1970s has been the question of what posture Britain should assume to the outside world. With some degree of simplification, but not I think distortion, we can identify three such postures. First, 'protectionism', a policy most closely associated with the Labour Party in the mid-1970s. This policy argued for the erection of import and trade barriers behind which fledgling British industry supported by public financial investment would be protected and allowed to grow. Second, a posture which favours further and more integrated links with the European Community, a policy which has been supported by a variety of factions from each of the main political parties. Third, an 'Atlanticist' posture which has a number of versions ranging from the pragmatic, which stresses the continuing close economic, military and cultural links between Britain and the United States, to that version, which, as assumed by Mrs Thatcher at least, echoes with Churchillian imperialist illusions, whereby Britain takes a leading position on the world stage as a representative of western interests. The details of these positions are not of concern here, rather they are identified in order to illustrate that all the main political positions in Britain recognize the importance of exogenous issues in determining the condition of Britain's domestic economy and policy. They also illustrate that countries such as Britain do have choices to make; there is no autarky in an increasingly internationalized world, but there are alternative strategies for dealing with such a world and the choice between these marks the limit of nation-state autonomy.

Further reading

A good introduction to and coverage of the historical background to the issues covered in this chapter are provided by Paul Warwick's article 'Did Britain change? An inquiry into the causes of national decline' (*Journal of Contemporary History*, Vol. 20, No. 1, pp. 99–133). This article is particularly useful in that it identifies the major themes of the controversy surrounding the decline of Britain in the late ninteenth century and traces them through to the post-1945 period.

The book edited by Steve Smith, Michael Smith and Brian White, *British Foreign Policy: Tradition, Change and Transformation* (London, Unwin Hyman; 1988), provides an accessible coverage of recent debates – philosophical and analytical – in political science on the subject of change in British foreign policy in the post-war decades.The introductory chapter, 'The analytical background', is particularly useful in this respect.

Finally, for an entertaining and detailed insight into the motivations and behaviour of a variety of politicians with different party affiliations, when faced with an international crisis, Anthony Barnett's 1982 article, 'Iron Britannia' (*New Left Review*, No. 134, pp. 5–96), on the Falklands/Malvinas conflict, cannot be bettered.

2 Britain's political crisis

Allan Cochrane

Contents

2.1 Introduction

2.1.1 Defining political crisis

There is a more or less commonly accepted interpretation of the politics of the post-war period in the UK which is probably familiar to most of us. It suggests that there was a consensus between the main political parties structured around the ideas and programmes of Beveridge and Keynes, endorsed in what has been called the post-war settlement, which finally fractured on the reefs of economic crisis in the middle to late 1970s. This interpretation is broad enough to attract the agreement of writers from a wide variety of theoretical and political traditions. It has not been the property of left or right, liberal or pluralist, Marxist or conservative, but has been shared and reinterpreted by each approach.

If there has been broad agreement that there was a **political crisis** of some sort in the 1970s, however, not only have the precise reasons for it been sharply debated, but the very nature of the crisis has itself been a matter of serious contention. One of the problems is that the notion of crisis has been significantly devalued by its over-use in the discussion of twentieth-century British politics. On the one hand in the contemporary writing of each decade the British political system seems to be lurching from one 'crisis' to another, yet at the same time the most striking feature of British politics over the longer period has probably been its remarkable stability. If the notion of crisis is not to be reduced to the trivial detail of everyday policies, as this or that Cabinet Minister is replaced or disgraced, or even as governments change, then it needs to be considered more carefully.

So one question which needs to be settled right at the start, before it is possible to consider whether there has been one in the recent past, is what a political crisis would look like. In many ways economic crises seem easier to define in objective terms – for example, in terms of falls in output or increases in unemployment. But it is difficult, even in discussing the economy, to distinguish between major crises and less important cyclical fluctuations. As the underlying argument of *The Economy in Question* (Allen and Massey (eds), 1988) suggests, what matters in making such judgements is whether or not a significant structural change (or set of structural changes) can be identified as arising out of the 'crisis' (see, in particular, the discussion of structural change by Allen in Chapter 3 of that book). Deciding whether structural change has taken place is not straightforward, even with the help of available economic statistics. As Massey (1988a) shows, it involves theoretical choices as well as empirical judgements.

This is equally, if not more, important in considering political crises, particularly if there is no *a priori* presumption that political crisis is a more or less direct and automatic consequence of economic crisis. No such assumption is made in this chapter. Since 1945 state and economy in the advanced capitalist countries have become increasingly intertwined in a way which makes it impossible sensibly to disentangle them, or sharply to distinguish between political and economic spheres. Even the rediscovery of market economics at the end of the 1970s was expressed through the endorsement of changing political leaderships – such as Reagan in the USA and Thatcher in the UK. O'Connor's description of the system as 'political capitalism' (O'Connor, 1987, p. 127) seems particularly apt.

According to O'Connor, theories of crisis which focus on economic explanations as somehow underlying the experience of wider social and political crises fail to acknowledge the significance of mass political democracy in the twentieth century. Mass democracy implies the need for a wider social consensus about the directions to be taken by state and economy. Unless this is achieved, there is a danger of political crisis – or '**legitimation crisis**'. For neo-Marxists, says O'Connor,

> **legitimation** depends on the capacity of the political system to secure a consensus of political policies from groups which either will not benefit or will be harmed by capitalist accumulation . . . the capacity to secure consensus is threatened when political parties and politicians who make claims that they are able to manage capitalism and accumulation successfully cannot in fact do so. (1987, pp. 110–11)

Economic crisis cannot be resolved without the involvement of the state and states have themselves been directly responsible in the generation of economic crisis. As Habermas has put it, 'the laws of the economic system are no longer identical with those analysed by Marx' in the nineteenth century, because of 'interference from the political system'. He argues that a new theory is needed which starts from 'the interaction of economics, politics and culture' (quoted in O'Connor, 1987, p. 134). Elsewhere, he suggests that 'if governmental crisis management fails, it lags behind the programmatic demands that it has placed on itself. The penalty of this failure is the withdrawal of legitimation' (Habermas, 1976, p. 69).

This analysis helps to provide a context for twentieth-century political crises, but it does not help a great deal in analysing the process of actual political crises. Once legitimation has been withdrawn, it is difficult to see how it can effectively be reconstructed, or how new forms of legitimation may be developed. Yet, as we have already suggested, it is in part by identifying a process of restructuring or structural change that it is possible to recognize a crisis. According to Leys, Habermas' model provides 'a checklist of possible sources of crisis in advanced capitalist countries in general', but it is not very helpful in analysing specific crises, and, in particular, that of Britain in the 1960s and 1970s (*Leys*, 1983, p. 25). Nevertheless, it is possible to develop a reasonable working definition of crisis. Like *Leys* (1983, pp. 25–6) I think it is useful to borrow some ideas from the Italian Marxist Gramsci although it is by no means necessary to be a Marxist to find these helpful. The definition drawn from these should be used as a guide rather than a universal model. It would be a mistake to impose it like a straitjacket on developing political events.

Gramsci suggests that in normal times the stability of state and politics in modern democracies is sustained by the relatively unchallenged permeation of a more or less coherent set of ideas throughout society which ties most members of that society by invisible, ideological, threads to existing social and political relations. Following this approach a crisis can be defined as a 'dissolution of the ideology that secures the consent of the mass of the population to the existing order' (*Leys*, 1983, p. 25). At this point for Gramsci, the crisis can be resolved either (and more likely) by the old dominant class restoring 'control by means of a new philosophy, new men [and, presumably, women] and new programmes; but an opportunity also arises to prevent this, to create a new "historic bloc" under the leadership of a new, more popular alliance of classes' (*Leys*, 1983, p. 25).

It is not necessary to share Gramsci's commitment to this second option to accept the force of his argument about political crisis. The key point for our purposes is that a crisis can be defined as the point at which existing political arrangements cannot continue as before and no longer have widespread and taken-for-granted popular allegiance. And the implication of this is that the resolution of such a crisis will take the form of **structural change** in which a changed set of alliances based on alternative philosophies becomes the basis for a new period of stability – or 'normality'. In the case of post-war Britain, as we shall see, the story is more one of rearrangement and restructuring from above than of challenge from below.

Some of the implications of using this definition of political crisis may not be immediately apparent, so it is probably worth spelling them out. It means that the focus of our discussion will largely be on political developments within Britain. That may seem obvious, but it should not simply be taken for granted. It has two main implications. The first is that the consideration of the international context tends to be handled through an approach close to that of *Brett* whose arguments are discussed in the previous chapter. In other words there is an implicit acceptance that the interrelationships between Britain and the rest of the world are largely reflected through changes in balances of economic and political power between states. It makes it more difficult to focus on the importance of general global trends and the ways in which Britain may relate to them. Secondly, and similarly, it encourages a focus on actual political developments – that is, on what political actors and state institutions do. It tends to draw attention away from more abstract discussions of political systems and their inherent strengths and weaknesses (such as those associated with Offe and Habermas).

2.1.2   Questions about crisis

In the debates about Britain's 'crisis' there has been a clear tension between those who stress political factors and those who emphasize economic influences. *Johnson* (1977, Ch. 1), for example, has argued that the post-war settlement was fundamentally flawed from the start in political terms, making promises which could never be fulfilled, and encouraging a personal reliance on state support, which in turn not only undermined Britain's prospects for economic success, but also threatened the legitimacy of its forms of democratic government. Others have suggested that the system only began to fall apart when the Keynesian element of the welfare state failed to deliver the goods in the face of world economic crisis and the sharpness of Britain's problems within it. In other words, economic failure brought political failure. As Ramesh Mishra put it, 'The state's ability to manage the mixed economy, of which the social welfare factor is an integral part, is in serious doubt. In many ways it is this loss of confidence that is at the heart of the crisis' (1984, p. xiii).

A second crucial question is the extent to which, following the formulation introduced in Chapter 1, the 'crisis' is understood principally as an endogenous (UK-based) phenomenon or one which is the consequence of exogenous political and economic pressures. The post-war settlement to which we have referred above needs to be seen both as a British settlement – between classes, between different interest groups – and a global one, between nations and national capitals as well as, potentially, between global classes, if one follows Wallerstein's arguments (see *Taylor*, 1989). Whatever the conclusion, it must be clear that exogenous factors cannot be ignored. If, for example, there are world-wide economic cycles (like those identified by Kondratiev and discussed by Harris (1988)) then the UK economy, too, will be affected. If there is a process of economic and political restructuring taking place at global level (reflected, for example, in the new international division of labour which Harris discusses or in the development of new dominant hegomonic powers which *Taylor* considers), then the UK's position will also be likely to change. If capitalism generally is entering a new phase (whether described as post-Fordism as discussed by Meegan (1988), or the move from organized to disorganized capitalism as Lash and Urry (1987) suggest) then the UK cannot escape the consequences.

A third issue which needs to be considered here is whether the term 'crisis' is at all appropriate to the post-war British experience. In a sense this is an underlying concern throughout this chapter, and there are a number of ways of formulating it. One would simply suggest that there has been a gradual process of organic change since the war, with few sudden jumps and no crises. Such an approach has its attractive features. As indicated above there does seem to have been a remarkable degree of political continuity since the war: elected government has succeeded elected government, the major political parties continue to debate with little threat of violent upheaval (outside Northern Ireland) and the unity of the UK state has survived. On the other hand, there has been a widespread feeling that major changes have taken place through the late 1960s and 1970s: that those years somehow marked a political watershed as well as an economic one. Just as it would be a mistake to see crisis behind every example of political conflict, so it might be to miss the onset of crisis simply because major state institutions have survived.

Another way of questioning any very sharply focused notion of crisis is to suggest that instead we have been witnessing a rather longer process of decline, to which the institutions of state and politics have gradually and subtly adjusted, while retaining continued links with the past. Britain's post-war experience can be understood, more positively, not so much as an adjustment to decline but to a changing world role and a changing economic base. One US commentator, after criticizing the descriptions of crisis to be found in the newspapers and magazines of the 1970s, has even suggested that Britain provides a tolerable model of the post-industrial society which other nations might choose to follow. Excluding Northern Ireland, he describes Britain at the end of the decade as 'a comfortable, decent, creative place, burdened with problems as are all industrial societies, but moving hesitantly towards a more civilized life' (Nossiter, 1978, p. 200).

This is *so* unlike the image of Britain which has come to dominate discussion that it is tempting simply to dismiss it. That, too, would be a mistake, since it is a valuable corrective to the rather careless use of 'crisis' as a term to be scattered around whenever problems of one sort or another are identified. On the other hand it also appeals rather too easily to another prejudice, widely shared in Britain, which stresses an effortless but probably illusionary continuity reflected in the widespread attachment to 'heritage' described by Nigel Thrift (1989), which makes it difficult to understand how substantial change is ever achieved. The idea of a longer period of change – commonly understood as decline – is a useful one, however, and can be fitted quite well into a crisis model, if the process of decline suddenly accelerates or requires a dramatic response from a political system which has changed at a different rate (see Gamble, 1985).

Instead of understanding political crisis as a simple process which occurs when certain clearly identifiable features and symptoms are present, it may be more appropriate to approach it through a model which stresses the importance of a series of interactions: so that we do not have to choose between political or economic causes; endogenous *or* exogenous causes; an immediate *or* long-term basis. In each period, it is important to consider the actual process of political development, instead of trying to read off some necessary conclusion from a given set of inputs into a theoretically derived model. In the 1930s, for example, despite high levels of unemployment (and international economic crisis) there does not seem to have been a major political crisis in Britain, while in the 1970s the onset of economic and political crisis seems to have coincided.

Activity 2.1

Looking back at Chapter 1, what do you consider to be the main features of the international context for political developments in the UK in the late 1960s and 1970s?

Summary of section 2.1

- As a working definition we start from the notion (drawn from Gramsci) that there is a political crisis when the old ideological 'glue' which binds society together through the institutions of the state loses its force and a new one is developed in the process of restructuring, whether from above or as the result of challenge from below.

- Three issues arise:
    - the relationship between economic and political factors in generating the crisis
    - the relative importance of exogenous and endogenous factors
    - whether there has been a 'crisis' in Britain at all, rather than a 'long decline' or adjustment to a changing world role.

- It is helpful to view the British 'crisis' in terms of a series of interactions between different factors rather than having a single cause, or even a simple moment.

2.2   When and what was the British crisis?

2.2.1   The crisis of the 1970s

Perhaps the extent of academic, journalistic and popular agreement that the 1970s saw some sort of political crisis should make us immediately suspicious, yet they do seem to have marked an important watershed or turning-point for British politics. Some of the key features of 'crisis' identified in our working definition were clearly present. It was widely acknowledged that it was no longer possible to go on as before, even if it was less clear what the alternatives were.

In his survey of Britain in the 1970s, *Guardian* journalist Norman Shrapnel says that they 'saw crisis become a daily condition of life' and that neatly sums up the dominant retrospective interpretation of the period (Shrapnel, 1986, p. 13). These were the years when it seemed that the social-democratic state was finally tested and found wanting. According to an editorial in the *Times*, Britain suffered from a 'depressing lack of purpose, lack of faith' (Nossiter, 1978, p. 11). The daily news was dominated by tales of strikes, factory closures and rising prices. State-sponsored **Keynesian** economic intervention failed to deliver the economic goods of growth and prosperity, and the Beveridge-inspired **welfare state** failed to deal effectively with problems of poverty, particularly in the face of rising unemployment and inflation. In part these failures might be explained in terms of the impact of world recession and the break-up of the international system described in Chapter 1, but it was Britain's particular version of the post-war settlement and the assumptions underlying it which were under assault.

Table 2.1 Governments of crisis: UK governments of the 1960s and 1970s

1959–64	Conservative government: Macmillan PM to 1962, followed by Douglas-Home
1964–66	Labour government: Wilson PM
1966–70	Labour government: Wilson PM
1970–74	Conservative government: Heath PM
1974 Feb–Oct	Labour minority government: Wilson PM
1974 Oct–1979	Labour government (minority government from 1978): Wilson PM to 1976, followed by Callaghan
1979–83	Conservative government: Thatcher PM

Leys graphically charts the developing crisis from the 1960s and into the 1970s (1983, Chs 5 and 6), stressing its interlocking elements as economic failure and political inadequacy came together. He indicates how the UK experience has to be understood in the context of international economic crisis and of relative economic decline. But he also argues that the economic crisis was largely an 'endogenous' one:

> What distinguishes the British experience, however, and underlines more clearly than anything else its 'endogenous' nature, is that in Britain the new crisis had already begun in the 1960s – a decade of unparalleled prosperity for the rest of the industrialized world. The worldwide accumulation crisis of the 1970s did not cause the British crisis, it only made it worse. (*Leys*, 1983, p. 66)

By the mid-1970s Leys notes that the failure of the two main political parties in terms of economic management led to declining electoral support for both of them. From a post-war peak of nearly 80 per cent of the electorate (97 per cent of those voting) voting for one or other of them in 1951, the figure was down to around 55 per cent in October 1974 (75 per cent of those voting) (Leys 1983, Table 5.1; Table 4.1 in associated Reader). *Leys* comments:

> This reflected more than loss of confidence in the parties' leaderships. The social-democratic values to which even the Conservatives had subscribed during the 1950s were losing some of their authority. The parties themselves, faced with the intractable problem of economic decline, became increasingly polarised. Political currents previously considered 'extreme' – the market-orientated doctrines of the 'new right' and the more radical socialist views of the 'Labour left' – gained ground in the parties outside parliament, and, in the case of the Conservatives, captured control inside the parliamentary party as well in 1975. (1983, p. 65)

2.2.2 The end of the social-democratic state?

Following the political confusion of the 1970s, it is tempting to view the election of the Conservative government in 1979 as marking a break with institutionalized arrangements of bargaining between state, big business and the trade unions and with the universalist welfare state which can be summed up as the British version of **social democracy**. In their place as an almost inevitable reaction, it could be argued, there was an endorsement of individualistic and market methods in economy and welfare. This is essentially the case argued by *Johnson* (1977; also 1987). For him the crisis of the 1970s was fundamentally a political one – a crisis of democratic government in the welfare state. In the late 1970s Johnson criticized what he saw as a dominant – consensus – belief in the 'providential power' of government, which encouraged a political system in which parties competed by offering greater and greater promises of economic and welfare benefits, both to the electorate and to major corporate interests (particularly trade unions). This either brought the political system into disrepute, because the parties and governments could not deliver the goods, or (still worse from his point of view) put intolerable strains on the economic system by the imposition of taxation or the growth of public borrowing to meet the demands. In a vivid comparison, he argues that successive governments of both parties had been persuaded

> ... to tolerate a steadily growing mortgage on the future in order to facilitate rising consumption standards and increasing public benefits in the present. More and more the political economy of the country has been adapted to principles which governed the domestic economy of that sweet and feckless woman, Madam Ranevskaya, in Chekhov's *The Cherry Orchard*. Surrounded by old retainers and importunate hangers-on she maintained a state far beyond what her income would support, struggling against change and the threat to the cherry orchard. Yet in the end it had to be chopped down and Madame Ranevskaya made way for that vulgar but successful capitalist, Lopakhin. (*Johnson*, 1977, p. 23)

Although writing from a position which would generally be regarded as being on the right, *Johnson* (1977) is highly critical of Britain's 'conservative political order' and suggests the need for 'deliberate attempts to re-fashion the rules of political order and to adopt new methods of political co-operation which in turn will compel those subject to them to see the world they live in differently'. The echoes of Gramsci's position in this formulation seem clear, and equally clear, too, is the call for structural change in the political sphere. Johnson espouses a break with the continuity of post-1945 British political arrangements, and in 1987 he confirmed that – for him – this break had taken place with the election of a Conservative government in 1979, with Mrs Thatcher playing the role of Lopakhin to the social-democratic cherry tree. That election brought 'far more than a mere swing of the pendulum in the two-party competition. Instead it brought far-reaching policy innovation combined with genuine conservatism in relation to institutions and political methods. By gradually redefining its role, the government regained its capacity to govern' (Johnson, 1987, p. 55).

This optimistic conclusion, however, which implies an almost logical necessity about the arrival of what has been popularly described as 'Thatcherism' is one which is not universally accepted. Some would argue – as *Leys* (1983) does, for example – that other choices are also on offer, although it is important to note that they have not (yet?) generated alliances capable of challenging those constructed around the agenda of the political right. It may also understate the continuity of state policy in attempting to find some way of restructuring in response to – or as a way out of – a longer period of decline.

2.2.3 The pressures for modernization

Another strongly argued critique of the politics and economics of the post-war period from the right (Barnett, 1986, Corelli rather than Anthony Barnett), suggests, like *Johnson* (1977), that the institutionalization of the Beveridge proposals meant that Britain was committing itself to a dangerous illusion, as a result of which welfare spending would be a growing drain on the productive sector – that is, the profits of private industry – 'uncontrollably guzzling taxes which might have gone into productive investment and spewing them out again indiscriminately to the poor and the prosperous' (Barnett, 1986, p. 141). He is particularly scathing about Beveridge and his supporters whom he dismisses as mere utopians – 'New Jerusalemists'.

Unlike Johnson, however, and most others on what has come to be called the 'new right', Barnett's argument places the 'failure' of 1945 in the context of earlier failure in the rearmament of the 1930s and the planning of the war economy itself. He suggests that the period of the 1930s and early 1940s marked the end of Britain as an independent power and confirmed it as a client state of the United States, without whose financial and industrial support Britain would have been unable to fight the Second World War. In this sense he places Britain's decline firmly in the international context, almost as a consequence of the rise of US power, albeit assisted by the responses of the British political establishment. Although not entirely consistent about this, Barnett argues that the key issue was industrial and economic **modernization** and he criticizes those within government and the state who were not prepared to take on industrial vested interests – employers as well as trade unions and workforces.

Once the problem is defined in this way, however, the state's role in the economic crisis and the nature of the political crisis arising from it need to be reconsidered. Instead of following a logic which says that post-war political history has been dominated first (up until the late 1970s) by the extension of the state and of state intervention into the economy and then by the rolling back of the state, it may be more appropriate to ask how the forms of state involvement and activity have changed. The *failure* of the state and hence the context of its restructuring may be a different one from that which is implied by Johnson's interpretation, and others which focus on the state's withdrawal from intervention as an explanatory factor (this issue is discussed further from the perspective of an economist in the next chapter).

These issues may become clearer if we consider an earlier period of state restructuring which is sometimes forgotten in the rush to characterize the *whole* post-war period as one of consensus. When Labour came to power in

1964 under Harold Wilson, its leader claimed to be breaking with a British post-war tradition of cosy arrangements within what was then often described as the 'establishment' (for example, Thomas, 1959). Then, too, questions were being raised about the state of British economy and society: it was a 'stagnant society' (Shanks, 1961), capital investment was low compared to that in Japan and Western Europe, already the rate of economic growth was lagging behind those of its main competitors, even if it was relatively high by historic (British) standards: 'The result was a feeling of profound concern and an acceptance of relative decline, which was taking place on a massive scale' (Sked, 1987, p. 3).

Although the programme of the new Labour government can be seen as continuing with past traditions in the sense that 'it assumed that social harmony was a permanent feature of British society' (Warde, 1982, p. 94), its promise was a rather different one. It stressed the state's role in the process of modernization, as Warde puts it, attempting to *restructure* consensus, rather than accepting its existing assumptions. Although Warde's argument refers principally to consensus within the Labour Party, it can usefully be extended to the wider political environment. The key slogans of the Labour Party stressed the need for a new technological revolution, linking science, planning and the state in a powerful set of images summarized in the, unfortunately apocryphal, promise of the 'white-hot heat of the technological revolution'. Warde quotes an enthusiastic Tony Benn from this period:

> What Britain needs today is more than modernization. What is wrong is that so much talent is wasted and so many opportunities are missed because people are not able to develop their full potential. The regeneration of Britain can only be achieved by releasing energy now bottled up by outdated traditions and methods and the maintenance of obsolete privileges. (Benn, 1965, p. 31; quoted in Warde, 1982, p. 97)

In the event Labour's promises of modernization bore only very limited fruit. There was little evidence of a developed link between science and the state, despite a major expansion of higher education through the 1960s. Attempts at national indicative planning soon foundered, with the ill-fated National Plan, and the early demise of the Department of Economic Affairs, although the increased importance accorded to the National Economic Development Organization survived until the late 1970s. Proposals for trade union reform outlined in the White Paper, *In Place of Strife*, were dropped in 1969 because of opposition in the Labour Party and trade unions and attempts to control inflation and increase productivity through a Prices and Income Board, accepted by unions and employers, were largely discredited as wages continued to rise with little apparent connection to productivity rates. The Industrial Reorganization Corporation (IRC) did succeed in encouraging some significant mergers within British industry (for instance, in electrical engineering and the car industry) which were intended to make the merged corporations more competitive. It achieved major rationalizations as older plants were closed, but its success was limited both because of the scale of the problem and because of its limited financial resources. The IRC model, however, was one which was taken up and developed in the 1970s through the National Enterprise Board, which also inherited the task of supporting some of its offspring – most notably British Leyland.

Returning to the points made by Barnett earlier, the task of state-led 'modernization' was acknowledged, but as in the 1930s and 1940s, there was little chance of carrying it through without challenging major corporate interests, in the form of major companies and trade unions. A contemporary commentator of the early 1960s argued that a major obstacle to change 'was the national hypocrisy about modernization and change. The fashionable belief among both parties for a long time was that if a country was to get moving it needed not a new financial policy but more fundamental changes in its industrial and business structure. Yet whenever any such structural change was proposed opposition immediately burst out from all sides' (Brittan, 1971, p. 290). Warde comments that, 'ultimately, capital and organized labour refused to co-operate with the government when their interests were adversely affected. The technical and administrative wisdom of state planning left the corporate interests cold' (1982, p. 118).

2.2.4 Towards a new settlement?

The point of this discussion is not to argue for or against the nostrums presented in the 1960s, but to indicate that even in the relatively recent past other strategies for modernization have been on the political agenda which did not necessarily imply the particular forms adopted in the second half of the 1970s and the 1980s. Indeed, if the task of modernization (and particularly economic modernization) is a central one for the British state, it may be that the changes introduced after 1979 should be seen as an initial shock, which heralds a more explicit and deliberate state-inspired programme of modernization in the future. Perhaps it is even buried beneath the surface of a politics which stresses individual initiative and enterprise.

This seems to be the implication of arguments developed by Keith Middlemas (1979, 1986), although he might not draw the same conclusions from the wealth of fascinating historical detail which he presents. Middlemas identifies a long-term trend or tendency in British politics (dating back to Lloyd George) of what he calls '**corporate bias**'. This implies the recognition of a set of corporate interests with a political legitimacy quite separate from that of the institution of representative democracy (see Middlemas, 1979, Ch. 13). Middlemas does not suggest that we are in any sense living in a corporate state like Mussolini's Italy (hence the emphasis on 'bias' and 'tendency'), but that the experience of British politics in the twentieth century can best be understood through looking at the changing balance between the state and representatives of big business and the organized workforce – as reflected today in the Confederation of British Industry and the Trades Union Congress, but also in less formally constituted organizations. 'Corporate bias', he says, is 'the tendency of industrial, trade union and financial institutions to make reciprocal arrangements with each other and with government while avoiding overt conflict' (Middlemas, 1986, p. 1). It 'presumes a common interest not only in avoidance of major sources of conflict but in the furtherance of a mixed economy' (1986, p. 5).

Like many other analysts of post-war Britain, Middlemas sees the '1944' settlement symbolized by Beveridge and Keynes, as a key moment. ('1944' because it pre-dates the election of a Labour government in the following year and thus implies a wider cross-party consensus.) Unlike Barnett, who stresses the disorganized nature of Britain's response to war and the need for increased (and more efficient) production, Middlemas argues that 'Britain developed in wartime a level of economic organization, technological innovation and efficient production without parallel in modern history, and did so almost without political or social conflict' (1986, p. 7). This was possible, he says, because of the ways in which the major corporate interests – and the trade unions, in particular – were integrated into the political system as 'governing institutions'. Addison also stresses the importance of war-time negotiation between these interests for the settlement finally arrived at later (Addison, 1975). Like many commentators, Middlemas believes that the form of this settlement was inherently unstable, even if that instability was not to become apparent for twenty to thirty years.

Schwarz neatly summarizes the analysis as follows:

> The picture which emerges is one which depicts the post-war bargain not only breaking with the past but becoming 'an organic part of the state'. Yet the upshot of Middlemas' analysis would suggest that it was a political contract built on an unsustainable economic basis, requiring the pursuit of impossible economic objectives, an instability constitutive of the post-war settlement itself. (1987, p. 115)

A crucial element of this instability, for Middlemas, was the position of the British settlement within the wider international one, described by Doherty. It was based on an assumption about the continued international economic strength of Britain symbolized by a commitment to sterling as world currency. In this sense the crisis could not simply be seen as an 'endogenous' one, and it was clearly also influenced by the outward orientation of key sectors of the British economy (see Harris, 1988). It has to be understood as part of an international system characterized by uneven development between the states which comprise it. Britain's crisis was also the consequence of the country's past position within that system and its relationship to changes within it.

> Given the initial agreement for reconstructing the economy with such a high degree of dependence on Sterling as a world currency . . ., attention became focused on the domestic economy, the gravitational pull of inflation, the 'exploitation' of the scarcity of labour by the unions and thus – by this stage of reasoning, inevitably – on the very possibility of sustaining full employment at all. This was the dynamic on which the settlement was based, triggering time

and again that irregular but long, reaction to the settlement itself which was to culminate in what we now call Thatcherism. (Schwarz, 1987, pp. 115–16)

The onset of political crisis, in this analysis, predates the late or even mid-1970s. For Middlemas the 1965–75 period is the key crisis period: 'Like an overloaded electrical circuit, the system began to blow more fuses than electricians could cope with in that dismal decade' (1979, p. 459). But, to continue with the analogy for a moment, for him the crisis cannot be resolved by the withdrawal of the 'electricians' (in the form of the state) from corporate arrangements or attempts to sustain the positive operation of the 'mixed economy'. On the contrary, that would be likely to bring continued instability. The importance of different elements in the 'governing institutions' may change from time to time, as one becomes more powerful at the expense of others, for example, because of shifts in their relative economic bargaining power (trade unions may be more powerful at times of full employment and employers' organizations at times of high unemployment: in Britain's case commercial and financial capital, too, may be more or less influential than industrial capital at different times). But, on the logic of Middlemas' argument, it is difficult to see how any of them can be completely disenfranchised without fundamentally disrupting unspoken assumptions about British politics and society, and bringing the promise of future uncertainty and conflict.

If this analysis is accepted, then the apparent exclusion of trade unions from the state sponsored decision-making in the 1980s has to be explained. It certainly looked as if they had been relegated from the ranks of the 'governing institutions'. One way of reconciling the developments of the 1980s with a longer-term indentification of 'corporate bias' may be to set them in a longer historical context. Instead of viewing the 1964–79 period as one in which increasingly desperate attempts were made to find some way of sustaining the post-war consensus in the face of failure, it could instead be seen as one in which attempts were being made to achieve a new settlement which rejected many elements associated with '1944', but continued to have at its centre the notion of a settlement and the acknowledgement of corporate interests not easily reflected in the structures of representative democracy or political parties.

From this perspective the various attempts to negotiate more or less open compromises by corporate methods through organizations such as the National Economic Development Council, the Industrial Reorganization Corporation and the National Enterprise Board and through arrangements such as the National Plan and the 'Social Contract' would be seen as attempts to shift the basis of the Keynes–Beveridge settlement, rather than attempts to prolong it. Middlemas (1986) charts the attempts of senior state officials to carry through reforms, to reflect what they (and he) perceived as the broader interests of society, to manage and restructure the settlement. According to him, they were the first to note the inherent flaws of '1944', although they – or their predecessors had been crucial to the development of that settlement, too. Unfortunately for the argument, however, this fails to account for the marked reluctance of these officials to contemplate restructuring of the state – reflected, for example, in the ignominious demise of the Department of Economic Affairs in the mid-1960s in the face of hostility from the Treasury. In any case, this group of officials – however far-sighted – effectively failed to achieve the restructuring they were looking for in the two decades of the 1960s and 1970s.

Part of the task was to renegotiate the dominant social understanding of the post-war settlement, according to which expectations of welfare, full employment and consumption continued to be high, while the possibilities of delivery were increasingly low. The attempted 'deals' failed not because of any lack of goodwill at national level, but because the organizations represented found it far more difficult to commit their members in the context of economic decline. Major capitalists firms showed a marked lack of interest in state-sponsored restructuring whenever it affected them directly; trade unions found it difficult to maintain incomes policies which restricted the wages of their members in times of inflation.

Within this framework, the key pressures facing state and politics in the United Kingdom in the 1960s and 1970s are clearly linked to economic issues. Moves to modernize state and economy went hand in hand. The implications of such an analysis for assessing the changes which took place at the end of the 1970s may be significant. Instead of seeing them as marking the end of corporatist arrangements at national level, perhaps they can be seen as offering a new basis on which such arrangements can be achieved – providing a shock to the system which forces the major participants to reconsider their positions over a longer period. The 1980s might be seen as a decade in which the ground rules were shifted and underlying assumptions changed, in particular about welfare spending, employment and trade union power, so that the negotiation of new compromises would be possible in the 1990s. This is not an issue to be developed further here, but underlies many of the questions considered in later chapters, where particular aspects of political restructuring are examined.

Activity 2.2

Leys, Johnson, Barnett and Middlemas all agree that there was some sort of political crisis in Britain in the 1960s and 1970s. But their interpretations of that 'crisis' vary significantly. Try to:

(a) identify the period in which the crisis had its origins and the nature of those origins; and

(b) indicate the nature of the crisis and its impact.

Key issues to take into account are:

- whether its roots were endogenous or exogenous
- whether its causes were primarily economic or political
- what the significance of the Keynes–Beveridge settlement was.

	Origins	*Impact*
Leys		
Johnson		
Barnett		
Middlemas		

What implications do you think these differences in historical analysis might have for the forms taken by restructuring to resolve the crisis identified?

Summary of section 2.2

- The late 1960s and the 1970s are widely recognized to have been a period of political crisis in Britain.

- Leys stresses a context of continued relative economic decline from which neither major party seemed able to escape.

- Johnson emphasizes the inherent weaknesses of the post-war settlement, identified with Beveridge and Keynes, which undermined the widespread acceptance of political democracy by encouraging the making of promises which could not be met. For him the election of the Thatcher government heralded a break with corporatist methods and a confirmation of economic individualism.

- Barnett stresses the failure of the British state in the 1930s and suggests that a more conscious state policy of restructuring and modernizing the economy is required. Labour's policies of the 1960s and 1970s and the Conservatives' in the early 1970s can be seen as attempts to achieve this, which foundered on an inability to carry the major corporate interests of business and unions with the programme.

- Middlemas suggests that the key political issue of the post-war period is the negotiation of a new settlement between these interests and the state, around which a wider programme of modernization can be taken forward. He implies that no single element of the corporate 'governing institutions' can be disenfranchised for an extended period if a mixed economy is to remain the basis of development in Britain.

2.3 The not so United Kingdom

2.3.1 The rise of the nationalists

If the precise form taken by Britain's crisis can only be understood by placing it in the context of uneven development on an international scale (as

Table 2.2   Votes for nationalist parties in Scotland and Wales (percentage of votes cast per opposed candidate)

	Scotland	Wales
1964	10.7	8.4
1966	14.1	8.7
1970	12.2	11.5
1974 (Feb.)	21.9	10.7
1974 (Oct.)	30.0	10.8
1979	17.3	8.1

This table may understate the extent of the voting shifts from the 1960s, because these figures reflect the share of votes in constituencies where nationalist candidates stood. The parties had candidates in more constituencies in later elections, so that in 1974 and 1979 the share of the vote is the same as the percentage of the (Welsh and Scottish) national vote. In 1966 their share of the national vote would have been about half the level it was in the seats where nationalist candidates stood.

Source: Leys, 1983, Table 11.1

Chapter 1 and the previous section have suggested), it is equally important to understand the significance of uneven development within the UK. One aspect of this (the importance of locality) will be taken up further in Chapter 6, but here we shall consider the importance of **nationalist** movements in reinforcing the sense of crisis associated with the 1960s and 1970s (see Table 2.2).

There was a major growth of nationalist parties in Wales and Scotland over this period. In the late 1960s nationalists won or came close to winning a series of previously safe Labour seats in parliamentary by-elections and local government elections in Wales and Scotland. Although their share of the vote in the 1970 General Election was low by the standards of the Labour and Conservative Parties it was substantially higher than its previous post-war peak.

In 1974, although Plaid Cymru had lost electoral support in Wales, the Scottish National Party replaced the Conservatives as the second party in Scotland in voting share, although the 11 seats it won still put it in third place in parliamentary terms. By 1977, for a time at least, opinion polls confirmed that it was the most widely supported party in Scotland (Drucker and Brown, 1980, p. 114).

The immediate challenge of the Welsh and Scottish nationalists seemed to fade in the wake of referendums held in March 1979 to consider proposals for devolution in the two countries. These referendums were slightly peculiar in the sense that not only was a majority in favour required for reforms to be instituted, but those voting 'yes' also had to exceed a 40 per cent threshold of those eligible to vote. In Wales this threshold was of little significance since the proposal was substantially defeated (only 20 per cent of voters voted 'yes'), but in Scotland there was a (small) majority (52 per cent of

Table 2.3 Referendum on devolution: March 1979 results (percentage of electorate)

	Wales			Scotland	
Yes	No	Non-voters	Yes	No	Non-voters
11.8 (20% of votes cast)	46.5	41.7	32.5 (52% of votes cast)	30.4	37.1

those who voted) in favour of devolution which was discounted because the proportion of the *electorate* voting 'yes' did not exceed the threshold (see Table 2.3). Whatever the peculiarities, however, it was impossible (even for nationalists) to pretend that there had been an overwhelming vote in favour of independence or home rule. In that sense the 'crisis' associated with the rise of nationalism seemed to have been resolved, although nationalism has come to stay as a political phenomenon in those countries and is increasingly reflected not only in the policies of the nationalist parties and the support for them, but also in those of the major political parties, apart from the Conservatives.

The significance of the new nationalisms for wider political processes in Britain is easily minimized. In principle the rise of nationalist movements appeared to have little to do with the undermining of the post-war settlement or the end of the social-democratic consensus, even if it coincided with the increasing failure of the unitary state centred on London to deliver the goods on welfare or economic issues. These movements were often – outside Scotland and Wales – popularly understood and presented either as inherently backward-looking, romantic and engaged in an almost irrational search for national roots in the context of global confusion, or as basically democratic rebellions against central control. Nationalist movements were understood as largely peripheral – adding to feelings of political crisis, but not centrally part of it in the same way as the others discussed in section 2.2

It is, however, appropriate to link them more explicitly, for two main reasons. First, because the failures of the United Kingdom state have helped to encourage nationalist responses, and the rise of the nationalisms has highlighted those failures. Indeed, in policy terms, from the 1930s on, the UK state defined the problems of these areas as regional economic problems, effectively encouraging the growth of area-based political alliances, without then being able to deliver any satisfactory solution to those problems. Secondly, although the nationalist responses seem to be rooted within the UK, they cannot be understood without reference to Britain's readjustments in the wider international arena. Looking at their development should help us to understand the position of the UK within that wider political and economic system.

An orientation towards nationalist-style solutions to economic and social problems clearly predated the explosion of nationalist politics in the late

1960s and early 1970s. But initially this was based on attempts to develop a 'regionalist consensus' which identified (UK) state intervention as a means of solving them (Rees and Lambert, 1979, in Massey, 1984, pp. 203–4). But the form taken by these politics changed dramatically in these decades in ways which reflected the wider strains experienced by the UK political system. The promise of regional policy could not be sustained which meant that alliances developed to put pressure on the centre for more assistance or regional aid began to make less and less sense. The old industries were in decline, and the new ones seemed to be of little relevance to the existing regional interest groups – whether unions or employers. Unemployment rose, population fell: the UK seemed increasingly to be defined in terms of England and the South East. The fracturing of regional consensus in Wales and Scotland heralded the rise of the nationalists – a legitimation crisis for the UK state at least in those two of its component nations.

Until the 1960s Wales, Scotland and Northern Ireland (as well as many of the English manufacturing regions) were still tied into the UK as an economic system: their staple industries continued to rely on past imperial connections and, in some cases, on defence orders from the state. But from the late 1960s the economic links between the regions and the UK state became progressively weaker. Doreen Massey charts the decline of employment in British manufacturing industry, and this is a decline which hit the economies of these areas particularly hard (Massey, 1988a). Overall levels of manufacturing output have declined, but what has been more important is a shift in the form of manufacturing and the ownership of the firms involved. Put simply, there has been a dramatic decline in large regionally based companies to the extent that most major employers are now either UK-wide or, more commonly, multinational (see Martin, 1988). The nationalized industries which took over some of the regionally based concerns, in ship-building, steel and coal, and even the car industry, have presided over major declines in both employment and output since the 1960s.

This has meant a gradual erosion of the links between key sections of the population in the sub-UK nations (and in the English regions) and key economic and political decision-makers. There are no longer regional 'ruling classes' to fit into the wider UK system and the basis of past arrangements linking trade union organizations, the state and industrialists has also been eroded because the basis of trade unionism has been changing too. This is so both because the stable base of organization in large workplaces has been eroded and because 'the increasing degree of external – particularly multinational – control poses new and different problems for working-class organization – the feeling of negotiating with ghosts, that those on the other side of the negotiating table have little more control over, or even knowledge of, decisions than have the unions' (Massey, 1984, p. 218).

The process of **uneven development**, in which economic and political restructuring builds on the foundations of past differential development, has both helped to set up and sustain national divisions *within* the United Kingdom and, more recently, to make devolution, autonomy or home rule real political and economic possibilities. The United Kingdom state has lost its pre-eminence. It has faded in importance. Its links with empire no longer have much to offer in terms of economic prosperity or political prestige although, as the example of the Falklands campaign in 1981 confirms, the unifying potential of empire can still be impressive. At least until the end of the 1970s there was no sustained and effective challenge to the suffocating and 'conservative' power of the United Kingdom institutions from within the existing political system, into which the working class had been accommodated via the Labour Party and the trade unions. Britain's new orientation to and involvement with the EC confirmed that it could no longer stand alone (or rely on a 'special relationship' with the US) and by implication this provided another institutional focus for the 'neo-nationalists' – towards Europe rather than London. In fact, it could be árgued that Wales and Scotland had greater claims to being 'European' than a state whose existence was predicated on the strength of its non-European empire.

At the same time as the United Kingdom state was failing to deliver economic prosperity and to generate political confidence, new economic possibilities seemed to be opening up for Wales and Scotland. They – as well as some of England's other regions – were becoming sites for multinational investment just as their traditional – United Kingdom – industries were moving into terminal decline. In the case of Scotland, the discovery of North Sea oil seemed to offer still greater hopes of economic independence, making it possible completely to bypass London. In the 1970s the growth of nationalism encouraged a degree of panic followed by realignment within Britain's main political parties. For the Conservatives the extent of adjustment was probably less far-reaching than for the Labour Party. Neither Scotland nor Wales had ever been a necessary source of electoral support for them (although they had always had a significant base in each). Despite an initial flirting with devolution under Heath in the late 1960s, the Conservative base lay in England and this has been increasingly accepted and reflected more and more sharply in electoral terms. For Labour, however, the rise of the nationalisms was, as Drucker and Brown (1980, p. 80) comment, 'more immediately threatening'. It even led to a split within the party in 1976 and the creation of a separate (and admittedly short-lived) Scottish Labour Party. More important, as a party which was highly dependent for votes on Scotland and Wales, new demands could not in the end be ignored, even if the 1970s looked like a series of attempts to do so, as different party factions fought for different solutions.

Yet these individual adjustments understate the significance of the nationalist challenge. It was not only important to the internal life of the Labour Party, but also had implications for the role of the parties as unifying forces within the UK – at least outside Northern Ireland. As Drucker and Brown argue, 'The parties are not simply the private vehicles of those who run them. They have a role in the constitution. One of the roles of the parties has been to unite the United Kingdom' (1980, pp. 80–1). The rise of the nationalists made this more difficult by exposing the local weaknesses of the

UK parties. In the end, it was even the central organizations of the UK parties which made the commitments to devolution: 'The local branches were too weak or too shocked – or too deferential to London – to make the commitment' (1980, p. 81).

2.3.2   Nationalism and the British crisis

Some, mainly Marxist, writers have seen the rise of nationalism as confirming a more deep-rooted basis for the crisis of the 1960s and 1970s, which they would argue has not yet been resolved.

Nairn (1977a and b), for example, sets the rise of nationalism in the context of a much longer history, stretching back to the seventeenth and eighteenth centuries. Following Anderson (1965), he stresses the **archaic** nature of the British state – its failure to escape from its absolutist legacy, its trappings of centralized power without democratic and popular legitimacy. Anderson complained that there had never been an effective bourgeois revolution in Britain (like that in France with a commitment to democracy and the removal of feudal constraints), nor had the industrial revolution of the nineteenth century brought the new industrialists to political power. On the contrary, the same (landed and English) aristocratic political elite had continued to rule, and to incorporate representatives of the new industrial bourgeois in a secondary capacity. As a result it is argued that the UK's political culture has served consistently to undermine and undervalue processes of economic growth. Despite some reference to the significance of imperial legacy, this is essentially an endogenous explanation. The emphasis here is on the 'exceptional' nature of the UK state. It is felt to be in crisis because of that. A similar argument is developed by Wiener (1981) from a non-Marxist perspective and is also discussed by Sarre (1989a). This elite is a British one, but it is also overwhelmingly an *English* one, and in many ways carries and encourages an English nationalism, reflected in Thrift's arguments (Thrift, 1989).

Nairn concentrates on the influence of this development on state formation. He argues that what he calls the 'Anglo-British' state system grew by absorption, making few concessions to the absorbed, particularly in the non-English nations of the UK. For him the crucial failure of the British state is that it was not transformed in the nineteenth century to reflect the changing class and economic relations of the industrial revolution. Instead a workable compromise was negotiated between the new industrialists and the landed aristocracy which allowed the free operation of the market without substantially changing the old rules of political conduct or encouraging dynamic attitudes to industrial growth: 'Although not, of course, an absolutist state the Anglo-British system remains a product of the general transition from absolutism to modern constitutionalism: it led the way out of the former, but never genuinely arrived at the latter' (Nairn, 1977b, p. 49).

This was a political compromise, but one which also rested on and reinforced existing economic relations. It was possible because Britain's industrialization began with little direct competition and British prosperity was taken for granted. More important, it was linked to a system of political and economic development which relied on Britain's imperial power. According to Nairn, the compromise resulted in:

> ... a clearly demarcated order of classes, in the stable form most appropriate to overseas-oriented exploitation. High social mobility, individualism, egalitarian openness, *la carrière ouverte aux talents*, restless impatience with tradition – the traits of dynamic capitalism were systematically relegated or discounted, in favour of those which fitted Britain's particular kind of empire. (1977b, p. 19)

If many of the arguments discussed in the previous section focus on the instability of and inconsistencies within the '1944' settlement which led to the development of the Keynesian welfare state, here we are talking of a much longer historical context for the crisis of the 1970s. According to this, 'modernization' has been on the agenda not since the 1960s, but since the nineteenth century when Britain's industrial capitalists faced their first major challenges from their Prussian and United States competitors.

The identification of the roots of Britain's political crisis in the late nineteenth century is not restricted to those who share Nairn's emphasis, although the extension back to the seventeenth and eighteenth centuries is less commonly accepted. Indeed, the end of the nineteenth century is almost as popular as the '1944' settlement among those looking for historical explanations for contemporary problems. Andrew Gamble talks of Britain's 'hundred years' decline' and argues that:

> Britain's career of industrial expansion was launched upon economic foundations that were similar to those of many previous empires, but its Empire was consolidated and reached its zenith under very different ones. When earlier empires that arose from a self-sufficient agricultural base collapsed, the imperial state was forced back to this base, once decline had reached a certain point. That possibility disappeared for Britain during the nineteenth century. At a certain stage of building its world power Britain abandoned such foundations, merging its future irrevocably with the wider world economy.
>
> All discussion of British decline must therefore start from this – the world economy that was the means of the British rise, which was transformed in the course of that rise, and to which Britain remains tied. (1985, p. xviii)

Like Nairn, Gamble suggests that the external orientation of dominant sectors of the British economy has been a basic explanation for Britain's decline. They would agree that the post-war decline of the British Empire and the replacement of Britain by the United States as a world economic (and political) power has helped to undermine the existing political arrangements at the same time as Britain's domestic economic difficulties have finally made it impossible, in any case, to sustain a world role for Britain. Each particular economic and political crisis takes place in the context of a much longer period of decline.

According to this analysis, the secular decline of the British economy

started in the 1880s and has continued over the past century. Over most of
this period, however, as Gamble notes and Nairn bemoans, 'the British state
has proved able to negotiate a gradual descent' (Gamble, 1985, p. xviii).
Indeed, despite points of greater and lesser strain and tension, perhaps what
is most remarkable is the extent to which change has been managed and the
United Kingdom's shift to second-class political and economic status has
been achieved with little upheaval and with many of the trappings of
imperial power intact, although a stress on the images and symbols of power
may only be a response to their disappearance in reality.

But there are major differences of emphasis between the two approaches.
These arise largely from Nairn's emphasis on the failure of the British state
to achieve (adequate) political arrangements in the nineteenth century,
while Gamble is more concerned to stress the roots of economic failure and
the political consequences of that. Gamble is also less concerned with
explanations which stress how 'exceptional' the British experience was.
Whilst he acknowledges that any analysis of Britain's crisis has to be set in
the context of changing international relations, his analysis suggests that
although the UK's position is unique it is the product of a continuing process
of uneven development rather than the result of a single (and endogenous)
historic political failure far in the past. There is an implicit assumption in the
writings of Anderson and Nairn on the UK that other countries have
followed a more orthodox route – are closer to the 'correct' model of the
capitalist state. Gamble makes no such assumptions: the UK may be unique,
but so are the other capitalist states, within a world characterized by uneven
development. Even the rise of nationalism, which Nairn identifies as a key
problem for the UK, is shared with a number of other European powers
including France and Belgium.

Nairn links what he calls the 'patrician' basis of the British political
orientation to the dominance of financial institutions based in the City of
London. He relates the power of those institutions back to the developing
political compromise of the eighteenth and nineteenth centuries, and argues
that attempts at modernization without a substantial political 'revolution'
were doomed to failure. Not because of the intractability of the economic
problems, but because of the inflexibility and archaic nature of the British
state and those who run it. Unlike Middlemas, he sees the leading civil
servants as obstacles to any resolution to the problem and equally imbued
with the ideologies of British 'conservatism'.

> 'Reindustrialization' is not really a question of economic policy in Britain. This
> is the characteristic empirical-minded error made by successive governments
> since 1945. It is, in fact, a call for revolution. More exactly, it is a call for the
> 'revolution from above' which the British state-system has been built upon
> denying and repressing ever since the Industrial Revolution. It is a call –
> therefore – which has not the most remote chance of being effectively ans-
> wered by the existing state, and the deeply rooted civil structures which sustain
> it. (Nairn, 1977b, pp. 34–5)

It is this which makes the nationalist movements so important for Nairn's analysis. The existence of 'subordinate' nations within the UK state system was seen as confirmation of its archaic nature, and the changing position of the UK within the wider international political and economic system also meant a changed position for those 'nations' within the UK. For him, the development of nationalism – the possible 'break-up of Britain' – also heralded the possibility of a 'modernization' of political life and social organization which might, in turn, offer the basis for some form of economic regeneration. But such change would, in his terms, be revolutionary: the crisis of the UK state would be resolved by its dissolution, and then, possibly, by its reconstitution on a new basis – possibly federal, possibly part of a wider European federation. And yet, at the end of the 1970s, the devolution debate seemed to have defused the major pressures for fundamental change and the Northern Ireland problem was increasingly marginalized in UK political debate, only returning to the agenda from time to time in response to the latest bombing campaign by the IRA.

There was certainly some restructuring of politics in Scotland and Wales, as the nation became a base for political debate. In Scotland the Conservative Party has lost substantial support at just the time when its support in England has seemed to be strongest. Miller notes that as early as the 1979 General Election Labour's lead over the Conservatives in Scotland was some 13 per cent greater than would have been expected after adjustments had been made for class differences between the two countries (Miller, 1981, p. 216). Within the orthodox structures of government, the Welsh, Scottish and Northern Ireland Offices have risen in political profile. The Northern Ireland, Welsh and Scottish Development Agencies all began to play an active (and relatively well-funded) part in managing and organizing the processes of economic change in their (national) regions. There has been a formal recognition in many ways that Britain is not a united kingdom – a unitary state brought together by the 'crown in Parliament' – but one in which different interests can (and must) be recognized in some way if some form of economic as well as political modernization is to be achieved. Certainly the various departments of state and development agencies are a long way from being institutions of emerging nation-states: they are hybrids, or rather means of reflecting and managing competing interests by the centre. In a period in which corporatism is said to be dead, they – particularly the development agencies – have provided avenues of corporatist negotiation on a different geographical scale. Unions, employers and the state meet together to determine the direction of development. In contrast to England, in Wales and Scotland even local authorities are recognized by the UK state and its agencies as important partners in development.

The extent to which there has been a substantial restructuring, however, remains open to question. Certainly Nairn continues to question such a view. And in the run-up to the 1987 General Election there was a great deal of debate in the Scottish press about the 'Doomsday Scenario', according to which if Labour won overwhelmingly in Scotland – which it did – but was faced with a strong Conservative government in London – which it was –

then pressure for a specifically Scottish solution and a more dramatic move towards home rule would increase. Tensions based on national divisions within the UK are likely to provide a continued basis for political conflict in the 1990s.

2.3.3   Restructuring the state in Northern Ireland

The case of Northern Ireland brings the nature and problems of the modernization process in the UK into sharp relief and so repays more extensive consideration. In some respects, the position of Northern Ireland is clearly exceptional. The nature of its politics is only one expression of this. In addition, manufacturing industry was hit much harder in the 1970s than the rest of the UK. Between 1973 and 1985 manufacturing output fell by 17 per cent, while output per worker rose by 41 per cent, so that manufacturing employment fell by 40 per cent (Rowthorn, 1987, p. 113). In the 'long boom' which followed the Second World War, the Northern Ireland manufacturing economy became increasingly dominated by external and often multinational capital – one estimate suggests that in the 1960s and early 1970s the increase in employment in foreign-owned firms was by far the highest among UK regions, and by 1975 it had risen to 26 141 from 4515 in the late 1950s (Teague, 1987a, p. 164). According to both Teague and Rowthorn, this made Northern Ireland particularly vulnerable to recession in the 1970s, and after 1975 the level of foreign investment fell sharply, larger plants were closed and new arrivals have been much smaller. The importance of multinationals has declined and within the economy, in terms of employment and output, attempts to attract 'new modern forms of international investment' have largely failed (Teague, 1987a, p. 172).

As far as the service sector is concerned, Northern Ireland has also faced major problems. In private services the growth of employment has lagged far behind that of the UK as a whole: 'In 1974, private services accounted for 20 per cent of all employers in the province compared with 26 per cent in the UK as a whole. By 1983 the gap had widened to 25 and 33 per cent respectively. In 1985, employment in private services actually fell' (O'Dowd, 1987, p. 192). The Northern Ireland economy has instead been increasingly reliant on public spending, both for public service employment and for direct income support. The gap between public service employment as a share of employment in Northern Ireland and the UK as a whole is virtually the reverse of that for private services – in 1983, the proportion of employers in the public sector in Northern Ireland exceeded that for the UK by 13 per cent (O'Dowd, 1987, p. 193). According to Rowthorn (1987, p. 118), 'Northern Ireland now resembles a vast workhouse in which most of the inmates are engaged and servicing or controlling each other'.

The process of state restructuring in Northern Ireland has to be set against this background, as well as the background, after 1968, of major internal political conflicts which spilled out of official structures of governments, first into the streets and then into violence.

The 'modernization' attempts of the 1960s did not pass Northern Ireland by. On the contrary, for the 'modernizers' Northern Ireland was a prime candidate for change and the implications of the ideology of modernization were clearly expressed in a series of official reports produced in the late 1950s and 1960s.

> Most of the reports were produced by teams of academics or industrialists, often British, whose understanding of Northern Ireland politics was to see it as an expression of an outmoded parochialism, laced with archaic religious and cultural attachments. Progress rested on an acceptance of the secular criteria of British social democracy; sectarianism in politics and administration could be an impediment to economic advance. (Tomlinson, 1980, pp. 106–7)

The development of a regional strategy was viewed as a means of more successfully integrating Northern Ireland into the promised, technologically based, capitalist, economic expansion. As elsewhere in Britain, regional policies were being developed to remove institutional obstacles and to attract investment by leading companies, particularly multinational giants, in what were seen as the advanced sectors of manufacturing (such as petrochemicals and related industries including artificial fibres, telecommunications, car assembly and components).

> Closer links with Britain through political and financial institutions, and the rationalization of administration within Northern Ireland, was what the industrialization required . . . All the development reports of the early 1960s shared these basic assumptions and a certain optimism that the state could be transformed reasonably smoothly for the task of modern government. There were motorways to be built, populations to be moved, skilled and professional workers to be produced, harbours and houses to construct and drains to be laid. (Tomlinson, 1980, p. 106)

The case of Northern Ireland, however, also shows in its sharpest form some of the reasons for the failure of the modernization process. Tomlinson (1980) charts the progress of local government reform, showing the importance of interaction between the (often London-based) reformers and the locally based politicians, who effectively controlled the process of reform. Technical considerations were said to be the basis of the administrative reform of local government in 1973, in a situation where councils had previously operated as a major channel for reinforcing the political dominance of Unionism. The stress was placed on service professionals and experts as a means of bypassing sectarian politics. The reforms opened up council representation to groups previously effectively excluded from representation in Stormont, from within both the Protestant and Catholic communities (they were accompanied by the rise of the Democratic Unionist Party and the Social Democratic and Labour Party and – since the early 1980s – the emergence of Sinn Fein as an electoral force). But at the same time, they also reduced the power of those councils. Major services, such as housing, education, libraries and social services, were transferred to

separate agencies directly responsible to the Northern Ireland Office. Overall local authority budgets were only ten per cent of those before 1973.

> In terms of the fundamental question of shifts in political relations, anti-
> Unionists who were denied a relative share of representation and power
> throughout the life of the Stormont government have benefited little from
> local government reform. While their chances of election and council control
> have been increased, it is a hollow victory to be in command of a minimal
> budget and relatively inconsequential services, such as street cleaning, manag-
> ing cemeteries and leisure centres. Nevertheless district councils remain
> important platforms from which Unionists ideologically declare the essential
> relationship of Protestants and Catholics to the state on a whole range of issues
> which are certainly not confined to prescribed council duties. (Tomlinson,
> 1980, p. 117)

According to O'Dowd the context for change in the 1960s and 1970s made
technocratic solutions impossible:

> Northern Ireland was established in 1920, not as the culmination of a move-
> ment to initiate economic and political change, but as an attempt to defend and
> preserve a social formation based on the uneven spatial development of
> nineteenth-century competitive capitalism, British imperialism and Protestant
> dominance. Despite the declining global role of British imperialism, the other
> two elements remained remarkably intact until the early 1960s, despite many
> vicissitudes. The key to this stability lay in the class and political relations
> between overwhelmingly Protestant industrial capital and skilled workers, the
> Orange Order and the Unionist state institutions. The general aim of defend-
> ing the Union was in the interests of nearly all sections of capital. Individual
> capitalists were heavily represented in all Unionist cabinets and even in the
> 1960s had frequent and easy access to Unionist ministers ... The other
> elements of the Unionist class alliance were firmly, if sometimes uneasily,
> integrated via paternalism and Orange clientelism in the workplace and state
> patronage and employment practices ...
> The initial acquiescence, and subsequent more positive support, of the
> British government for this unique form of devolution was also central to its
> impressive stability. The legal and administrative terms of devolution served
> to minimize the political articulation of class conflict within Unionism. Reve-
> nue raising, a potential area of conflict, was largely a matter for Westminster.
> The local administration was largely responsible for expenditure, within broad
> guidelines laid down by the central state and this helped to lubricate the
> mechanisms of political patronage.
> One factor, however, appeared at once to threaten political stability while
> helping to maintain the political integration of Unionism. The 'democratic'
> viability of the state meant ensuring the permanent minority status of Catholic
> Nationalists; on whom the Partition settlement had been imposed in con-
> ditions of civil war between 1920 and 1922. Nevertheless ... neither the
> Unionist state nor any major sector of (Protestant) manufacturing depended
> crucially on the 'manipulation and control of Catholic labour mobility or
> suppression of Catholic political and trade union organization'. Catholic
> labour, especially males, were poorly represented in manufacturing industry,
> and over-represented in construction, agriculture and services in semi-skilled
> and unskilled occupations. They were also heavily over-represented among
> the unemployed and among emigrants ... The Catholic middle class was
> mainly composed of farmers, teachers, clergy and small businessmen, largely
> servicing their own 'community'. Under these conditions, the maintenance of

Unionist economic dominance could be left to the operation of 'market forces'. Yet, Catholics remained, numerically at least (33 per cent), a substantial disaffected minority, with consistently higher birthrates. They continued to oppose the legitimacy of partition by constitutional, and occasionally by violent means. They even had numerical majorities in many areas west of the Bann. Thus the detailed *political* control of the Catholic population, outside the workplace, seemed to be of paramount importance to the survival and stability of Northern Ireland. Herein lay the final and crucial specificity of devolved government, that is, its responsibility for security via the courts, police and paramilitary B-Specials, all of which were closely identified with the Unionist Party. The technocratic or social democratic compartmentalization of 'economics', 'politics' and legal coercion had little purchase in Northern Ireland. (O'Dowd, 1985, pp. 148–9)

One consequence of this experience was that there was little chance of mobilizing some sort of broad national consensus, on the Welsh or Scottish models, behind a policy of regionally based economic regeneration and state restructuring in the form of quasi-corporate development agencies. The role of the United Kingdom state in Northern Ireland since the late 1950s has been double-sided: on the one hand to reorganize the local economy to reflect wider economic changes, making it safe for capitalist expansion; and on the other to sustain the political stability (and even promote the legitimacy) of the state itself, which has frequently involved responding to 'popular, and often territorially based, class and sectarian pressures' (O'Dowd, 1985, p. 160; see also *O'Dowd*, 1989). The existing regional state structure – Stormont – failed to deal with these tasks, because it was so clearly identified with existing relations of political power and was incapable of satisfying the demands either of local industrial interests or of the wider political base of Unionism in the Protestant working class. Nor was it able to keep the lid on protest from the excluded minority, without risking unacceptable levels of repression. It was for this reason that direct rule from London was instituted in 1974.

The new institutions developed in the 1970s and extended in the 1980s, show the continued importance of Northern Ireland as a site for political experiment, since they confirm the wider shift identified by Middlemas, albeit at a different level. A whole series of attempts has been made to ensure representation for particular groups – including industrialists, professionals and 'experts', as well as different sections of the Protestant and Catholic communities – while reducing the importance of democratically elected representative institutions. There has been a conscious process of state restructuring to deal with political crisis, both internally and since the mid-1980s in terms of developing relationships with the rest of Ireland. The process has been a long drawn out one, however, so far with little evidence of significant success. The crisis of the UK state in Northern Ireland has not been resolved.

Nor, perhaps, has the wider crisis of the United Kingdom state as a whole. Like its component parts, the United Kingdom's state restructuring can only be understood in the context of the long period of its construction and, over the last century or so, its decline or weakening. In this sense, it may be mistaken to focus – as the modernizers of the 1960s did – on out-dated institutions which, by implication, can be relatively easily swept aside in the path to progress; or – as the 'new right' have – to focus on the structures of the post-war period – the institutions of the Keynesian welfare state. Structural change to meet the changed realities of Britain's new political and economic position are likely to have to go deeper, to be more than simply a reflection of and adjustment to a general process of decline.

Summary of section 2.3

• The growth of nationalist movements was also a part of the political crisis of the 1960s and '70s, challenging the assumptions of the UK-wide Keynesian welfare state.

• The old mechanisms which tied the nations of Scotland and Wales to the UK began to break down in the 1960s, as the Empire became increasingly incapable of delivering the economic or political goods. There was a move away from imperial markets and an increase in multinational investment which encouraged the development of different economic and political roles which made the UK an unstable whole.

• Nairn argues that the contemporary United Kingdom state can be understood as a product of the effective endorsement of an archaic political system in the eighteenth and nineteenth centuries in which the new classes of industrialization (both industrial capitalists and the working class) were absorbed by that system and the (patrician) values which underlay it. He stresses the political aspects of the system and its exceptional nature. 'The break-up of Britain' offers the prospects of a more fundamental reorganization of state, society and economy.

• Others, such as Gamble, emphasize the economic roots of decline and its interrelationship with political malaise. Uneven development, rather than exceptional archaism, is a crucial element of the analysis.

• The fundamental restructuring hoped for by Nairn did not take place in the 1980s, but in Scotland and Wales there has been a more modest process of restructuring which seeks to link regional interests (or the regional representative of national and even multinational concerns) to the state through sub-UK agencies which seem to have a degree of autonomy from the centre, and are not subject to any local electoral control.

• In the case of Northern Ireland, the process has been more complex, since the threat to the wider UK state and the degree of economic crisis has been sharper. But there, too, despite the difficulty (perhaps impossibility) of the tasks, attempts have been made to identify corporate interests with which to negotiate, at the same time as the importance of local, elected, 'democratic' structures has been downplayed.

Activity 2.3

Return to the definition of crisis outlined in section 2.1. To what extent is it consistent with the long-term view of underlying crisis implied by Anderson and Nairn?

2.4 Conclusion

The starting-point for much of the discussion in this chapter has been an acceptance that there was a political crisis in the UK in the 1970s, at least in terms of the definition drawn from Gramsci and outlined in section 2.1. The main features of that crisis which are considered in this chapter include: the acknowledged failure of the state to live up to its promises in terms of welfare or economic growth; the increasing inability of major corporate political and economic interest groups to bargain effectively over key issues; the growth of nationalist movements in Scotland and Wales and of instability in Northern Ireland; the decline in electoral support for the governing political parties; and a change in political rhetoric and programmes from an emphasis on welfare to an emphasis on market mechanisms (the developing crisis is discussed in detail in *Leys*, 1983, Chapters 5 and 6).

But three main alternative (if not always entirely inconsistent) views of crisis have also run through the chapter. The first, which has been largely illustrated from the work of Johnson, has stressed the extent to which it is a **crisis of social democracy** and the state constructed in the post-1945 period. The strength of this approach is that it seems to explain the success of 'Thatcherism' at the end of the 1970s with its stress on individualism and the market as alternatives to the apparent failures of collectivism and state economic management. It identifies major tensions in any system which relies on the 'providential power of government', when the government does not actually have the power to deliver.

The weakness of the approach, however, is that it makes it difficult to understand why the social-democratic path was chosen in the first place. It tends simply to be viewed as a mistake, which became self-perpetuating and institutionalized. This is encouraged by the historical period which has been chosen, since starting in 1945 makes it more difficult to set these issues in a longer historical context. One of the reasons for the particular form taken by the 'post-war settlement' may be the need to take some account of problems generated over a longer period.

This is the implication of the arguments developed within the second approach, which identifies what might be called a **crisis of modernization**. In this chapter that approach is mainly exemplified by Barnett and Middlemas, but it could also be associated with the Marxist analyses of Gamble and Leys. For Barnett, the '1944' settlement can be seen as a means of avoiding the harsh realities of life as a second-class power, acknowledging the dominant role of the USA, to which the UK was now merely a client, and in that respect his analysis is closer to Johnson's. For Middlemas, however, it presented the possibility of a longer-term set of negotiations and accommodations between major corporate interests to achieve the commonly desired end of increased prosperity within a mixed economy. Like the others, Middlemas saw some basic flaws in the 'settlement' actually achieved, which were to cause its breakdown from the late 1960s on, but this could only be the precursor to a more developed and effective 'settlement' in the future. This new 'settlement' would be the final resolution to the crisis – this rather than the success of market approaches and 'Thatcherism' would bring the restructuring of political alliances predicted by Gramsci. The success of 'Thatcherism' in the 1980s according to such an approach (although Middlemas does not himself develop it in this way) might be seen as ephemeral, insofar as it is depicted as a victory for the market over political decision-making, but it might instead be setting the foundations for a new round of negotiations between major corporate interests.

The strength of such an approach in its broad historical sweep, which allows one to draw back from the immediacies of day-to-day politics and to identify longer-term trends. Its weakness is that it is difficult to be sure about its analysis of the present. At the time of writing, for example, there appear to be few cases of continuing (or revived) corporate bargaining at national level, with the possible exceptions of the National Economic Development Council which seems to have become effectively marginalized. At local and regional level (for example, through urban development corporations and regional development agencies) there are some signs of alternative approaches, but they remain relatively small in scale. If anything, the external orientation of British capital identified by Middlemas, Gamble and Leys has become more marked in the early 1980s, to the extent that the finance sector has tended to squeeze out other major groups, without even needing any formal institutional representation – except, perhaps, through the Bank of England.

The final approach which can be labelled a **crisis of archaism**, is associated primarily with Nairn. His stress on the fundamental flaws not only of the '1944' settlement, but of those in the seventeenth century which went unchallenged (or at least were ineffectively challenged) in the eighteenth and nineteenth centuries, helps to explain the longer-term stability of the UK political system. Even in the context of a significant political crisis in the 1970s, instead of fundamental change, there was a more modest set of readjustments which left the state intact, and, as Doherty reminds us, even brought reference back to glories of the imperial past to go alongside a renewed commitment to free-market economics and attempts to reduce state spending. These were hardly new ideas around which to form an alliance like that indicated by Gramsci, but were certainly strong enough in the absence of serious rivals at the end of the 1970s and in the early 1980s. The weakness of Nairn's approach, however, is twofold. First the stress on 'exceptionalness' is unconvincing, since it is difficult to find any state which is not exceptional in comparable ways, and it would be better to set the UK within a wider framework of uneven development. And, secondly, the 'crisis' to be drawn from this analysis is so extended and long drawn out that it never seems to be resolved, yet it also never seems to be too much of a problem.

Perhaps it is useful to see it as presenting a context within which more immediate political crises take place and helps to explain why, in the UK at least, such crisis also tend to include elements of nationalist upheaval.

In this chapter we have looked at some aspects of the British political crisis of the 1960s and 1970s and indicated some of the attempts to resolve that crisis. There are still major debates about how some of the underlying tensions can be dealt with. The crucial lessons to be drawn from our arguments, however, are, first, that it is important to set debates about crisis and restructuring in a broader historical context, and, secondly, that the balance between exogenous and endogenous factors is not an easy one to draw. Using the notion of uneven development outlined in the series introduction, it is important to understand the interaction between past development, which helps to generate national political systems, and external shifts which are also shaped by relationships with and between existing national political structures.

Similarly, the balance between political and economic factors is difficult to determine in abstract terms. It is necessary to consider developments in all their complexity to grasp which are the most important influences in any particular case. Certainly it may help to start with some general rules; even if the analysis often ends up very similar as it is modified to deal with greater complexity. For example, although Nairn starts with a concentration on the consequences of a political compromise, and Gamble with a view of underlying economic factors, their analyses of the political crisis of the 1960s and 1970s share many key features, in which each acknowledges the significance of factors stressed more strongly in the writing of the other. Similarly, Leys stresses the endogenous nature of the crisis, but does so only in the context of an analysis which acknowledges that importance of understanding Britain's changing position within a global system.

The language of crisis has been endemic in the twentieth-century political history of Britain, without any major state restructuring having been achieved. As Middlemas suggests, even the growth and expansion of the Keynesian welfare state after the war and the extension of corporate bias in the 1970s can be seen as the most recent expressions of a process which began in the first decade of the century. If, however, the acknowledged 'long decline' and its management by political and administrative elites has been the background to political events, more recently – in a period dating from the late 1960s – it seems that a new set of exogenous shocks made the maintenance of the old regime more difficult to sustain.

In the remainder of this book, we shall be considering not only whether the social-democratic state has been in crisis, but whether it is being replaced by a whole new political environment and set of political relations. In other words, if we can agree that Britain experienced a political crisis in the 1960s and 1970s, we still need to consider a little more carefully what the response to that crisis has been: whether there has been a political realignment to preserve the main features of Britain's state and politics or whether there has been a realignment capable of significantly restructuring them.

Further reading

The most interesting of general discussions of the British crisis are already referred to in the chapter, but would repay more extensive consideration. Both Leys' *Politics in Britain* (London, Heinemann; 1983) and Gamble's *Britain in Decline: Economic Policy, Political Strategy and the British State* (London, Macmillan; 1985) are clearly written and theoretically informed. They are also both written from within the Marxist tradition, and if you want a less partisan (but also rather less exciting) survey, Sked's *Britain's Decline: Problems and Perspectives* (Oxford, Basil Blackwell; 1987) is worth looking at. In *The Context of British Politics* (London, Hutchinson; 1984) Coates usefully brings together debates about economic, social, cultural and political change.

If you want to follow up any of the debates about neo-Marxist theories of crisis, Chapters 4 and 5 of O'Connor's *Theories of Crisis* (Oxford, Basil Blackwell; 1987) summarizes them relatively briefly although it is worth remembering that he has his own particular point of view in the debate to put across. More developed discussion of political developments in Northern Ireland since the late 1960s is to be found in Arthur and Jeffrey's *Northern Ireland since 1968* (Oxford, Basil Blackwell; 1988) and *O'Dowd* (1989). The latter is a brief and helpful survey.

3 Continuity and change in state economic intervention

Simon Mohun

Contents

3.1   Introduction

The relationship of the state to the economy is a highly controversial subject. Through the 1980s it has been a major theme of the Conservative Party's strategy in government that state interference in the free workings of **markets** is generally deleterious in its effects. Allowing markets to work freely (and at the same time focusing policy on reducing rigidities in the functioning of markets) is held to be sufficient to raise UK growth rates, to reduce unemployment, and generally to break out of the consensual interventionist straightjacket which was responsible for what is seen as the dismal economic record of 1945 to 1979. Previously, however, in the aftermath of the inter-war years, it was generally recognized that the state had a positive duty to intervene in the economy to support the level of aggregate demand and thereby ensure full employment, and to ensure sufficient welfare provision to eliminate poverty. Each view in its time was the 'common sense' of the period, but both views cannot simultaneously be correct.

This chapter is written from the point of view of an economist. It is structured around the question:

*   How do markets work and what are the consequences for the role of the state in the economy?

This is a theoretical question, and in order to provide an overall perspective on the phenomena in question the next section outlines some statistical and historical background on trends in state expenditures. Section 3.3 then considers recent economic history from the standpoint of methodological individualism, a theoretical understanding of state and economy based upon aggregating up from individual behaviour. However, within this individualist framework, there are two different understandings of how markets work, which are sufficiently different and cause sufficient controversy one against the other as to necessitate separate treatment. These are the 'market pessimist' and the 'market optimist' views. The former dominated policy from the 1944 Beveridge Report through to 1970 and then more falteringly until around 1976; the latter then dominated policy hesitantly until 1979 and robustly thereafter.

Section 3.4 outlines a Marxist interpretation of how markets work and what the role of the state is. Here the emphasis is on a very different theoretical approach, and the section concludes with an Activity in which you are asked to apply this approach to account for recent UK experience concerning the state and the economy. This is followed by a short conclusion.

3.2   Trends in UK state expenditures

Around one person in five of the UK working population works for central or local government, and between 1976 and 1986 this proportion remained roughly constant. Of these 5.3 million people, around 55 per cent are employed in local authorities and 45 per cent in central government, and they contribute by their economic activity around 17 per cent of Gross Domestic Product (GDP).

The most frequently used statistic to describe government economic activity is government expenditure, which in its most inclusive form is 'general government expenditure', defined as the sum of all current and capital expenditures, and net lending, of central government and local authorities. This aggregate includes 'transfer payments', the redistribution of resources from one section of the population to another (such as retirement pensions, unemployment benefits and sickness payments, child benefit, supplementary benefit and housing benefit), and has to be financed out of taxation and borrowing. It is the movements in this aggregate which were a major focus of stated government policy in the decade following the late 1970s.

Table 3.1 gives a rough indication of post-war trends in general government expenditure after allowing for inflation. These figures are annual averages and conceal two peaks, in 1968 and in 1975–76. Following a small peak in 1968, attempts were made at the end of the 1960s to reduce government expenditure (by deferring for two years the raising of the school leaving age, by delaying a general increase in social security benefits, and by accelerating the withdrawal of British armed forces east of Suez). Government expenditure in real terms was reduced in 1969, but thereafter increased in real terms quite rapidly to a much larger peak in 1975–76. In the second half of 1976, after negotiations with the International Monetary Fund, the government revised its expenditure plans for 1977–78, reducing them (more or less across the board) by one billion pounds, and raising a further half-billion via the sale of government-owned shares in the British Petroleum Company in 1977–78. However, in the event, actual expenditure in 1977–78 was around four billion pounds less than the revised plans had indicated at the beginning of 1977, a massive underspending coinciding with the introduction of cash limits. Hence general government expenditure in real terms fell sharply from its 1975–76 peak in 1977, but thereafter began to increase again, surpassing its mid-1970s peak in 1980, and increasing steadily, but at a lower rate, through to 1985, then showing a small fall in 1986.

Table 3.1 Approximate average annual rates of growth in real general government expenditure (per cent)

1950–59	2.75
1960–69	4.50
1970–79	3.00
1980–86	1.25 including offsetting privatization proceeds
1980–86	1.75 excluding offsetting privatization proceeds

Source: Central Statistical Office, *Economic Trends*, October 1987

Figure 3.1   General government expenditure as a percentage of GDP, 1963–64 to 1986–87

Source: *Central Statistical Office,* Economic Trends, *October 1987*

If general government expenditure is expressed as a percentage of GDP, then the growth rates of the two can be compared. From less than 15 per cent before 1914, the figure rose to just under 50 per cent during the First World War, fluctuated around 25 per cent during the inter-war years, rose to around 60 per cent during Second World War, fell to around 34 per cent in 1950, and, with the exception of a small rise at the time of the Korean War, remained at around 34 per cent until 1960. The figure then rose to 36 per cent in 1964, and thereafter its behaviour is traced (for financial rather than calendar years) in Figure 3.1. Thus the figure peaks in 1967–68 at 42 per cent, drops back to 40.5 per cent the following year and remains roughly constant until 1973–74, when a sharp rise begins, peaking at 48.5 per cent in 1975–76. There then follows a sharp fall over two years to 42.6 per cent in 1977–78, a steady rise to nearly 47 per cent in 1982–83, and then a decrease from 46.2 per cent in 1984–85 to 44 per cent in 1986–87. In these figures, which exclude privatization proceeds, the influences of the recession of the mid-'70s following the first oil price shock, and the recession of 1979 to the early '80s are plainly apparent. It is also quite clear that from 1982–83 onwards, general government expenditure was growing less fast than GDP.

Activity 3.1

Are the general election results of 1964 (Labour victory), 1966 (Labour victory), 1970 (Conservative victory), 1974 (Labour victory), 1979

(Conservative victory) and 1983 (Conservative victory) sufficient to explain the trends indicated in Figure 3.1? (Remember that movements in either general government expenditure or GDP or both may explain their changing ratio.)

We now turn to the different theoretical accounts which give this statistical background meaning.

3.3   Individualism, markets and state economic intervention

3.3.1   The theoretical backdrop

An approach to social phenomena in terms of **individualism** begins with the individual as the fundamental unit of analysis, and explains market behaviour in terms of the choices individuals make given the constraints they face. In these choices, each individual is presumed to be the best judge of his or her own interests, a presumption which can be traced back at least as far as Adam Smith:

> It is not from the benevolence of the butcher, the brewer, or the baker that we expect our dinner, but from their regard to their own interest. We address ourselves, not to their humanity but to their self-love, and never talk to them of our own necessities, but of their advantages. (1776; 1970 edn, p. 119)

Now if all individuals act selfishly, it would seem obvious that the overall outcome of all such behaviours must be anarchy and chaos. However, economic theory shows that, on the contrary, provided that certain conditions are met, individual selfishness is compatible with a state of equilibrium, a state of balance in each market with demand no greater than supply. This is not conceived as a *process* whose *outcome* is an equilibrium; rather it is a statement that, under certain conditions, when all individuals behave selfishly there nevertheless *exists* a set of prices such that all individuals are doing what they want to do and all markets are in equilibrium. And since all individuals *are* doing what they want to do, this state of affairs cannot be improved upon, in the sense of making any one better off without at the same time making somebody else worse off (a welfare criterion taken from the work of Pareto, hence known as '**Pareto efficiency**').

Adam Smith used the metaphor of 'an invisible hand' to explain how atomistic competition based on selfishness works for the public good. But there are very specific conditions which have to be satisfied for this result to obtain. These include private ownership of everything, all consumers and producers sufficiently small relative to the size of the market that no one has the power to alter the market price by his or her own actions (i.e. price-taking behaviour), no barriers in any industry to the entry of new firms, costless information available to all, constant returns-to-scale technologies in all industries (if all inputs are altered proportionately, output alters in the same proportion) and so on (*Helm*, 1986). Only when these conditions are satisfied is competitive equilibrium Pareto-efficient.

This result (called 'theorem' by economists) shows how individual-istic self-seeking behaviour is compatible with socially desirable outcomes. The former characterizes participation in markets, the latter the concerns of the state. Consequently, the state's role in the economy can be related to the extent to which activities are provided by markets and the nature of the market processes involved. For the presumption is that, wherever possible, all activities should be provided by competitive markets. Where markets do not do this very well, they should be helped to do it better, and only in those cases in which markets do not provide certain activities at all should state provision occur.

These propositions are in general terms non-controversial. The contro-versies arise over the nature, extent and consequences of state intervention, positions taken being so different as to amount to very different understand-ings of how the economy as a whole functions. It is to these controversies that we now turn.

Activity 3.2

Consider the UK economy in terms of three spheres of activities:

(a)   those activities provided solely by markets, with minimal, if any, state intervention;

(b)   those activities provided by markets, but not very well, so that there is considerable state intervention;

(c)   those activities not provided at all by markets, so that state provision is the norm.

How would you classify the following activities from the standpoint of 1860, 1960 and 1990: military defence, health care, education (nursery, primary, secondary and tertiary), housing, railways, telecommunications, electricity supply? Why do you think activities might have shifted from one sphere to another?

	1860	*1960*	*1990*
Market			
Market imperfect, so state intervention			
State			

3.3.2 Market failure: the approach of market pessimists

The theoretical background just outlined is obviously very abstract. In particular, the conditions required for the theorem to hold are not remotely satisfied in reality. Markets are by no means the 'perfect' constructs required by the theorem: private ownership is not universal; many markets are characterized by degrees of monopoly with elements of price-making (rather than price-taking) behaviour the norm; many industries have significant barriers to the entry of new firms; information is not costless, and often is just not available at all; not all technologies have constant returns to scale; indeed the list is potentially endless. In general, we can say that markets do not work as the conditions for the theorem require: that is, there is '**market failure**'. And wherever there is market failure, there would on *prima facie* grounds appear to be a case for optimally directed intervention by government to correct for that failure.

The perception that market failure was significant and that invervention was required to correct for it was the major underpinning of public policy from 1945 at least until 1970 or so. This is the case at both microeconomic level (individual firm, industry, market or consumer) and macroeconomic level (the economy as a whole), the two combining in a broad consensus concerning provisions of the welfare state, the mix of public and private ownership, and the overall coordination of the economy (surveyed by *Helm*, 1986). Here we focus briefly on microeconomic interventions, and discuss macroeconomic interventions in section 3.3.3 below.

Direct intervention: nationalization

Nationalization was one of the most significant responses to market failure. A public corporation in theory could use pricing and investment policies to mimic the welfare efficiency of perfectly competitive markets; alternatively, instead of the economic inefficiency of unregulated, profit-maximizing, privately owned firms, public corporations could maximize welfare directly. Thus Herbert Morrison proposed,

> The public corporation must not be a capitalist business ... It must have a different atmosphere at its board table from that of a shareholders' meeting; the board and its officers must regard themselves as the high custodians of the public interest. (Morrison, 1933, cited by Kay and Thompson, 1987, p. 185)

Between 1946 and 1949 most of the fuel and power industries were nationalized and so, too, were large sections of the transport and communications industries. As a group, nationalized industries in 1960 produced about 10 per cent of national income, employed about 8 per cent of the UK labour force and invested about 18 per cent of total gross fixed investment. Predominantly they were either industries which provided a service considered vital, or they were industries whose output was an input into manufacturing industry rather than directly meeting consumer demand.

Policy towards the nationalized industries was developed through successive White Papers in 1961, 1967 and 1978. These various White Papers
attempted to establish pricing and investment rules whose rationale was
sought ultimately in rules which would apply were the nationalized industries perfectly competitive. However, ad hoc interventions by government
on matters other than those established as objectives were frequent, altering
previously agreed plans and strategies and sometimes interfering with
detailed operating decisions. Pricing and investment rules were not in
practice the analogues of perfect competition rules, and the nationalized
industries were not treated as, and did not behave as, the 'high custodians of
the public interest'. Rather, they increasingly came to be seen as state
monopolies; and while few queried the necessity of regulating monopolies,
the abandonment of the Morrisonian concept implied that there was no
necessity that these monopolies be *owned* by the *state*, and indeed that they
would benefit from disentanglement from short-term political interference
by the state.

Direct interventions in private industry

In theory, the process of competition in the long run determines the structure of industry via growth, mergers, bankruptcies and so on. But if market
incentives and sanctions are slow to operate, if financial institutions are
unresponsive to the needs of industry, and if both social and private costs of
transferring inputs from one use to another are thereby increased through
such market failure, then there is a strong case that the government should
assist the process.

In these terms, specific industries helped in the private sector during the
1960s were predominantly the cotton industry (government-aided contraction in the face of competition from the Asian Commonwealth), the aircraft
industry (amalgamations forced by declining purchases by the government
as the industry's dominant consumer) and the shipbuilding industry (subsidies and amalgamations in the face of foreign competition in order to protect
employment, preserve a defence capability and compete with other shipbuilding countries, most of which subsidize their own industry).

More generally, in 1966 the Industrial Reorganization Corporation was
established to promote rationalizations and mergers throughout the private
sector, and assisted in some major mergers in the largest merger wave since
the 1920s. However, it was abolished in 1971 as the incoming Conservative
government placed more faith in the efficacy of competitive forces in
fostering reorganization and efficiency. Open-ended support for companies
was abolished and market forces were to be allowed to kill off 'lame duck'
firms. But concern over the situation in Rolls-Royce and Upper Clyde
Shipbuilders led to the celebrated U-turn restoring government intervention
in 1971. The 1972 Industry Act gave powers to grant financial support, on a
selective basis, to industry, much in the spirit of the previous 1968 Industrial
Expansion Act, and included provision for grants in exchange for state

shareholding (first used in Labour's rescue of British Leyland (BL) in 1975). Under the 1972 Act a large number of firms and industries were helped, including shipbuilding, computers, machine tools, motor cycles and wool textiles. Having entered office in 1970 with a pledge to reduce direct, detailed intervention in industry, the Conservatives left office in 1974 having increased such intervention and promoted its legitimacy. Initially the incoming Labour administration enthusiastically continued this tradition, although as with its record in the 1960s, there remained some distance between its rhetoric and its achievements. Thus the National Enterprise Board (NEB) was established in 1975 to promote industrial reorganization, through investing in profitable projects, with some initial propaganda about extending the public sector to embrace 100 (subsequently reduced to 25) of the largest UK companies. But in practice the NEB generally confined itself to dealing with the securities and other property in public ownership which had been transferred to it (such as Ferranti, Rolls-Royce and BL).

Industrial interventions were largely motivated by the UK's poor overall economic performance with respect to competitors. Regional policy was also important and so too were policies with respect to advanced technological and defence-related industries. Mottershead remarks with respect to these policies for the years 1960–74;

> They have usually been associated with 'crisis' interventions, and the most commonly cited have been the preservation of regional employment (shipbuilding and textiles), aiding the balance of payments (shipbuilding, aircraft and aluminium), supporting technology (aircraft and computers) and protecting home from unfair foreign competition (shipbuilding and textiles). In many instances a combination of these motives was apparent and frequently the government claimed the support would be temporary . . . (Mottershead, 1978, p. 479)

To this list since 1974 could be added the attempt to maintain mass-volume car production at British Leyland (subsequently BL, then Rover Group, then a subsidiary of the privatized British Aerospace). In all of these 'crisis' interventions, temporary support assumed more permanent dimensions, and no intervention can unambiguously be regarded as successful. Internationally competitive shipbuilding, computer manufacturing and mass-volume car companies were not established and hence such interventions had little effect in improving overall UK economic performance. The problem was precisely the 'ad hoc' nature of the interventions, unstructured either by any overall strategic planning or by any attempt to facilitate and smooth the changes dictated by market forces.

Competition policy

If there is significant market failure, an alternative to direct intervention is for the government to act as referee, to police the competitive process, and in general 'to hold the ring for competition'.

Legislation along these lines has differed in emphasis according to which government is in office, with the Conservatives tending to stress the economic benefits of competition, and Labour the dangers of monopoly. Policy originated in 1948 with the Monopolies and Restrictive Practices Act, whereby the Monopolies Commission was set up to investigate situations in which one firm (or group of firms acting together) controlled more than one third (later one quarter) of the market. Various pieces of legislation followed, extending the policy to cover the investigation of mergers and of restrictive practices, and culminating in the 1973 Fair Trading Act which consolidated existing law, and codified and extended protection for consumers. Modified by 1976 and 1980 legislation, the 1973 Act was still the basis of policy in the mid-1980s.

Until around 1970, references to the Monopolies Commission were mainly industries with a single dominant firm; thereafter there was more concern with oligopolistic industries (in which groups of firms had a market share of over 25 per cent) on the grounds that competition in such industries was perhaps too weak to force firms to resist or absorb cost increases. The Commission's powers were, however, weak and could not deal with restrictions on competition that were anything other than explicit; moreover large-scale interventions radically to shake up what Kay and Thompson characterize as 'the comfortable oligopolistic structures that characterize many important sections of British industry' (Kay and Thompson, 1978, p. 199) were never conceived as necessary.

In 1965 the Monopolies Commission was given powers to investigate proposed mergers and to recommend prohibition on public interest grounds. Until the early 1970s government policy tended to promote rather than restrain mergers in the name of industrial restructuring in pursuit of economic growth. From 1965 to 1973 government departments considered some 875 mergers or proposed mergers. Of these, eighteen were referred to the Monopolies Commission: five concerned newspapers (and were therefore a statutory reference) and were approved; of the other thirteen only six were forbidden. But there was no coherent strategic policy either for or against mergers – mergers originating in the market being by and large encouraged with little consideration of specifically competitive criteria. The Commission was more hostile to the few large mergers proposed during the rest of the 1970s decade (particularly horizontal mergers), but merger references were increasingly divorced from straightforward competitive criteria of judgement (Lonrho–House of Fraser: suspicion of and distaste for ambitious entrepreneurs; Enserch–Davy Corporation: the issue of foreign investment; bids for the Royal Bank of Scotland: fears that Scotland would suffer; and so on). Moroever, little regard was taken of anti-competitive arrangements falling short of full merger, such as minority share acquisition coupled with tacit rather than explicit anti-competitive agreement.

Market pessimism: a summary

If markets do not work effectively, and there is substantial market failure, then public interest and private interest will diverge. One approach to this is nationalization, whereby managers of nationalized industries are instructed to pursue welfare-maximizing rather than profit-maximizing policies. It is hard to argue that this has been a great success in the UK. A second approach is to regulate private industry with a structure of incentives and constraints such that the private interest will coincide with the public. While cartels and resale price maintenance have largely disappeared, and large horizontal mergers have been prohibited, competition policy has otherwise had little impact. Finally, it is hard to argue that the record of specific industrial interventions has been anything other than dismal in its success. Overall, no serious attempt has been made to mimic the structure of perfect competition, and from 1945 up to the late 1970s no overall strategy dictated government microeconomic interventions.

Yet market failure does call for substantial intervention. '**Market pessimists**' emphasize that active state intervention is required to correct for the failures of real-world markets; indeed market failures are so pervasive as to render the scope of government intervention to correct for them very great indeed – arguably much greater than has ever existed in so-called market economies, at least outside wartime. If the free working of competitive markets is to yield a Pareto-efficient outcome, massive intervention is necessary to perfect the competition which the result requires. But the historical record strongly suggests that when intervention has occurred, it has been characterized by *chronic regulatory failure*.

Activity 3.3

Why do you think that monopolies might not be desirable from society's point of view? (Hint: what can a monopoly do that a perfectly competitive firm cannot?) Can you think of any arguments in favour of monopoly? (Hint: how do the large drugs companies justify their profits?) How should society regulate monopolies, if at all? What problems might arise and why?

3.3.3 The macroeconomic experience: from market pessimism to market optimism

Thus far, the argument has considered the historical record of microeconomic interventions by the state. Running parallel to such policies was a broader macroeconomic consensus concerned with managing the economy as a whole. This consensus was essentially established in reaction to the experience of the 1930s: a capitalist economy seemed incapable of providing employment for all those who wanted to work. Consequently after 1945 it was broadly common ground between the major UK political parties that the state had a positive duty to intervene in the economy, in pursuit of full employment, higher growth rates, stable prices and an adequate balance of payments position. Policies used were fiscal (taxation, borrowing and expenditure) and monetary (supply of money and credit, interest rate and exchange rate), and the whole became known as the **Keynesian** approach to demand management, both complementing the microeconomic supply-side policies outlined above and providing their overall context.

But what was achieved was not impressive, at least in terms of international comparisons. Attempts to accelerate growth rates persistently foundered on balance of payments difficulties, and full employment policies appeared to generate inflation; overall, policy became known as 'stop–go', and led to a significant deterioration in living standards relative to other member states of the Organization for Economic Cooperation and Development (OECD). Thus from 1957 to 1967 the growth rate of UK GDP was only 65 per cent of the average rate for member states of the OECD; from 1967 to 1978 it was only 60 per cent of the OECD average, and from 1973 to 1978 only 45 per cent. Other indicators, such as those for inflation and for unemployment, reveal the same record: a performance significantly worse in the UK than in other advanced capitalist countries.

Thus from the early 1970s there was growing disillusionment with the techniques of managing the economy through Keynesian policies. The emphasis accordingly changed as the 1970s progressed, from a belief that active government intervention was desirable to a belief that it was not, and unemployment problems were increasingly seen not in terms of a failure of overall demand in, and coordination of, all markets in the economy, but rather in terms of the functioning of one specific market, the labour market. Thus by 1975 Samuel Brittan was writing that,

> Orthodox demand management has been based on the view that governments have the power to fix the amount of unemployment at a politically chosen level by monetary and fiscal policy. The most fundamental of the 'monetarist' contentions is that governments do not have such powers. The minimum sustainable level of unemployment is, on the contrary, determined by the functioning of the labour market. Attempts to push the unemployment percentage below this sustainable level will lead not merely to inflation, but to an increasing rate of inflation and ultimately to currency collapse. (cited in Keegan, 1984, p. 42)

As is clear from this argument, the alternative to Keynesian demand management was sought in '**monetarism**'. The basic tenets of monetarism can be summarized as follows:

• If left to itself the economy is stable. Instabilities are generated by the erratic policies of governments, partly because of the erratic nature of politicians and partly because of the variable and unpredictable lags in policy implementation.

• Insofar as there are instabilities which are *not* generated by government policy, flexible prices in competitive markets create a natural tendency towards equilibrium which irons out such instabilities. This equilibrium is characterized by 'the natural rate of unemployment', determined in the labour market, at which all inflation expectations are fully realized and all unemployment is voluntary.

• Changes in the rate of growth of the money stock in the long run determine changes in the price level. Inflation is caused by governments printing too much money, and can be eliminated by controlling the money supply.

Monetarism assumes, first, that individuals optimize, in price-taking, competitive markets, and, secondly, that markets clear, for if markets are not in equilibrium, there are profitable trading opportunities which are unexploited and, if that is the case, individuals cannot be optimizing. Only autonomous shocks can disrupt the economic system, and these shocks are then identified as instabilities in the monetary system, one major source being government monetary and fiscal policy. The policy implication of the theory for demand management is, then, that *monetary and fiscal policy be passive, based on pre-announced rules which everyone knows and understands*.

Thus markets can be treated *as if* they were perfect, and to the extent that they are not, government intervention must be directed solely towards working *with* market forces. Instead of demand management, the focus of government policy should be on the supply side, the freeing up of market forces. With monetary policy controlling credit and hence inflation, the role of fiscal policy is restricted to providing those tax incentives which stimulate individual enterprise and initiative.

3.3.4   Failures of intervention and the approach of market optimists

Side by side with the transition from Keynesianism to monetarism was a growing recognition that the regulatory failures, engendered by microeconomic policies to correct for market failure, could not be ignored. Whereas market pessimists stress the failure of real-world markets to approximate the competitive ideal and the consequent necessity for intervention, **market optimists** stress that intervention is only likely to make things worse.

Market optimists contrast the information and incentive requirements necessary for successful state intervention with those of the price mechanism. In a market mechanism, market participants need only know their own preferences and the relevant market prices on the demand side, or their own technologies and the relevant market prices on the supply side. Hence informational requirements for efficient choice are minimized; moreover, choices *will* tend to be efficient in a market system, because other choices will result in reductions in utility to consumers, and in profit to producers. By contrast, non-market allocation has no such inbuilt incentive mechanism, and the difficulties of devising an enforcement mechanism with appropriate rewards and penalties both for those who have to formulate the rules, and for those who have to implement them, are enormous. Thus the information economies of the price mechanism, and the incentive mechanism embodied in it, combine for market optimists to suggest that reliance on markets will in general achieve a more efficient allocation of resources than that effected via any form of state intervention.

This argument has long been used against central planning as a means of resource allocation, but the experience of state intervention at both macro and micro levels in the UK since 1945 has led to its generalization as an argument against *all* forms of state interference with the market mechanism. Even if we are concerned only with regulating markets (rather than replacing them with planning), those who do the regulating have to have sufficient information to define objectives, and then have to ensure that incentives are such that those who are regulated achieve those objectives. Market optimists argue that these requirements are in practice impossible to fulfil, and point to the historical experience outlined above as evidence. This is a pragmatic argument that the inefficiencies resulting from imperfect markets, from market failure, are likely to be less than the inefficiencies resulting from the interventions of an imperfect state, from regulatory failure. And as such, it can only be argued on a case-by-case approach. For if the advantages of economies of information and inbuilt incentive mechanism are to be achieved, the information given by the prices to the market participants has to be 'correct'. But if prices are distorted by market imperfections, such as monopoly, or asymmetries of information among participants, then reliance on such prices is hardly conducive to economic efficiency; indeed, the converse – the distortions are likely to be amplified.

Nevertheless, the historical experience of macroeconomic failure and of regulatory failure generated the presumption by the end of the 1970s that state intervention generally made things worse. Market pessimists had been forced to retreat from the high ground they had held in the 1950s and particularly the 1960s in the face of both macroeconomic and regulatory failure, and policy by the end of the 1970s was increasingly informed by market optimism. While Keynesianism had been effectively displaced by monetarism by 1976–77, with associated restrictions ('cash limits') on government expenditure programmes, this displacement was not wholehearted; enthusiasm for a market optimist approach was not apparent until the election of a Conservative government in 1979 which explicitly committed itself not to repeat the microeconomic regulatory failures and the macroeconomic demand management failures of its predecessors. In place of the former, it embraced privatization and deregulation, and in place of the latter it combined monetarism with the pursuit of structural alterations in the functioning of the labour market. Rather than an ad hoc, piecemeal and pragmatic approach, this combination of policies effectively elevated market optimism into an overarching principle.

Privatization

Privatization means several different things. First, there are sales of central government-owned land and buildings. Secondly, raising five times as much revenue in 1986, there are sales of council houses by local authorities. Between 1979 and 1983, nearly 600 000 housing units were sold; more than 400 000 have been sold between 1983 and 1987; and a further one million units are planned to be sold by 1992. More than 90 per cent of units sold have been purchased by their tenants, and units were sold in the period 1979–83 at an average discount of 42 per cent. In the financial year 1987–88, the average discount is expected to be 47 per cent (according to *The Observer*, 25 October 1987). Local authority asset sales are forecast by the government to raise £3.5 billion in 1987–88 and £3 billion annually thereafter to 1990–91.

The third aspect of privatization is harder to quantify and concerns the 'contracting out' of services so that they are privately rather than publicly financed. According to Yarrow, contracting out

> ... implies the establishment of more complex arrangements than those surrounding housing sales and it requires the continuing involvement of public authorities in contract enforcement and renewal. Nevertheless, by early 1984 over fifty local authorities had each privatized at least one service using this method. The services most commonly 'contracted out' have been various types of cleaning (street, offices, schools, hospitals, etc.) and refuse collection, but others have included pest control, catering, architectural services, grass cutting, provision of parking facilities, laundries and housing repairs. (1986, p. 326)

This, however, was all on a small scale by the mid-1980s. For local authorities, around 4 per cent of refuse collection services were put out to tender, and half of these were supplied by private contractors; for the health service, 11 per cent of laundry services, 2 per cent of cleaning and 0.5 per cent of catering were supplied by private contractors (figures cited by Kay and Thompson, 1987, p. 199).

The final and perhaps the most visible aspect of privatization is the whole or partial disposal of publicly owned bodies to the private sector as going concerns, together with the whole or partial disposal of public stakes in private companies. Revenues of £3.8 billion were raised in 1986, for example, and companies sold by 1987 included British Aerospace, British Petroleum, Cable and Wireless, Sealink, Jaguar, British Telecom, Britoil, British Gas, British Airways and the British Airports Authority, plus a host of smaller concerns. As with sales of council houses, discounts also applied to the stock market flotations of public sector corporations; according to an *Observer* report of a seminar held in January 1988, 'Treasury ministers reiterated that public sector corporations must be sold at 20 per cent less than their real worth to attract investors' (*The Observer*, 31 January 1988). By the late 1980s plans were in train for the privatization of the electricity industry, the various water boards, the National Girobank, British Steel and, more distantly, British Rail. Consequently the government was forecasting that privatization share sales would raise £5 billion every financial year from 1987–88 to 1990–91.

The privatization programme illustrates the way in which the reaction to regulatory failure has elevated the substitution of private ownership for public into a principle which economic theory cannot justify. For the product and capital markets in which the larger privatized enterprises operate are highly imperfect. There is hardly a credible takeover threat, or bankruptcy threat, to British Telecom or British Gas, for instance. Kay and Thompson remark that

> ... where privatization involves a new regulatory framework – as in telecom-munications – there may be a possibility that performance in non-competitive areas will be improved by it, although that has yet to be demonstrated. Where, as in gas, it involves only the creation of a new regulatory institution, expec-tations must be very low. The weakness of the privatization programme, then, is that it is not rooted in an analysis of why nationalization had failed, as distinct from the assertion that it *has* failed. The view that, since nationalized industries are unsuccessful, private ownership must be better is a slogan rather than a coherent industrial policy. (1987, pp. 206–7)

The privatization programme was not only an expression of the ideology of market optimism; it was also part of the more general programme of reducing government expenditures. At the time of writing (mid-1988), it is likely that sustained further reductions in government expenditure will require an extension of the run-down of public sector corporations to the general government sector itself. This will involve the reduction of employ-ment by general government, and a reduction in the growth of expenditures (relative to GDP) on education, health and social security, and housing (items which in 1986 comprised some 60 per cent of all government expendi-tures). Cuts in public provision and the replacement where possible of public provision with private provision are part of the general trend towards encouraging 'the enterprise economy' and 'individual self-reliance', of which the privatization programme is a part.

The labour market

On pre-1982 definitions, male unemployment more than quadrupled from 1970 to 1985. On OECD standardized definitions, male unemployment (in percentage terms) in the UK in 1984 was almost double that in France, Germany, Italy or the US. By 1985 male employment in the UK was lower than it was in 1911. This increase was principally in two jumps, 1974–76 and 1979–82, of which the latter was the major one. Total unemployment rose from 4.8 per cent of the working population (excluding HM Forces and the self-employed) in June 1979 (about 1.2 million people) to 15.7 per cent in March 1986 (on the same basis of recording, about 3.8 million), excluding around 670000 workers on special employment and training schemes in early 1986. This increase in unemployment was almost entirely due to an increase in the duration of unemployment – those becoming unemployed in the early 1980s on average remained so for a year. This striking increase in long-term unemployment was concentrated in a small proportion of the population (in any year some 3 per cent of the labour force account for 70 per cent of the total weeks of unemployment).

Now according to monetarist philosophy, if unemployment exists at all, its causes must be sought in market failure in the labour market. This could take a number of forms:

- payments to the unemployed might be too high relative to wages to induce people to work;

- there might be floors to wages which prevent them falling sufficiently to induce employers to increase hirings;

- the skills of the unemployed might be inappropriate to the skills required by employers;

- monopoly power might be exercised (by trades unions) to maintain wages at higher levels than would be sustainable in a genuinely free market.

In the first half of the 1980s legislation was pursued in all of these areas, the long-run goal being to establish a market in which individual employee contracted with individual employer over hiring and remuneration. Thus, corresponding to the above forms of market failure:

- the replacement ratio (between income when unemployed and income in employment) was reduced by measures such as taxing unemployment benefit, and abolishing the earnings related component of unemployment and sickness benefit, forcing a greater reliance on supplementary benefit;

- employment protection legislation was reduced, and various safeguards to workers in low-paid employment were abolished (for example, the removal of 500 000 workers under 21 from regulation by the Wages Councils, and the repeal of both the Fair Wages Resolution of 1946 and its extension to non-governmental employment in 1975);

- there was a series of measures to encourage training and employment and proposals that the schemes be absorbed into a national training programme;

- the Employment Acts of 1980 and 1982, and the Trade Union Act of 1984 were intended to reduce union power, making it more difficult to call and to successfully pursue a strike, and indeed more difficult for unions to organize and to retain members. In addition, the government carefully prepared for – indeed arguably provoked – a dispute with the National Union of Mineworkers in 1985, whose rhetoric at the time was one of industrial struggle, and then used the resources of the state to ensure the NUM's humiliating defeat as a public lesson to all.

Together with the end of any macroeconomic commitment to full employment, all of these measures are directed at establishing a 'new realism' in industrial relations, with a restoration of management's 'right to manage', which would facilitate an 'enterprise culture'.

Market optimism: a summary

If by the mid-1970s the failures of interventions structured by market pessimism were apparent, what can be said by the late 1980s concerning the policies informed by market optimism?

First of all, we should not expect the removal of rigidities in the function-ing of markets to be a short-run affair. There *has* been some acceleration of productivity growth (particularly in 1982–83), but this could have been associated with the upturn of activity in the business cycle as the economy recovered from the trough it reached in 1981. It is worth noting (Metcalf and Richardson, 1986, p. 286) that if unemployment was to fall to 2 million between 1985 and 1991, some 2.6 million extra jobs would have to be created in that period, or some 1400 jobs a day. The previous six-year fastest post-war growth rate was only 750 jobs a day, between 1959 and 1965, or just over half the rate required. There have been periods in the past when employ-ment has risen sharply (thus a rise of 2 million from 1933 to 1937), and by the late 1980s it remained to be seen whether policies aimed at correcting market failure in the labour market could repeat this experience.

Secondly, there was some evidence of changes in the structure of the labour market, but it is open to different interpretations. For example, was the reduced trade union militancy of the early 1980s attributable to the success of trade union legislation, or was it merely an obvious consequence of historically high levels of unemployment? Mayhew provides some inter-esting summary judgements on the effects of policy on the labour market by the mid-1980s:

> At present there are very good jobs and there are very bad jobs, and a whole spectrum between these two extremes. But there is no obvious dividing line separating people into two distinct segments, between which immobility is particularly marked. Yet we may well be starting to see the emergence of two more strongly distinct groups than the labour market has hitherto witnessed ... On the one hand, there will be a group of workers who are well paid, in secure employment and with 'career prospects' and possibly well represented by 'reformed' unions. On the other, there will be a group who are poorly paid, in casual or short-stay employment and with no careers. Some signs of this are apparent. (Mayhew, 1985, p. 78)

He cites as evidence the widening income gap between low paid and high paid, the increase in subcontracting, the growth of employment in small firms, and processes of technical change which might be destroying 'middle-ranking' jobs (see also Allen, 1988b).

Thirdly, there were severe distributional implications of policy towards the labour market and policy towards unemployment and income support of the poor. The gibe that the poor had to be made worse off to persuade them to work harder but the rich had to be made better off in order to persuade *them* to work harder has a certain justice to it, for a succession of tax-cutting budgets made the rich substantially better off, while policy towards social security and above all the unemployed substantially worsened the relative position of the poor. By 1983, for example, some 2.8 million people were living in families with incomes below the supplementary benefit level. Indeed, taking all people with incomes within 40 per cent of supplementary benefit level (often described as being 'on the margin of poverty') this figure rose from 22 per cent of the population in 1979 to 30.5 per cent (or 16.4 million) in 1983 (Atkinson, Hills and Le Grand, 1987).

Finally, we must recognize that market optimism cannot be understood solely as a perspective in economic theory of the free workings of competitive markets. Equally important is the associated political philosophy. This political philosophy is individualistic in exactly the same way that economic theory is individualistic: the liberty (or freedom – the two words are treated synonymously) of the individual is paramount. Liberty is defined negatively, as the absence of coercion of any one individual by another and, in particular, the absence of coercion by society or by the state except in so far as intervention is required to ensure negative freedom for all. What is important is to establish the widest possible area in which each individual is free from coercion by others, and from coercion by the state. This approach is the same as that of an economic theory which proposes that any interference in the functioning of free markets, other than that required to support or maintain their free functioning, is to be condemned as a restriction on individual freedom. In summary, the combination of an individualist political philosophy founded on negative freedom and an individualist economic theory founded on optimization in competitive markets in equilibrium, provides one basis for understanding the changing role of the state in the economy. *Helm* (1986) outlines a similar interpretation of 'Thatcherism' in these terms with slightly different emphasis.

Activity 3.4

Return to Activity 3.2 at the end of section 3.3.1. In the light of the discussion of section 3.3 as a whole, would you tend more towards market pessimism or market optimism in deciding what classification is most desirable today? Why?

3.4 Marxism, the economy and the state

3.4.1 An introduction to the Marxist approach

Individualism defines the functions of the state in terms of provision of what the market cannot provide, and in terms of supplementing what the market cannot do well; otherwise the state is concerned merely 'to hold the ring for competition' by defining the rules under which markets can operate freely. Negative freedom or negative liberty is thereby maximized. We have seen that the difference within this framework between market pessimists and market optimists concerns whether state intervention in general improves any existing state of affairs. In both approaches, however, individuals are treated as free and equal. They are presumed each to have an initial endowment of resources, and are free to trade, or not, as they please. But suppose those endowments are such that one small group of individuals owns all the means needed for production, and the remaining much larger group has no asset other than its capacity to work. If that is the case, then mutually beneficial trade can occur. But now there is a crucial asymmetry between the groups, For individuals who have nothing but their capacity to work cannot choose meaningfully not to work at all. All they can choose is to whom in the smaller group to sell their working capacity. Conversely, people in the smaller group can indeed choose not to work, for they can live off the labour of the larger group. The latter's lack of access to resources forces them into the market. This is the basis of the **Marxist** critique, which centres on the way in which access to means of life and means of labour in a market economy based on private property restricts the liberty or freedom of the many for the benefit of the few, and at the same time proclaims the liberty of the few in the name of all.

The Marxist approach argues that the relation of the individual to the means of production – whether access is only gained through the market by the sale of the capacity to labour, or whether it is gained directly through ownership – is sufficiently important that all individuals who have the same relation can be aggregated and treated as one. Define groups of individuals in the same structured relation to the means of production as 'classes', as capitalist class (the smaller group) and working class (the larger group). Then take the total output produced by the working class, subtract the consumption requirements of the working class, and what remains is the surplus product (i.e. surplus to the consumption requirements of the producers themselves). This accrues to the capitalist class. In order that a surplus product be produced at all, the working class must work for longer than is necessary to produce its own consumption requirements, that is, must perform surplus labour. A society in which the fruits of this surplus labour are appropriated by the producers themselves is called 'communism', a precondition for which is when producers control the means of production themselves, and hence, because definitionally there is only one class, there are no classes at all. All other societies are characterized by situations in which the fruits of the surplus labour of the producers are appropriated by some other group, or class. Class antagonism, or class struggle, accordingly structures the history and development of all non-communist societies, and they cannot be understood except in these terms.

Hence the critical question for Marxism concerns how one class maintains its domination over the other, how one class extracts surplus labour from the other, and how this extraction is reproduced through time. In slave societies and feudal societies, this extractive process is fairly evident, but in capitalist society it is not at all obvious, and a major task of Marxism is to expose how and why surplus labour takes the form of a sum of money called 'profit'.

Class societies are in general determined by a particular pattern of property relations and the class struggle surrounding them. Major historical transformations occur when one pattern of property relations is superseded (generally violently) by another: these transformations are often concentrated in a political transformation of the state (i.e. a 'revolution'), although economically they take longer to effect and may precede, or be implemented as a consequence of, political struggle. The dynamics of this are not relevant here; what is important is the implied role of the state in the analysis. In general, the state in the Marxist account is seen as the political instrument of the ruling class, an instrument which advances and defends a particular pattern of property relations.

But analysis of the *capitalist* state cannot be left in these terms, because, unlike the situation in pre-capitalist societies, economic activities are separated from political activites (just as a 'private' sphere is separated from a 'public' sphere). The extraction of surplus labour in capitalism does not (usually) require the political coercion associated with feudalism or slavery. Rather, it happens automatically via the market mechanism. So what requires further elaboration is the sense in which the capitalist state is the political instrument of those who own the means of production, and the way in which the market is their economic instrument. For capitalist society is one in which, first, class relations are systematically reproduced by the market mechanism and, secondly, the state protects the existing pattern of property relations from any market failure in this regard.

Activity 3.5

Contrast the meaning of 'market failure' just outlined with that of 'market failure' of section 3.3.2. For whom is it a 'failure' in each case?

3.4.2 Markets and Marxism

Members of the working class require a certain quantity of resources to survive and reproduce themselves, but can only find such resources through market processes. Specifically, workers have to sell whatever resources they have in order to gain the money required for market access to consumer goods, and the only resource they have to sell is their capacity to work, or their 'labour-power'. This is sold for a wage. The purchaser, the capitalist, purchases this potentiality and 'consumes' it by organizing its combination with the means of production (material inputs and instruments of production) and hence its realization as actual work performed in a production process. But commodities of greater value are produced by the actual work performed than the capacity to work costs the capitalist. How units of time become sums of money is not relevant here. All that is important is that the working class works for longer than the time necessary to produce the commodities it needs to survive. On translation into sums of money, the working day divides into paid labour time in which the working class produces commodities of equivalent value to the wage, and unpaid labour time appropriated by the capitalist class as profit. The ratio between unpaid labour time and paid labour time in the aggregate defines the rate of surplus value, or rate of exploitation.

Why should workers involve themselves in such exploitation? The Marxist answer is that they have no choice, for it is only through working for capitalists that workers survive at all. And why should all profit accrue to capitalists? The historical process of coercion whereby the mass of the population is separated from the means of production – typically the separation of the peasantry from the land and the herding of landless peasants into the nascent cities – creates the necessity for a worker to sell his or her labour-power in order to survive. Labour-power therefore becomes a commodity, with property rights accruing out of its possession to its owner. Just as when the capitalist purchases a loaf of bread and is then free to consume it in whatsoever manner he or she chooses, so when the capitalist purchases labour-power the same is true. The fact that the 'consumption' of labour-power in production has the peculiar property of creating more value than it itself possesses is merely the good fortune of its owner, the capitalist. The injustice involved is *not* the injustice of the *individual* transaction, for no injustice is there involved. (It is this, for Marxists, that explains why individualist theories maintain their attraction and their power, for they are in one sense true.) The injustice that is involved is the *class* injustice whereby one class is compelled to work for a period for another, for free, in order to gain access to a subsistence base that it has produced itself but which has been expropriated from it.

It is the market mechanism which reproduces and hence perpetuates this situation. This means that markets in Marxist theory function quite differently from the perspective that individualism provides, particularly in its market optimist variant. Whereas for market optimists markets work via the diffusion of resources across vast numbers of participants, perfect competition being the norm and monopoly the exception, for Marxists the situation is the opposite. Markets function so as to concentrate resources in the hands of the capitalist class; workers leave the production process as they enter it, with no asset other than their potentiality for work; and the competition that exists is not between large numbers of small participants but between small numbers of large participants, with a tendency for the numbers to decline and the size of participants to increase.

Accordingly, for Marxists, markets are free, in the sense that individuals can choose whether or not to participate; all participants are equal before the law; equivalents are exchanged and nobody gets something for nothing; and yet despite all of this, class exploitation exists. For the extraction of surplus labour-time occurs *in production*, but it depends upon workers being forced into the labour *market* (more properly, the *market* for labour power) to gain monetary access to consumer goods. This perspective on markets then determines how Marxists understand the state.

3.4.3   Markets and the state

Within the framework of individualism, the state is basically a neutral referee holding the ring for competition, and disputes within individualism concern how most appropriately to organize a framework for competition. Neither market pessimists nor market optimists question the state's neutrality. In contrast, a Marxist approach regards the way in which the state relates to markets as the way in which the state advances, protects and reproduces the class exploitation of workers by capitalists. Appearances to the contrary, the state is a class state, and not a state of all the people. Appearances suggest that the state is separate from the production processes of society, but just as capitalism requires freedom and equality before the law for the unfreedom and inequality of exploitation to occur, so too the capitalist state is not external to the structure of class exploitation but is an important part of it.

For the reproduction of class relations requires certain types of activity by the state over and above the obvious ones of maintaining a monetary system, formulating and maintaining a legal system which defends the existing structure of property rights, maintaining coercive forces to defend the status quo from external and internal threat, and so on. These other activities are broadly twofold: first, to regulate the value of labour-power; and, second, to represent to all capitalists their common class interest and thereby to act as the vehicle whereby general class interest dominates the disparate interests of different fractions of the capitalist class.

The value of labour-power

The (money) value of labour-power can be defined in a number of ways. One way is to see it as the monetary equivalent of the time taken to produce all of those commodities which the working class needs to reproduce itself – food, clothing, housing, transport etc. Clearly, there is a lower limit to the value of labour-power, defined by biological subsistence. But a major portion of the value of labour-power comprises what is conventionally recognized at a particular time as being necessary, and in the long run this is the subject of class struggle. Alternatively, the (money) value of labour-power can be defined as that monetary equivalent of society's total product which in the course of class struggle accrues to the working class. Either way, if the value of labour-power over time rises faster than unpaid labour-time can be increased via productivity changes (by decreasing the time it takes to produce commodities for a given working day), or more generally if the cost of investment rises faster than the returns to which it gives rise, then the mainspring of capitalist accumulation is threatened as profitability falls.

Now consider the activities of the welfare state. The taxation and social security system affects the amount of money workers have to spend; certain goods and services are subsidized, such as housing; certain services are provided free or at greatly reduced cost, such as health-care. All of these activities have a bearing on the value of labour-power; so too does the quantity and quality of state provision for the non-working population – children, the elderly, the sick, those physically or mentally handicapped and so on. These activities must all be financed, and they can only be financed out of surplus labour-time. This at once suggests the possibility that at particular times the scale of state expenditure on welfare provision might hinder the processes of capital accumulation and economic growth.

The state as collective capitalist

The way in which capitalists realize the unpaid labour they have extracted from workers is through the competitive sale of their commodity outputs. The phenomenon of capitalist competition is an extremely important one, for competition acts as a coercive force on each individual capitalist, impelling continual innovation and technological advance as a matter of survival. But if capitalists are in competition with one another, the expenses incurred in ensuring an adequately educated and healthy workforce, for example, will not be voluntarily shouldered by any one of them. A similar argument holds with respect to the maintenance of a legal system to defend capitalist property rights, a police force to implement such laws, and an army to defend against subversion from within and to maintain whatever posture is deemed appropriate on the international arena. Capitalist competition requires a state to enforce upon all capitalists the provisions required by all but provided by none.

This implies that the state be separate from, or distinct from, the capitalist class as a whole, for otherwise it could not mediate between different and competing capitalist interests, let alone represent their common interest. It is this separation which encourages the belief that the state represents *all* individuals equally, which permits working-class reforms to be won, which allows room for manoeuvre, and which enables varieties of strategy. Policies can be attempted and reversed, and mistakes can be made.

But in all of this, what structures overall development are trends in surplus labour-time in production. Whether in the national or the international arena, only market forces provide the necessary discipline towards that economy and technological innovation which allows for the expansion of surplus labour-time, and only such sustained expansion can provide resources for investment, capitalist consumption and state expenditures without imperilling growth and profitability.

3.4.4   Trends in state economic policy

The account presented so far has been logical rather than historical. Marxist accounts of capitalist history are structured around the Marxist theory of crisis, whereby periods of sustained accumulation contain the seeds of their own demise, and are followed by periods of dislocation and restructuring which in turn lay the foundations for renewed accumulation.

The theory of crisis is based on a number of interrelated propositions:

• that competition forces technical advances upon capitalists as a condition of their survival;

• that technical advance typically involves tendencies towards greater levels of mechanization per worker;

• that such mechanization involves a proportionately greater expenditure on inputs than the increase in profits to which it gives rise, resulting in a falling rate of profit;

• that a falling rate of profit generates a series of measures which work in the opposite direction, principally the reorganization of production via the creation of unemployment, the reduction of the value of labour-power, the bankruptcy of individual capitalists and so on;

• that these measures lay the basis for a restoration of profitability;

• that this cyclical fluctuation of the rate of profit is structured by particular waves of technical advance and their subsequent exhaustion.

The focus is therefore on longer-term movements in the rate of profit, which are illustrated in Table 3.2.

Activity 3.6

Sketch a historical account within a Marxist framework of the relation of the state to the economy in the UK, analogous to the account of section 3.3 within an individualist framework. You should bear in mind:

(a) the international context:

• the long boom in the international capitalist economy from 1945 to 1970 or so, against which background Keynesian demand management policies were deemed successful;

• the international orientation of British capitalism towards the protected markets of colonies and ex-colonies, the low levels of domestic investment that this encouraged, and the problems encountered in international competition when world markets were liberalized from the 1950s onwards;

• the petering out of the long boom in the late 1960s and the stagflation of the 1970s;

• the restructuring of the world economy from the 1970s with the establishment of a new international division of labour and of a new role in that division for financial markets, the agents of transformation being primarily the multinational corporations and the international banks;

(b) the domestic context:

• the combination of the domination of capital over labour with the

Table 3.2   Rates of return before interest and tax at current replacement cost (percentages)

	All industrial and commercial companies		Industrial and commercial companies excluding North Sea[1]		Manufacturing companies	
	Gross (a)	Net (b)	Gross (a)	Net (b)	Gross (a)	Net (b)
1960	11.8	13.7	11.8	13.7	12.2	14.8
1961	10.6	11.7	10.6	11.7	10.6	12.3
1962	9.9	10.7	9.9	10.7	9.8	11.1
1963	10.4	11.5	10.4	11.5	10.2	11.7
1964	10.9	12.2	10.9	12.2	10.5	12.1
1965	10.5	11.5	10.5	11.5	10.0	11.2
1966	9.6	10.1	9.6	10.2	9.0	9.7
1967	9.6	10.2	9.7	10.3	9.1	9.8
1968	9.7	10.3	9.8	10.4	8.9	9.5
1969	9.7	10.1	9.8	10.2	9.1	9.8
1970	8.9	8.9	8.9	8.9	8.0	8.1
1971	9.1	9.1	9.1	9.2	7.3	6.9
1972	9.3	9.5	9.3	9.5	8.0	8.1
1973	8.8	8.9	8.8	8.9	7.8	8.0
1974	6.2	5.1	6.3	5.3	5.3	4.3
1975	5.5	3.9	5.6	4.2	4.4	2.8
1976	5.9	4.3	5.7	4.3	4.7	3.2
1977	8.0	7.4	7.4	6.7	6.4	5.7
1978	8.4	7.8	7.7	7.1	6.5	6.0
1979	8.0	7.4	6.6	5.6	5.4	4.3
1980	7.4	6.3	5.4	3.8	4.7	3.0
1981	7.3	6.1	4.8	2.8	4.2	2.3
1982	8.3	7.7	5.6	4.0	5.2	4.0
1983	9.3	9.3	6.2	4.9	5.5	4.4
1984	10.1	10.7	6.6	5.6	5.9	5.1
1985	10.7	11.5	7.8	7.2	6.6	6.4
1986	9.7	10.0	8.8	8.9	7.3	7.5
1987	10.5	11.3	9.6	10.2	8.3	9.2

Industrial and commercial companies and manufacturing companies based on national accounts data.
[1] North Sea exploration and production activities.

Basis of estimates

Profits

(a) Gross operating surplus on UK operations, i.e. gross trading profits less stock appreciation plus rent received.

(b) Net operating surplus on UK operations, i.e. gross operating surplus less capital consumption at current replacement cost.

Capital employed

(a) Gross capital stock of fixed assets (excluding land) at current replacement cost, plus book value of stocks, in UK.

(b) Net capital stock of fixed assets (excluding land) at current replacement cost, plus book value of stocks, in UK.

Source: Department of Trade and Industry, *British Business*, 30 September 1988

compromise of capital with labour represented by nationalization and the welfare state in the 1945–50 era;

● the repeated attempts to alter this balance through attempted 'reform' of the trades unions from the late 1960s onwards;

● the pressure for market provision of welfare and educational pro-grammes in the 1980s, programmes originally conceded during the Second World War, but funded with increasing difficulty after the petering out of the post-war boom.

You should think about crisis theory particularly in relation to a comparison of the trends of Table 3.2 with the trend of Figure 3.1. Finally your account should be as sharply focused as possible on the Marxist account of how markets function, considering ways in which pressures on profitability may have encouraged changing state policies. *Leys* (1983, Chs 5 and 6) provides a useful background to this exercise.

3.5 Conclusion

We have examined three different answers to the question of how markets work. Two of these are variants within the same framework of individualism and focus on the issue of whether state intervention in general improves any existing situation.

● For market pessimists, markets are imperfect, in disequilibrium, and require coordination. Market failure is pervasive and requires active state intervention in order to improve social welfare.

● For market optimists, markets by and large work as if they are perfect, in equilibrium, and hence adequately coordinate themselves. State interven-tion only leads to regulatory failure and hence should be minimized.

The third answer to the question of how markets work is set within a Marxist framework, and is rather different from considerations of whether markets work well or badly, and whether their functioning can be improved by the state.

● For Marxists, markets work to reproduce class relations of exploitation, and whether the state steps in to reinforce such relations in particular areas is a historically contingent question depending upon, first, class struggle as it determines and is determined by the role of accumulation and the necessity for restructuring and, second, the response of the state to such economic imperatives.

While there are some points of contact between market pessimism and market optimism, because of their common basis in individualism, there is none between individualism and Marxism.

● For individualism, social cohesion and harmony is achieved through the pursuit of selfish gain; and the state articulates the national consensus which emerges out of competition.

● For Marxism, society is conflictual, with class struggle structuring and determining all significant phenomena; the state is a class state, but with appearances which legitimate a status quo which could not long survive the withdrawal of the consent of the majority to be denied non-market access to the means of production and consumption.

In order to understand the relation between state and economy, some choice must ultimately be made between these competing perspectives.

Further reading

A very readable account of the change in emphasis in macroeconomics from the early 1970s to the 1980s is *Mrs Thatcher's Economic Experiment* by W. Keegan (Harmondsworth, Penguin; 1984). More analytical perspectives are contained in *The British Economic Crisis* by K. Smith (Harmondsworth, Penguin; 1986). One Marxist approach to the welfare state is given by I. Gough in *The Political Economy of the Welfare State* (London, Macmillan; 1979) and controversies within Marxism about the state and its relation to society are surveyed by B. Jessop in *Theories of the Capitalist State* (London, Martin Robertson; 1982). *Leys* (1983, Chapters 5 and 6) looks specifically at the development of different state strategies in Britian. This chapter has concentrated mainly on economic interpretations of state-economy relations. It has not looked closely at the spatial impact of changes in these. Useful background to this is to be found in Martin (1988), and *Lovering and Boddy* (1988) look specifically at the spatial impacts of defence spending.

4 Restructuring the state: the case of local government

Allan Cochrane

Contents

4.1   Introduction

After a period of apparent – and perhaps misleading – political stability in the first twenty-five years following the Second World War, the 1970s seem to have marked some sort of turning-point for the British political system. But the direction taken at that turning-point is less easy to identify. In the previous chapter Simon Mohun considered one aspect of the problem, exploring different interpretations of the changing relations between state and economy in the post-war period. Here we shall be looking rather more closely at changes within the state system itself, considering ways in which it has been restructured or, perhaps more accurately, was restructuring itself, in response to crisis.

A key concern will be to explore the extent to which there has been **structural change** in this area. In other words the issue is whether there has been a gradual process of change based on clear continuities with the past or an accumulation of changes in a relatively short space of time which has fundamentally altered the structures of the UK state. In another context Allen and Massey (1988, p. 2) develop the notion of *periods* of structural change to describe this process, and one of the central questions around which this chapter is organized is whether the UK state has recently passed through (or is still passing through) such a period.

These issues will be developed by looking in some depth at one particular aspect of the UK state – namely, local government and its position within the wider state system. Local government has been chosen as a case for further exploration not only because of its inherent interest as an object of study, but also because of its remarkable centrality to debates about the changing UK state in the 1970s and 1980s, reflected in policy discussion, academic debate and a continuing series of legislative 'reforms' and official reports. For much of that time, local government acted as an arena through which wider political debates about the state were conducted.

Local governement was a crucial element of the social-democratic or Keynesian **welfare state** so laboriously constructed after the war. As *Rhodes* (1985) notes, sub-national government in the UK has developed extensively because until the 1970s it was the prime vehicle for building the welfare state. Although most existing powers and responsibilities over the delivery of health services and the production of utilities, such as electricity and gas, were effectively removed by post-war nationalization, within the welfare state the role of councils was substantially increased, building on responsibilities some of them had already claimed in the inter-war period. There was a massive expansion of public housing (which was even called *council* housing); responsibility for personal social services (such as children's welfare and provision for the old) grew dramatically; the growth of education budgets and responsibility for (almost) universal primary and secondary education gave local education authorities very high profiles in the lives of ordinary people; and the introduction of a nationally organized town and

Table 4.1   Local authority expenditure as a
percentage of national income and public expenditure,
United Kingdom

	Gross domestic product	Public expenditure
1950	9.1	25.8
1960	10.3	27.8
1970	13.3	30.7
1973	14.6	33.7 (peak)
1974/75	15.9 (peak)	32.2
1978/79	12.8	28.2
1981/82	12.0	25.6
1983/84	12.6	27.7
1985/86	11.4	26.4

Sources: Newton and Karran, 1985, Table 1.7; *Local
Government Trends* (CIPFA, 1987), Tables 4.2 and 4.3
(from 1974/75, figures are for financial years)

country planning system suggested a major new influence over
development.

The discrediting of the post-war system in the late 1960s and 1970s,
discussed in Chapter 2 and charted by *Leys* (1983, Ch. 5 and 6), was also
reflected in the position of local government within it. In the years up to the
mid-1970s, local authority expenditure rose steadily, and apparently inexor-
ably, as a proportion of national income (up to 1975) and as a proportion of
public spending (until 1973) (see Table 4.1). After declining sharply up to
1979 its share of both stabilized in the first years of the Thatcher government, only to fall once more into the late 1980s.

The changing financial fortunes of local government have been accompanied by substantial organizational change. Since the late 1960s there has
been a series of overlapping periods of local government reform, each of
which helps to illustrate some key theoretical debates about the state. These
periods can crudely be labelled as those of modernization (1966–76), centralization (1975–85) and fragmentation (1983 onwards). Although it would be
a mistake to see them as watertight compartments, or to pretend that issues
raised in the first were not also relevant to the third, this division is helpful in
indicating broad trends and key differences, which will be explored in the
sections which follow.

4.2   Modernization (1966–76)

4.2.1   The search for efficiency

The dominant critique of **local government** as it existed in the 1960s was relatively straightforward. The old system, with its urban district councils, rural district councils, municipal boroughs, county boroughs, the London County Council and other County Councils (the 'shire' counties), was perceived as ramshackle and illogical: incapable of efficiently delivering the services required by a welfare state in the modern age. Despite ritualistic genuflections from time to time towards the value of local democracy, it was assumed that the purpose of local government was more or less consensually agreed to be the local delivery of a set of services enshrined in centrally determined statutes. And, certainly, it was difficult to find any substantial difference in approach between authorities on the basis of party political control. Sharpe and Newton (1984), for example, set out to identify differences between the spending patterns of urban councils (county boroughs) in the 1960s on the basis of party political control, and by the use of extensive statistical manipulation they succeeded in doing so. But perhaps what is most noticeable from this and other research is that the differences seem marginal. Labour councils tended to spend relatively more and be more committed to spending on social services than Conservative councils which spent a higher proportion of their budgets on education, but the bulk of spending was similar and handled through nationally organized professionals rather than locally based politicians.

By the second half of the 1960s the machinery of **local democracy** was being presented in official reports as one of the sources of problems for the effective operation of local government. John Dearlove has neatly summarized the dominant views of the period: 'Most commentators have *described* the system as democratic, inefficient, subject to massive and increasing central control, and dominated by councillors (and officers) of declining calibre' (1979, p. 22). This was reflected in a series of official government reports and White Papers, which offered the prospect of a still greater expansion of local authority spending and responsibility but only on the basis of substantial reorganization to provide greater efficiency and improve the calibre of councillors and officers. The assumption was that the creation of larger authorities (with larger budgets) would attract less parochial (more managerial) councillors and also make it possible to attract a different sort of officer, less tied to the narrowness of existing departmental boundaries with a management style closer to that of the major corporations in the private sector. An indication of the direction and degree of interest can be given by listing the series of reports produced at the time (and generally known by the name of the person who chaired the relevant committee):

• Report of the Committee on the Management of Local Government (1967) (Maud Report);

- Report of the Committee on the Staffing of Local Government (1967) (Mallaby Report);
- Report of the Royal Commission on Local Government (1969) (Redcliffe-Maude Report) (among the research studies undertaken for the Royal Commission were one on Economies of Scale in Local Government, another on the Performance and Size of Local Education Authorities, and a third on Aspects of Administration in a Large Local Authority);
- Report of the Royal Commission on Local Government in Scotland (1969) (Wheatley Report);
- Report of the Review Body on Local Government in Northern Ireland (1970) (Macrory Report);
- The New Local Authorities: Management and Structure (1972) Report of the Study Group on Local Authority Management Structures (Bains Report);
- The New Scottish Local Authorities: Organization and Management Structures (1973) Working Group on Scottish Local Government Management Structures (Paterson Report).

The overall message drawn from these many reports was that technical efficiency needed to be improved, management given an increased importance and decision-making streamlined. The 1970 White Paper on the reform of local government in England expressed these concerns simply and clearly:

> Unless local government is organized to meet the needs of the future, and in particular is organized in units large enough to match the technical and administrative requirements of the services which it administers, its powers must diminish, and with it the power of local democracy . . . Radical change is overdue. And only if such change occurs, and local government is organized in strong units with power to take major decisions, will present trends towards centralization be reversed, and local democracy secure its place as a major part of our democratic system. (HMSO, 1970, paras 10, 97; quoted in Dearlove, 1979, p. 23)

These concerns provided the basis on which major local government reorganization took place in the early 1970s in England, Scotland and Wales. In England the Local Government Act (1972) redrew the boundaries of local government and created a mixed system, in which major metropolitan areas retained powerful district councils whose responsibility included education, housing and social services, while in non-metropolitan areas education and social services were the responsibility of county councils, which also had the tasks of strategic (structure) planning. In the metropolitan areas, the newly created counties were left with strategic responsibilities, and responsibility for the police and fire services. The main tasks of the non-metropolitan districts were concerned with housing and basic services such as street cleaning and refuse collection. In London, the Greater London Council had similar responsibilities to the metropolitan counties, but the Metropolitan Police came directly under the Home Secretary, while through the Inner

London Education Authority – which also included representatives from the Inner London Boroughs – it was directly involved in education within inner London. In outer London, the individual London Boroughs alone were responsible.

Although the results of reorganization and the distribution of responsibilities which arose from it may sound confusing, the system was clearer than before. And the principles underlying it, despite short-term political bargaining over boundaries, were relatively simple, too: to have major services, councils had to have populations large enough to sustain an efficient delivery system; to have strategic planning functions, still larger bodies were needed, to reflect the need to attract technically adequate staff and to interest political leaders of a sufficiently high calibre.

Outside England, apparently, there were no areas suitable to be given metropolitan district status. In the Local Government Act (1972) Wales was organized on the basis of non-metropolitan counties, so that none of its major cities had education or social services functions, while the Local Government (Scotland) Act (1973) brought similar results to Scotland. But there the county equivalents covered very large areas and were called regions rather than counties. In addition there were three island authorities (covering the Western Isles, the Shetlands and the Orkneys) not included in any region. Cities such as Glasgow and Edinburgh were placed in the same sort of category as non-metropolitan districts in England although they had populations larger than the more rural regions and all the island councils. (Table 4.3 (in section 4.3.1) shows the structure of local government in Great Britain and the distribution of functions between different councils in 1987. The only change since 1974 is that the metropolitan counties and the GLC were abolished in 1986, so that their functions have largely been distributed between their component districts and boroughs or transferred to newly created joint boards.)

Although the changes were presented as *local* government reform, the main criteria which underlay the new legislation seemed to be national in origin. Local governments were to become more efficient and effective parts of a national system. The reorganization in England recognized some important variations between areas, for example in (not always successfully) attempting to distinguish between metropolitan districts (such as Sheffield, Birmingham and Manchester) and non-metropolitan districts (such as South Northamptonshire and South Bedfordshire). Places such as Nottingham, Southampton, Bristol and Middlesbrough, however, continued to stick out, having been labelled non-metropolitan, yet with population sizes and political traditions which suggested a different status. And in Scotland and Wales because there were no equivalents to the metropolitan districts, major urban centres were left as part of much bigger administrative areas with which they sometimes had little in common.

A clearer, if implicit, recognition of the importance of uneven development can be seen in the nature of the reforms which took place in Northern Ireland. As the Macrory Report pointed out in 1970, Northern Ireland 'is smaller than Yorkshire and has a population of 1.5 million ... the rateable value of the entire province is only £14m. In contrast the rateable value of the City of Leeds alone ... is nearly £22m: and many of the proposed unitary authorities in England will have rateable valuations of £20m, £30m and even £40m' (quoted in Tomlinson, 1980, p. 109). And for reformers from above – based in Whitehall rather than Northern Ireland – the past operation of local democracy was seen as part of the problem. The Macrory Report favoured a move (away from elected county councils) towards area boards, made up of appointed experts and other 'public-spirited individuals' with only a minority representation of elected councillors. This report presented this as 'a suitable combination of professionalism and popular representation'. But the dominant theme of the Macrory recommendations with respect to the distribution and control of services between Stormont (the Northern Ireland Parliament which has since 1971 been replaced by direct rule from Westminster) and local government was to emphasize the role of service professionals and experts, since ' "sensible" and "spontaneous" social democratic politics were absent' (Tomlinson, 1980, p. 114). The result today is that few important functions (measured in terms of expenditure) are handled by local government in Northern Ireland: most, like housing, are instead the responsibility of non-elected quangos or, like education, of area boards. The particular position of Northern Ireland in a sense encouraged the development of the 1970s programme of reforms to one of their logical conclusions with a stress on the techniques of management rather than electoral politics. (Local government reform in Northern Ireland is discussed more fully in Chapter 2, section 2.3. See also *O'Dowd*, 1989.)

In England, Wales and Scotland the new local government systems which finally came into operation in 1974 appeared to confirm a new status for local government, which was also reflected in significantly increased salaries for the chief officers of the new councils. Local government, as the Bains Report commented, was 'not limited to the provision of services. It is concerned with the overall economic, cultural and physical well-being of the community' (Study Group on Local Authority Management Structures, 1972, p. 122). The task of councils had apparently become the management of urban change, and this implied a move away from old fragmented forms of decision-making with a plethora of committees and sub-committees and unpredictable interference from councillors, towards a more integrated system. New management approaches and political structures swept through local government. Almost all the new councils soon had chief executives instead of town clerks – even if the person employed remained the same. Corporate management appeared everywhere, with the development of joint management teams of chief officers, central policy units and sometimes a series of interlocking interdepartmental working groups to cover joint areas of work and policy. On the councillor side and paralleling the creation of management teams, most councils set up policy and resources committees, to allow leading councillors an overview of the council and, in principle at least, force them to move away from narrow service committee interests and department loyalties. The new councils were to be managed, like business corporations, as single entities with overall strategies, rather than an accumulation of individual decisions made by separate departments or committees.

The connection between these reforms and the **modernization** strategies discussed in Chapter 2 should be clear. They stressed notions of strategy, planning, professional skills and modernity, while moving away from traditional forms of fragmented, professionally specialist, administration and political organization. This was reinforced by a number of other changes which took place at roughly the same time. Large generic social services departments, which arose from the proposals from the Seebohm Committee on Local Authority and Allied Personal Social Services (1968) were set up at this time. The Town and Country Planning Act (1968) and Town and Country Planning (Scotland) Act (1969) introduced a system of structure and local plans, apparently endorsing a vision in which planning departments of different authorities might integrate their development strategies into a coherent network, supervised by the Department of the Environment, the Welsh Office and the Scottish Development Department within the Scottish Office. Responsibility for these plans was divided between the tiers of local government after reorganization so that counties, metropolitan counties and the Scottish regions were responsible for the structure plans, which were understood, at first at least, to be of strategic importance, providing the framework within which local plans might be prepared by district councils.

4.2.2   The case for structural change

The extent of local government reorganization and managerial reform in the UK at the beginning of the 1970s makes it very tempting to argue that a structural change was taking place. This is a view which has been popular among some analysts of the period. According to Benington (1976), this was the time when local government became 'big business'. In her book on the local state Cynthia Cockburn develops this idea by suggesting that the main criticism to be applied to corporate planning in local government was that it was a method borrowed from the private sector and was thus inherently anti-democratic, implying control from the top and attempts to manage the community (the reproduction of labour power), as well as the workforce (in the process of production) (Cockburn, 1977, pp. 6–18). In addition, 'not only could new planning processes forge a closer link between the interests of business and government, the very style of corporate management, the language that both partners were now speaking, brought them closer together' (p. 19).

Dearlove (1979) seeks to develop a rather more sophisticated analysis in his discussion of reorganization, but his conclusion is similar. He focuses on the 'coded' language of the official reports with their complaints about the 'calibre' of officers and councillors. As Dearlove explains:

> The concern about declining councillor calibre embodies a bitter lament that a variety of changes have conspired to result in a situation in which there is now a less close and direct relationship between economic power, social status, and the political control of local government than was once the case in the Victorian age when local government enjoyed the leadership of businessmen and local notables. Business groups consider that in some places 'decline' has reached such a pitch that local political power has become almost totally divorced from economic power and may even be working against its interest ... In effect, the concern to increase calibre embodies a concern to recapture the social relations, style of politics, and class of leadership, that existed before the franchise was extended and before the working class rose to some sort of local political power through the Labour Party. (1979, pp. 104–5)

In retrospect, it is now rather easier to see that the cases made for the identification of structural change at the beginning of the 1970s were exaggerated or, at least, rather premature. The analyses of both Cockburn and Dearlove imply a relationship between business and local government which did not exist at the time and could not easily be generated, whatever the ambitions of civil servants in the departments of central government, or of individual chief executives. In most areas of local government activity, the main concern of business organizations was that councils should operate as cheaply as possible and interfere as little as possible with their operations through planning controls. Longer-term relationships had generally only developed where particular business interests were more or less directly involved. The construction and development industry is best known for this and there were notable scandals in the 1970s which linked architects (such as John Poulson), who were highly dependent on local authority orders, to key local politicians (such as T. Dan Smith), who had some influence over their allocation. Without introducing questions of legal impropriety, Dunleavy (1981) charts some of the links between the London Borough of Newham and major construction companies. But these linkages were highly instrumental. They existed because councils were – until the early 1980s at least – a major source of orders and remain, as planning authorities, agencies whose decisions could significantly influence the profitability of development schemes.

Links of this sort are intuitively likely to be stronger when local government has a major construction programme, with orders to distribute, or when large-scale development is on the cards and council co-operation is needed to ensure its success. But they hardly suggest that a major structural change has taken place.

Other links between business and local government were more informal. Saunders (1979, Chapter 8) charts a whole series of social and committee contexts through which leading councillors, local businessmen and managers from national companies tended to meet. He argues that this helped to create an overall 'community of interest' shared by business and council which made direct and formal interconnection largely irrelevant. In the case of Croydon, which he studied, the main business interests directly represented on the council were those connected with property and development. (Newton (1976) noted a similar phenomenon in Birmingham, although there the building trade was highly represented.) Although Saunders stresses that the individuals concerned did not gain directly from this, the period of his study was one of major commerical development in the borough. There was little in the way of negotiation or managed change of the sort which might be expected from the Cockburn model. Instead the council's role seemed to be facilitative. And a need for a more structured set of relationships was not recognized.

Evidence of closer and longer-term institutional arrangements between business interests and local government at this time is far more limited. Flynn's (1983) assessment of developing relationships in planning is cautious. He considers attempts by county councils to set up 'industrial liaison groups' through which firms were able to express their concerns over planning processes and procedures, and planners tried to influence the behaviour of firms. And there were also attempts to generate significant consultation in the structure planning process. But the links were not consistent or sustained, in part perhaps because it was unclear what the general discussions could be expected to deliver for particular firms and structure plans, in particular, soon gained a reputation for being of little relevance for actual processes of development. Similarly, although King (1985) is able to identify some links between the Leeds Chamber of Commerce and the council's developing economic strategy in the 1970s, they do not develop fully until the 1980s, and the links identified seem to be more of form, in terms of meetings and forums for discussion, rather than of detailed negotiation. Sheffield, too, had such links (even before reorganization) formalized in an Industrial Development Advisory Committee, involving representatives of industry, trade unions, central government departments as well as the city council, and in the late 1970s Nottinghamshire set up an economic forum involving similar groups (Johnson and Cochrane, 1981, p. 171). But such links remained tentative and seem to have been of little relevance to policy development even if the symbolism was important. It would be a mistake to suggest that there were no direct links between business and local government at this time and, indeed, it may be justified to acknowledge that they were becoming more important and more regular through various forms of consultation. But they were not sufficiently close to sustain Cockburn's analysis, particularly in the field of urban policy and the management of local communities. Cockburn's own research in Lambeth actually highlighted the difficulties of managing community groups because their ambitions rarely fitted with those of the council.

Similarly, in retrospect Dearlove's prognosis of the reorganization of local government does not survive close inspection, although like Cockburn much of what he says hits important targets. One of Dearlove's central theses is that local government reform was intended to take power away from representatives of the working class in local government and return it to representatives of the economically powerful. At one level, of course, it is difficult to assess this claim since none of the *supporters* of reform ever made it. As we have seen he argues persuasively that the issue of councillor 'calibre' was a coded way of raising it. But circumstantial evidence suggests that his case is weaker than he would allow: in particular, there is little evidence before the late 1970s of substantial party political conflict within local government. Gyford argues that the dominant form of Labour politics before then was 'municipal labourism' in which officers and politicians were allied to make 'local government's contribution to the post-1945 welfare state' (1985b, p. 5). And if undermining the left was the intention of the reforms, then it must be said that they failed dismally. By the end of the 1970s there was substantially *more* conflict between central and local government than there had been before and, by the early 1980s, not only was Labour in control of almost every urban council – even when very weak at national level – but in some places the controlling Labour groups had swung dramatically to the left. In a few cases they were even using corporate planning techniques to reshape the political face of their councils in ways never envisaged by the Bains or Paterson Reports. Gyford (1985b, p. 27) goes so far as to suggest that local government reorganization was one of the reasons for moves to the left outside London, where older councillors were replaced not by the hoped for technocrats waiting in the wings, but instead often by representatives of Labour's new left.

The ambitions of the modernizers, themselves, seem to have been exaggerated and to have encouraged commentators to believe more substantial change was taking place than was actually implemented. British local governments have not yet shown any marked ability to effectively manage change outside their own organizations. Whatever the aspirations of the corporate planners, most of the attempts to develop corporate objectives and goals (whether in structure plans or corporate documents) have ended up as bland statements of intent, which are either unachievable or virtually meaningless. The actual work of most councils continued to look more like the product of incremental growth and fragmented decision-making than of corporate policy-making.

4.2.3 Assessing the theories

These retrospective criticisms of Cockburn and Dearlove are largely based on evidence which has accumulated since their books were written. They are not fundamental criticisms of analysis or method, although they begin to raise wider questions about theoretical approaches. Put simply, it might be fair to ask whether their underlying theories of the state (or local government) can be appropriate if they lead to conclusions which are contradicted by empirical evidence.

Cockburn's analysis starts from a view of the local state (which includes local government, but also other locally based state agencies including offices of central government departments) as having a functional role within capitalism, principally concerned with **capitalist reproduction**. This is not only expressed through direct welfare, housing and educational provision to families which helps to ensure an adequate supply of suitable labour, but also in the reproduction of wider ideologies of popular consent which make it difficult for the rule to see the possibility of any other form of economic and political organization. The state's primary role, she says, is 'continually to reproduce the conditions within which capitalist accumulation can take place' (Cockburn, 1977, p. 51) and the local state is part of this greater whole. The 'state preserves a basic unity. All its parts work *fundamentally* as one' (1977, p. 47), even if from time to time its various parts seem to be moving in different directions.

This neo-Marxist theoretical underpinning encourages Cockburn to look for changes in the requirements of capitalist production to explain what is happening in the sphere of local government. Having found the key to changes in terms of the need to manage the politics of reproduction more effectively, she tends (in theory, at least, since her own empirical analysis is rather more flexible) to follow the perceived logic through, so that the conclusion is that local government is being reorganized more or less in line with changes in the organization of major capitalist enterprises. Unfortunately, as we have seen, such an approach suggests a more complete, less messy and more fundamental change at the time of her study than seems to be justified by the continuing history of the 1970s. It is almost as if the direction of change is determined in advance (by theory) and then events have to be fitted into that pre-ordained model.

Dearlove's approach shares some features with that of Cockburn, but is less directly Marxist influenced. Like her, he tries to set local government within 'the context of the encompassing political economy', but he also argues that Cockburn's approach, by presenting local government as an instrument of capital makes it 'unproblematic and so renders any detailed study of it almost superfluous' (Dearlove, 1979, p. 217). He suggests, instead, that local government reorganization took place precisely because local government is not 'a simple instrument of either the central state or dominant interests' and so has some room for political manoeuvre (1979, p. 221). 'The persistent concern to increase councillor calibre through reorganization', he says, 'makes it equally clear that the essential object of reorganization has been to make local government more functional for dominant interests, by restructuring it so as to facilitate their direct control of its expenditure and interventions' (1979, p. 245).

Dearlove starts from an understanding of changes in local government as part of a struggle between different groups 'to control public power' (1979, p. 105). In principle, of course, the conclusion of such a struggle need not be as straightforward as Dearlove implies in his own study. Even if the *intention* (however identified) of reorganization was to shift power away from local working-class representatives, the results could be, and (in the 1970s at least) probably were, different. But at the level of *theory* Dearlove's approach seems more helpful than Cockburn's in a number of important respects. Above all it succeeds in escaping from criticisms of political economy approaches for being determinist and allowing little scope for political intervention, yet it continues to stress the importance of changes in the priorities and organization of capitalism. It attempts to give some meaning to notions of relative autonomy at local level and encourages the consideration of actual political processes in determining what is possible.

One problem which remains, even in Dearlove's formulation, however, is that it tends to present options in rather too clear-cut a fashion. Reorganization is fitted into a model which already exists without sufficient attention always being given to those parts which do not fit very well. For example, in order to argue that reform was intended to remove power from working-class representatives it becomes necessary to exaggerate their power, and the differences between authorities controlled by different parties, as well as the influence of community groups of various sorts (pp. 235–6). Similarly, it becomes necessary to read back some of the concerns of the later 1970s about levels of spending into the reports which fed into the 1972 legislation (for example, p. 243). At the time those concerns were far less significant than they were to become in the late 1970s, and reorganization was actually accompanied by a substantial increase in local authority spending.

One of the main strengths of both Cockburn and Dearlove is their concern to place changes in local government within a wider 'political economy' context. But this also seems to make it more difficult for them to look at changes generated from within the state system itself, whose importance is stressed by *Rhodes* (1985). He argues that after the Second World War central government depended heavily on local government for the implementation of its policies on welfare. This, he says, resulted in the development of service-based (vertical) linkages between civil servants at the centre and officials at local level on the basis of what he calls **policy networks**. The importance of these networks was, in turn, reinforced by the increased professionalization of these service areas. He stresses the ways in which the period from the early 1960s to the mid-1970s saw the effective by-passing of local elites, including councillors, because of the development of other central-local linkages. According to him, 'policy-making in British government became characterized by professional bureaucratic complexes based on specific functions: a series of vertical coalitions or policy networks in which central dependence on sub-national government (SNG) for the implementation of policy was complemented by SNG's dependence on the centre for financial resources. Fragmentation between functions within the centre went hand in hand with centralization within policy networks' (*Rhodes*, 1985).

The strength of Rhodes' arguments is that they allow a focus on interests and negotiations within the state. They imply that the state – and groups within it – have their own interests which may be pursued separately from any changes in the structures of British capitalism. There is no *a priori* assumption that the state (whether local or national) acts either as an agent of capital or in response to pressures from other classes. Insofar as a 'logic' unfolds, it is one which follows from the organization and structure of the state itself, rather than the requirements of capital. Of course, the state is not insulated from economic pressures or political demands from the working class and other groups, but this analysis suggests that it will respond to them in ways which are to its own advantage, which may not coincide with the narrowly defined interests of capital or other political forces.

There is a balance which needs to be drawn here, however. Even if one acknowledges the significance of the state itself as an agency, there is a danger that it may be given a role which is too sharply independent. As far as local government is concerned the extent and direction of change to which it has been subject since the 1960s are difficult to explain mainly in terms of the state itself.

Here Cockburn and Dearlove seem more convincing again – at least in terms of their focus on broader tendencies of change, which also seem relevant to the continuing shifts that have taken place up to the late 1980s. In particular, both argue that reorganization was part of an attempt to adjust systems of representation to fit with the social and economic structures of the late twentieth century. In doing this, they make it easier to understand why some form of local government continues to survive as more than simply a creature of the centre. Cockburn stresses the need to use community approaches to local authority management to involve and incorporate groups in urban areas which might otherwise increasingly question and even threaten the operations of the state. Such incorporation is, for her, a necessary corollary of a continued erosion of popular control over local government. Dearlove focuses on the pressures to encourage the direct involvement of business interests at local level. The changed nature of business – the shift to corporate organization and the break between the location and ownership of industry – means that old, more or less direct methods of incorporation on the Victorian model cannot be sustained or renewed. There are few modern equivalents of the great nineteenth-century urban capitalists like Cadbury, Rowntree, Boots, Lever, Chamberlain, Salt and others, who lived near the factories and were directly involved in local politics and urban development in one way or another. Instead, some institutionalized system of representation may be required, with some similarities to the 'corporate bias' identified by Middlemas (1979) at national level, and discussed in Chapter 2. One of the problems for local government is that it is easier to see how this might work at national level where the interests are clearer and more easily identifiable. The national economic and political environment is likely to be far more important for most companies, particularly since they will tend to be nationally or even transnationally organized. This may help to explain why Dearlove's conclusions were premature, but the issues he identifies come back as key concerns in the 1980s and 1990s.

Activity 4.1

Rhodes' approach seems to play down the importance of 'local' politics because of its stress on the state system and relations within it. What significance do you think Cockburn and Dearlove would attach to local politics in explaining the changes of the early 1970s?

Cockburn

Dearlove

Summary of section 4.2

● In the late 1960s official reports wanted to make local government more efficient by:

  – rationalizing the confusing structures, boundaries and distribution of responsibilities between authorities

  – increasing the size of local authorities so that they could undertake strategic tasks and attract a higher 'calibre' of officer and councillor

  – introducing new methods of management, particularly corporate management.

● Some commentators – particularly Cockburn and Dearlove – have argued that this was a period of structural change in which local government became more clearly tied to the interests of capitalism and closer to business interests.

● The argument for this is not convincing, because relations with business remained informal and instrumental and local governments were, for a time, more rather than less troublesome for the centre. Corporate management did not make councils more managerial.

● The theories themselves seem partly to blame for this inaccurate assess-ment. In both cases the theory becomes more important than the development being investigated, so that the evidence is made to fit, instead of being used to test, the theory.

● Cockburn's approach is more determinist than that of Dearlove, who stresses the importance of political conflict around local government as one of the reasons for the reforms.

● By setting local government reform in a wider 'political economy' context, Cockburn and Dearlove help to explain change, but may exaggerate its significance. Rhodes, by focusing on shifts within the organizational structures of the state, is able to identify some reasons for longer-term stability, but is less able to explain the extent of change since the late 1960s.

4.3   Centralization (1975–85)

4.3.1   Financial controls and legal controls

In 1975, just after reorganization had finally been implemented, and in the context of a great deal of criticism about its unexpected costs, Tony Crosland (Secretary of State for the Environment) announced that cuts were needed in local government spending: 'We have to come to terms with the harsh reality of the situation which we inherited. The party's over' (quoted in Crosland, 1983, p. 295). The years of steady expansion were over, although achieving the hoped-for cuts was not to be as easy as the centre expected.

The second half of the 1970s and the early 1980s were dominated for local government by a series of changes in funding arrangements and rules on spending. The importance of this should not be missed: one aspect of growing local government spending in the first thirty years after 1945 was that the balance between sources of funding shifted dramatically. The increased role of councils in the local administration of a nationally organized welfare state had meant that an increased proportion of local spending was funded by central government grant, as well as centrally approved loans for capital spending. Both the rates (then the only locally determined tax, levied on property and based on the capitalization of rental values) and fees and charges declined as a proportion of income, while grant became more important. After the mid-1970s, however, the proportion of local spending funded by central grants fell sharply, and continued to fall into the 1980s. This is shown in Table 4.2.

These changes were, of course, initiated from the centre. They were not products of local decision-making. Within central government in the mid-1970s, Rhodes stresses the 'pre-eminence of the Treasury and the treatment of *local* expenditure as a matter for national decision' (1986, p. 239). The Department of the Environment (DoE, the central government department with overall responsibility for local government in England) was, he says, trapped into the position of being both the advocate of local services within the centre and the guardian of the purse-strings as far as local government

Table 4.2 Proportion of 'relevant' local government
expenditure payable as grant (percentages)

	England and Wales	Scotland
1967/78	54	–
1971/72	57.5	–
1975/76	66.5 (peak)	75.0
1977/78	61.0	68.5
1980/81	61.0	68.5
1982/83	57.1	66.7
1983/84	52.8	61.7
1987/88	46.3	–

This table overstates the proportion of actual local
authority expenditure covered by grant, because
'relevant' expenditure is defined by central government
and actual spending is higher.

Sources: Hepworth, 1984, p. 55; Titterton and Wade,
1984, p. 30 (updated from *Local Government Trends*,
CIPFA, 1987)

was concerned (in that respect the Secretary of State acted as a sort of 'mini
chancellor') (Rhodes, 1986, p. 238). In the context of the mid-1970s and
later, this meant that the DoE's role increasingly became that of policing the
spending of local governments. The Scottish and Welsh Offices were in
similar positions. Indeed, Goldsmith argues that on finance, 'the Scottish
Office has been the pioneer for the Imperial core, seeking and using greater
controls over local government' than was the case in England (1986, p. 168).
(See also, for example, Midwinter, Keating and Taylor, 1983.)

The context for this shift in direction was to be found in wider pressures to
reduce state spending and, above all, levels of state borrowing to finance
such expenditure. There have been many different attempts to explain these
pressures, in terms of capitalist crisis (or the fiscal crisis of the state (O'Connor, 1973)); or the state acting as a leech on productive sectors of the
economy (most strongly argued in Bacon and Eltis, 1976); or simply in terms
of monetarism (outlined in Gamble, 1984, pp. 145–9; *Leys*, 1983). But
whatever the explanation, there can be little doubt that local spending
became a target for central control.

As the proportion of central support began to fall dramatically, local
authority dependence on it became clearer. Until the late 1970s, however,
the centralization was largely limited to tighter control over overall levels of
grant and the imposition of 'cash limits' which meant that no (or little)
account was taken of inflation. Those councils which wanted to could make
up for lost grant by increasing rate levels, and many did so, so that overall
levels of spending did not fall significantly. Some indications of future policy
moves, however, were to be seen in the increasingly tight controls on capital

spending including the introduction of Housing Investment Plans (HIPs) which meant that individual councils had to agree the pattern of their housing capital spending with the Department of the Environment. The Inner Urban Areas Act of 1978 also encouraged a more detailed consideration of urban programme spending through partnership and other arrangements, which involved central departments more directly in decision-making on local spending.

If the direction of change was already clear by the end of the 1970s, the *pace* of change accelerated dramatically in the early 1980s. A series of reforms, heralded by the Local Government Planning and Land Act (1980), developed further controls on capital and current expenditure. This Act introduced a new block grant in England and Wales and included a formula which penalized councils which spent more than a previously determined limit. Grant was removed from those authorities, so that any increase in spending brought a fall in income and, therefore, implied a further increase in rates to make up for that loss. Now councils were to be targeted individually, rather than as a group. This was taken further with legislation which limited rate levels as well as spending. The first steps in this direction were taken in Scotland where, for the first time in 1982/3, individual authorities were targeted for 'excessive and unreasonable expenditure' in what was popularly called a 'hit-list' (see Midwinter *et al.*, 1983), and legislation on 'rate-capping' was enacted in England in 1984, enabling central government to set a maximum rate level for particular councils – just as later (in 1988/9) the community charge (popularly known as the poll tax) and the uniform business rate were introduced there before the experiment was extended to England and Wales. In 1985 a further Act was passed which went beyond controlling the operation of existing local governments, when the Greater London Council (created in 1965) and metropolitan county councils (created in 1974) were abolished and their responsibilities transferred either to borough/district councils or to joint authorities of various types.

4.3.2   The defence of local democracy

Most academics involved in the study and teaching of local government lined themselves up behind the councils which they perceived to be under threat, in a centrally inspired attack on local democracy and local autonomy. The main criticisms directed against the legislation of the first half of the 1980s were 'that decentralized democratic decision making in the form of representative local government is an essential element of the country's political and government system ... we believe the government's proposals to limit local authority rates and expenditure levels are a major threat to this' (SAUS, 1983, Conclusion). As the title of another book written by two leading academics in the field made clear, they saw themselves as presenting 'a "case for" local government' (Jones and Stewart, 1983).

The implication of their arguments was that a major restructuring was

Table 4.3 Principal functions of local authorities in Great Britain, 1987

	Metropolitan		England and Wales Non-Metropolitan		Greater London	Scotland		
	Joint Authority	District Councils	County Councils	District Councils	Borough Councils	Regional Councils	District Councils	Island Councils
Social services		•	•		•	•		•
Education		•	•		•[1]	•	•[2]	•[2]
Libraries		•	•		•	•	•	•
Museums and art galleries		•	•	•	•	•	•	•
Housing		•		•	•		•	•
Planning – strategic			•		•	•		•[2]
– local		•[4]		•	•		•	•
Highways		•	•		•	•		•
Traffic management		•	•		•	•		•
Passenger transport[6]	•		•			•		•
Playing fields and swimming baths		•		•	•		•	•
Parks and open spaces	•[5]	•[5]	•	•	•	•	•	•
Refuse collection		•[5]		•	•		•	•
Refuse disposal	•		•		•	•		•
Consumer protection		•	•		•	•		•
Environmental health[7]		•		•	•		•	•
Police[3]	•		•			•		
Fire[3]	•		•			•		•

1 Outer London = London boroughs. Inner London = Inner London Education Authority. (From 1989 education throughout London becomes the responsibility of the London boroughs.)

2 Except in Highlands, Dumfries and Galloway and Border regions, where the function will be regional.

3 There are Joint Police Forces and Joint Fire Brigades in some areas. In London the police authority is the Home Secretary and the Fire and Civil Defence Authority controls the Fire Brigades.

4 Strategic planning in metropolitan districts is co-ordinated by a joint committee of the districts in each former metropolitan county area.

5 In metropolitan areas, refuse disposal may be either a joint authority or a district council function.

6 Passenger transport in London is carried out by a separate body, London Regional Transport.

7 Regional and Island councils in Scotland control water and sewerage, in addition to the usual environmental health duties.

Source: Chartered Institute of Public Finance and Accountancy, *Local Government Trends*, CIPFA, 1987, p. 6

taking place. Indeed, in their most extreme form, it was suggested that the legislation of the 1980s heralded the end of local government as an independent sphere. Although the immediate context for the 'attack' on local government was pressure for overall reductions in public spending and local government spending in particular, few of those writing about it have accepted this as a major explanation, partly because the evidence that levels of local government spending are of major significance to the economy are limited, and the arguments that state spending in itself discourages private investment are also weak. Newton and Karran argue that 'the case for the present degree of control is built on shabby theory and lacks empirical support. As one economist puts it, the cost of this form of monetarism' is 'the erosion of local democracy which has accompanied the move towards greater centralized control of public spending decisions. On macro-economic grounds there is little justification in exacting such a heavy toll in the form of lost local autonomy (Jackson, 1982)' (Newton and Karran, 1985, p. 124). A great deal of the argument against central controls has stressed that local government has shown a greater ability to reduce spending than the departments of central government and even the Audit Commission – in the early 1980s – has acknowledged that the operation of central rules may actually have encouraged increased levels of spending and a reduction in the accuracy of information feeding into the centre (Audit Commission, 1984).

But, if the end-result of the changes has not been significantly to reduce spending, it remains to be determined what it actually has achieved and what has been at stake. Duncan and Goodwin argue that:

> . . . the centralization of local government is not merely an issue of macroeconomic and financial policy. The desire to control public spending does not necessitate the detailed and blanket control of local authorities sought by the Conservative government – still less if it is public *borrowing* that is crucial (as monetarist doctrine would have it). Indeed, some of the Government's actions are counter-productive or at least peripheral to this aim. Rather, we claim, it is the political objective of removing local government's autonomy that is at issue. This has both a short-term and a long-term objective. In the short term, the centre can make cuts in public service provision and enforce its own policy aims in every local area. In the long term, alternative political and policy positions can be weakened – there will be no government framework to give them any institutional voice or credence.

Although Duncan and Goodwin develop a particular analysis of local government which explains its existence largely in terms of uneven development and the representation of differentiated local social relations (discussed extensively in Mark Goodwin's chapter which follows), their conclusions here would have been shared far more widely both by academics in the field of local government studies and by many local government politicians (such as Blunkett and Jackson, 1987). For them, the main explanation of national policy – at least in its centralization phrase – was that it was designed to undermine resistance to the wider political strategies of the Conservative government. More broadly, it was placed in the wider context of the continuing ambitions of central government to control local independence.

Underlying this interpretation are echoes of Dearlove's. Local politics is understood as being difficult to manage from the centre, because it reflects locally generated demands, through local democratic institutions (including political parties, community groups and other local interest groups).

In its various forms, this is probably the dominant interpretation of the reforms of the 1980s, and implies a fundamental change – a structural shift – in which local government becomes far weaker and central government becomes virtually the sole political power.

4.3.3 Alternative explanations

There are a number of major problems with this interpretation of events, however, which makes it difficult to accept it as an entirely adequate explanation. First, like Dearlove, it still seems to exaggerate the localness of local politics and the extent to which they ever presented a substantial obstacle to the programmes of the centre. In a sense the abolition of the GLC and the metropolitan counties and the successful implementation of the 'rate-capping' legislation, while presented as examples of **centralization**, can also be seen to confirm the relative weakness of local governments. Despite widespread opposition to abolition expressed in opinion polls it is difficult to discern any significant backlash in the 1987 general election – indeed the increase in the Conservative vote in London seems to have been higher than elsewhere.

O'Leary (1987) argues that attempting to identify general trends revealed in the attack on local government may be a mistake, since it ignores the importance of political style within government. His own analysis of the abolition of the Greater London Council stresses that it was 'a policy folly rather than a rational decision . . . the government embarked upon a major initiative as an unintended ill-considered by-product of its other policies' (1987, p. 212). He concludes that it was the consequence of a political style – a belief that 'Firmness, the resolute approach, is considered essential even in defence of the indefensible; consensual, rational approaches to decision-making, tedious incrementalisms are regarded as excuses for doing nothing. A dramatic political style is required to rectify Britain. The price of such a style is repeated unintended and counter-productive outcomes for its supporters' (1987, p. 214). In principle, perhaps, such an analysis could be integrated within those outlined above. But it would undermine the essential certainty of an approach which sees the abolition of the GLC as an integral part of an attack on local autonomy. O'Leary would be more sceptical.

Rhodes' analysis, too, suggests a rather less dramatic set of changes and makes fewer claims to the essential democracy of local government. It sets developments in a longer context of negotiations and bargaining between levels of government. He argues that: 'the financial relationships between central and local government can also be characterised as a complex set of interactions involving a range of government institutions and placing a premium on networking skills ... The relations between central and local government are too often seen in an oversimplified light. The intricate pattern of linkages is both a constraint and a source of opportunities' (Rhodes, 1981, pp. 28 and 34).

This certainly seems to fit the experience of local government up until the early 1980s. Reductions in levels of central government grant did not mean that councils had lost control of their spending. The impact of cuts was dulled by a return to the use of rates as a source of funds and, in some cases, a shift to increasing income from charges. Probably the most important means of evading the intentions of the centre was the increased use of what came to be called 'creative accounting'.

At first, this largely involved the search for loop-holes in central government legislation: if, for example, the rules suggested that future grant depended on spending in a particular year, then it was possible with little difficulty to prepare the accounts to show that spending had been higher or lower that year (whichever was the required answer), More important, perhaps, as time went on, it become common for councils and their treasurers to seek new sources of funding which were not covered by the rules or were covered by different rules. The accounting convention which divided spending into revenue (current) and capital expenditure was particularly susceptible to manipulation. So, for example, moves were made to turn revenue spending (i.e. which had to be paid for out of current income – grants, fees, charges and rates) into capital spending (i.e. which could be paid for from loans raised from banks and other financial institutions). Spending on housing maintenance was frequently capitalized in the late 1970s and early 1980s. Another increasingly common way round the rules at the time was to engage in lease/lease-back arrangements, which became more and more complicated as the rules surrounding them tried to plug loop-holes, until they were finally outlawed in 1987. Under these schemes, which had first been developed in the 1970s as a means of raising capital from the private sector for new development, for example, on office and shopping complexes (i.e. as a means of avoiding constraints on capital spending), council property was sold on a long lease to another agency and then leased back for shorter periods until the long lease expired. They were often, in effect, used as ways of borrowing money from commercial banks at slightly higher rates than the commercial market and those guaranteed by the government-sponsored Public Works Loan Board.

For the purposes of our argument here, it is not necessary to understand all the ins and outs of these various schemes, nor to grasp the increasingly complex rules of the centre invented to limit them. By the mid-1980s there were very few people who would have pretended to understand all the ramifications of Grant Related Expenditure Assessments, rate-capping or capital controls. Local government finance was a labyrinth, (possibly) understood by the experts, but a complete mystery to most of those involved in local government (officers and councillors) and certainly to the electorate. But the extent of the schemes should make us cautious about identifying radical structural change too readily even in the wake of the legislation so severely criticized in the 1980s. And too sharp a division between central and local government may also be misleading.

Rhodes' analysis stresses the continuity of central–local relations in the post-war period. He charts an unfolding if uncertain logic which goes back to the way in which the welfare state was put together after the war, as pieces were tacked on in a rather haphazard way to existing state institutions. Rhodes argues that the organization of both central and local government was characterized by functional divisions (along service lines, such as education, social services or planning) so that links between levels were also on functional (rather than territorial) lines through policy networks, including professionals as well as politicians. He stresses the complexity of interrelations and points to an increase in the importance of territorial politics (i.e. based on a local government area) at just the time when – in the face of severe economic problems – local (welfare) expenditure has become an increasingly important element in central (economic) planning. The tensions were bound to create difficulties, which came to the fore as national problems of economic management became clearer, even if they were not simply the consequence of those problems (*Rhodes*, 1985). The conclusions drawn from the arguments of Duncan and Goodwin would point to an increased process of centralization and the erosion of an existing local autonomy. But Rhodes' view is rather different. He would deny that any clear direction can be identified. Instead he suggests that the centre has always used local government (and other sub-national governments) to serve its own political interests 'whether the example is the construction of the welfare state, the modernization of sub-national government or the containment of public expenditure. If central actors have not been literally squalid, the results of their actions have been a mess through their failure to comprehend the differentiated nature of the system' (1985, p. 55). The implications of this would seem to be that 1975–85 did not see a process of structural change, but simply the latest in a series of chaotic attempts by central actors to use local government as a means of achieving their ends, without any appreciation of the range of different interests reflected in its various policy networks, and which are also linked by various routes to the still disaggregated parts of the centre.

There is, however, a potentially very important theoretical weakness in the approach adopted by Rhodes, because it is difficult to see how any other conclusion could be generated by it. The focus on a complex process of negotiations appears to exclude the possibility of structural change. Conclusions will tend to be in terms of shifts within the system itself – adjusting the balance between groups, levels and interests of different times. Any structural change – that is one which changes the rules of the game on the basis of which bargaining takes place – would have to come from outside the system. Arguably just such a change took place in the early 1980s, and the pressures encouraging it could only be understood in the context of shifts in the wider political economy.

Both Rhodes and Duncan and Goodwin, in their different ways, make it possible to identify some dynamic for change. Put simply, the failure of economic management at the centre and the onset of economic crisis set a context in which the continued survival of a relatively independent or autonomous sphere of politics, reflected in the institutional form of local government, became less likely. At precisely the same moment at which central government concerns to reduce spending on the welfare state became dominant, it became *more* difficult to ensure that local authorities would do what was required. They were under increased (local) pressure to respond to the demands of their residents for welfare support. Indeed, the increased concentration of central government on local government spending helped to increase its political profile, locally as well as nationally, at just the time when reorganization had created authorities with major staffing and financial resources, authorities more powerful than the patchwork quilt of councils which they replaced.

The conclusion to be drawn from one theory is that attempts to restructure the welfare state helped to generate forms of 'territorial' resistance (Rhodes), while from the other, this is merely the latest in a continuing series of attempts by UK central governments to overcome and control the differentiated demands of a series of local governments with their own local bases of political support (Duncan and Goodwin). In Rhodes' formulation, the nature of the **'territorial' resistance** may be defined in terms of the interests of local government professionals, as well as the local populations. They, too, have an interest in sustaining levels of welfare spending (and even existing forms of delivery), possibly to a greater extent than local consumers of services. This tends to be underemphasized in more 'localist' approaches like those of Duncan and Goodwin. But they are able rather more easily to explain the strength of local resistance and the loyalty of local electors to politicians apparently under attack from the centre. As Mark Goodwin shows in the next chapter, they are able to uncover and explore a rich world of local politics.

Activity 4.2

Local government spending has fallen significantly since the middle 1970s both as a proportion of state spending and of national income. But it has remained at levels comparable to those of the 1960s. How do you think Rhodes and Duncan and Goodwin would explain this and how would they differ? Factors to take into account include: the role of policy networks and professionals, the independent basis of local politics, the intentions of government.

Rhodes

Duncan and Goodwin

Summary of section 4.3

● From the mid-1970s local government spending was under severe pressure from the centre as more and more complex rules were developed to keep it under control.

● Many academics (including Newton and Karran, Duncan and Goodwin) have suggested that the official explanations for this pressure were unconvincing, since the control of local finance is argued either to be irrelevant to the needs of the economy or, even, counterproductive.

● Instead, they have explained it in terms of political conflict over the programmes of central government (particularly after the election of a Conservative government in 1979) or longer-term central–local tensions, in which the centre is concerned to minimize the pressure generated by the existence of local political autonomy. According to this approach, because local governments have their own political bases, they are always potential rivals to the centre.

● Others have been unconvinced by the search for an overall – and underlying – logic, linking the various local government reforms. O'Leary, for example, has argued that the abolition of the GLC is best understood as an act of 'policy folly'.

● Rhodes sets the period of 'centralization' in a longer-term context of negotiation and bargaining between levels of government since the war. This seems to fit quite well with the detailed process of manoeuvring which characterized the early period of financial centralization. But it fits less well with a situation in which the 'rules' under which the negotiation takes place are regularly changed to the extent that the nature of the 'game' may itself have been changed.

• Rhodes' analysis leads to a conclusion in which no clear direction of change can be identified: policy-making has been 'chaotic'. Duncan and Goodwin identify a more coherent direction of change, pointing to an erosion of local autonomy.

4.4   Fragmentation (1983 onwards)

4.4.1   Breaking up is hard to do

The era of 'centralization' brought rather uncertain conclusions for the local government system. The centre proved incapable of controlling levels of local spending to the extent which supporters of restraint had hoped, but local governments also came to accept new parameters beyond which they could not stray. Those few councils which sought substantially to exceed government guidelines were brought sharply into line. The trench warfare of the early 1980s was replaced by more subtle forms of guerrilla conflict, in which the guiding principles are no longer so straightforward, yet the consequences of change may be rather more significant, to the extent that the '80s as a whole might justifiably be seen as a period of structural change.

Three main features of change can be identified: changes in the tax base; the growth of privatization; and the growth of non-elected local governments.

The changing tax base

The domestic rating system, which provides around 11 per cent of local government income in England, is due to be replaced by the community charge (or poll tax) in England, Scotland and Wales by the end of the 1980s. Instead of local taxation being based on property values, it is to be based on a flat rate per capita charge levied on all adults, with limited rebates for some groups. Accompanying this shift is the introduction of a uniform business rate whose level is to be centrally determined, with the income also collected centrally and then redistributed in the form of government grant according to a centrally determined formula. This replaces non-domestic rates (i.e. property taxes levied on commercial, industrial and other business premises), whose levels have previously been locally determined and raised about 17 per cent of local government income in England (1984/85 figures, Douglas and Lord, 1986, p. 15). The end-result of this will be to increase dramatically the proportion of local income which is funded by government grant, since the only sources of local income will be the community charge (poll tax) and specific fees and charges for planning applications and the use of leisure facilities, for example. In the 1990s over 75 per cent of local spending will, in effect, be funded through central government grant.

Privatization

An underlying theme of change since the early 1980s which has sometimes been buried in the overall conflict over spending levels has been a move towards the **privatization** of services: that is, the replacement of previously direct local government provision by the provision of services by commercial enterprises under contract to local authorities. This has taken a number of forms and has not spread as widely as some of its supporters might have hoped.

The various support and maintenance activities which could relatively easily be 'contracted out' were early targets. Direct labour housing construction and maintenance departments of local authorities (DLOs) now have to compete with commercial tenders for much of their work. Since 1980 DLOs have had to make a return of 5 per cent on capital. Although DLOs have survived, Stoker (1988, p. 186) notes that there was a 22.5 per cent fall in numbers employed between 1980 and 1985 and a 17.7 per cent fall in value of output over the same period.

Some councils have been more eager than others to develop 'contracting out' schemes. Despite a boom in interest in the early '80s, with one hundred and fifty authorities considering contracting out in the years 1982/83, only thirty-seven actually did so. The value of contracts in 1986/87 only amounted to £120 million (Stoker, 1988, p. 186). In many cases, according to Stoker, the threat of privatization was used by councils to 're-establish firm control over their in-house staff and trade unions. The tendering process has in a number of cases been used by local authority managers to reassert their right to manage' (1988, p. 187). But legislation in 1987–88 has also brought an increase in moves towards more explicit privatization by making competitive tendering compulsory for a wider range of activities, including refuse collection, street cleaning and vehicle maintenance.

This probably underestimates the extent to which there has been a wider shift away from direct council provision, however. The limitations on council spending have encouraged a search for other ways of providing services. There has, for example, been a marked reduction in direct council provision of homes for the elderly and a concomitant increase in privately run homes. There has been a move away from the use of children's homes towards more developed foster care and some private sector provision. In the field of housing where central financial controls have made housebuilding by councils almost impossible, there has been a marked increase in partnerships with housing associations and many councils have also sought to encourage low cost housing through equity share schemes with the private sector.

From a slightly different perspective, there has been a shift in emphasis among some councils towards seeking to influence the wider environments within which they find themselves rather than concentrating on direct service provision. This has been particularly noticeable in the areas of local economic policy and equal opportunities. In the former, agencies such as local enterprise boards, or economic development units, have attempted to encourage firms to develop or invest with the help of limited assistance from councils – attempts have been made to 'lever' additional funds from the private sector (Clarke and Cochrane, 1987). In the field of equal opportunities, the notion of contract compliance has been borrowed from the USA by some councils: the idea behind this is that a condition of local authority purchase from its suppliers may be expressed in terms of key employment practices, including the recruitment of ethnic minorities and women, and reasonable access for them to promotion within the enterprise. Government legislation has sharply reduced the scope for this, but a number of councils are still interested in developing it as far as they can.

Other forms of privatization have been closer to the dominant forms identified at national level by Mohun. The sale of council houses to sitting tenants has (as Hamnett, 1989, notes) helped to shift tenure patterns significantly, particularly when coupled with the lack of housebuilding in the public sector. And the deregulation of bus services following the 1986 Transport Act has dramatically changed the nature of public transport which is now either privately owned and managed (outside London) or run in direct competition with the private sector, with severe limitations on possible subsidy.

The growth of non-elected local governments

The standard model of local government since the war has been of multifunctional authorities with an elected council supervising the direct provision of services. As the previous point suggests, the 1980s saw a decline in the direct proportion of services directly provided, whether by the extension of activity into new areas (such as economic development) or by the privatization of existing services. Alongside this there has been a move towards non-elected and usually specialist forms of local government.

In the 1970s there were already some moves in this direction, reflected in the formation of regional agencies, such as water authorities and health authorities (Duncan and Goodwin, 1988, Ch. 7). Although their significance as regional political institutions has been undermined – in the case of water authorities by proposals for privatization and in the case of health authorities by a series of financial and managerial initiatives which have encouraged a shift towards private sector (market-type) decision-making (Pollitt, Harrison, Hunter and Marnoch, 1988) – there has been a growth in regional state institutions in other policy areas. The joint boards created in the wake of the abolition of the metropolitan county councils in England to cover such actitivies as strategic planning, fire and police services, for example, point in this direction, while the major development agencies in Wales and Scotland (and Northern Ireland) also suggest that regional bases for political negotiations remain important. Regional bodies of this sort encourage the representation of interests *as* interests, rather than their fragmentation through electoral politics. In the case of the development agencies, for example, although they are explicitly market-oriented and sometimes presented as examples of the neo-liberal, non-interventionist virtues (Moore, 1986), they also negotiate with representatives of business and communities (represented by local councils) to develop agreed programmes.

But these changes are not just taking place at regional level. Some of them are specifically oriented towards more identifiably *local* areas. The urban development corporations first introduced by the Conservative government in 1981 are one example of this. These corporations are non-elected and, although an attempt is made to ensure some representation of different interests at board levels, their tasks are clearly defined in advance in terms of development and infrastructure. The early and best-funded corporations (such as the London Docklands Development Corporation) were clearly intended to bypass the local authorities in their areas, using their own planning powers and financial resources to achieve changes which would allow private sector property development to take place. Although councils have often been appointed to sit on the boards, more recently they have been more open to direct local authority involvement: in the case of Shef-field in 1988, for example, there was a substantial degree of negotiation over representation from the start. But the key point remains the same – to achieve development the constraints of electoral politics need to be avoided, so that effective decisions can be made and negotiated with key industrial and commercial interests.

The initiative for bodies of this sort has not only come from the centre. Stoker (1988, Chapter 3) identifies a much wider trend in this direction. In the field of local economic policy, this is particularly clear, because of the development at local level of a series of public/private partnerships. The move towards these has come from more than one direction. There has certainly been central government encouragement: bodies recognized as enterprise agencies are entitled to various tax concessions and become part of a wider national network. And there has been some encouragement from within industry, reflected, for example in Business in the Community (BiC), founded in 1982 and sponsored by firms such as IBM and Marks and Spencer as well as supported by the DoE and the Manpower Services Commission (later the Training Commission, itself absorbed by the Department of Employment in 1988). BiC has the objective of encouraging the growth of enterprise agencies and 'bringing together groups of local companies to work in partnership, together and with their local authorities' (quoted in King, 1985, p. 206). Local governments have eagerly become involved, both because such agencies appear to offer new opportunities for development and because they may have legal powers (for example on financial assist-ance) which exceed their own. They may also give increased access to other sources of finance. Some councils have also set up local enterprise boards (many of which are now organized on a regional basis) which operate at an arms-length from the councils and are separate legal entities with a commitment to working with financial and commercial agencies to encourage local investment. Although initially set up in direct opposition to the policies of the Thatcher government, the implications for local government structures are similar, with a move away from direct electoral representation towards a greater concern for the representation of functional interests.

Other areas in which non-elected local government has increased in importance go right to the heart of the post-war system, in particular in reforms proposed for housing and education. In the field of housing there has been and is likely to continue to be a major growth in housing associations, particularly after provisions are implemented which will allow council tenants to opt out of council control and into housing associations or tenancy with private landlords. In some cases local authorities have even set up their own associations to deal with this, although since many housing associations are organized on a regional and increasingly even a national basis, *local* input is likely to diminish over time. In education, although legislation promises increased power to parents and the opportunity for schools to opt out of local education authorities, it also promises a greater power for head teachers and, in the case of City Technology Colleges, a greater direct input from industry. The reorganization of the Training Commission has already shifted decision-making on post-sixteen training towards non-elected decision-making forums, often with the enthusiastic involvement of colleges which see them as sources of additional funds.

It it is accepted that these moves *are* taking place, and there seems little doubt that they are, the question remains as to what significance they have, and what they imply. There are two main ways of interpreting them and these will be discussed below.

4.4.2   Towards increased freedom of choice?

These changes can be viewed as one aspect of a potentially liberating move towards an increased role for the market and in this sense the reform of local government may be understood as a part of a wider restructuring of the state to achieve the same ends. According to Barry,

> The market at the moment appears to be on the threshold of a new era of intellectual popularity. This is not merely the result of changes in fashion that inevitably occur in the social sciences, but has perhaps more to do with the observed failures of alternative social and economic arrangements. A properly understood market process is not just a generator of economic welfare, it is also protection for liberty and an efficient method for the realization of many desirable social goals. (1987, p. 171)

Just as the post-war local government system can be understood as a key element of the social-democratic consensus developed in that period, so it has been argued that 'what is needed is a new municipal culture' to fit the changed social and economic realities of the late twentieth century (Walker, 1983, p. 10). Arguably it is this aim which provides the 'ideological coherence which holds together the various initiatives and pieces of legislation' (Stoker, 1988, p. 251) introduced by the Conservative governments of the 1980s.

The strongest critiques of local government as it was in the 1970s concentrate not on its localness, but its position within a national system and, above all, use it as an example of what its critics see as the failings of bureaucratic decision-making. According to this analysis the existing municipal culture is one which stresses uniform provision, with little choice for the consumer and which has been driven largely by the demands of the producers. In that sense, local government is only a special case of bureaucratic choice organized through the state. Walker's critique of the 'municipal empire' stresses that it 'is not local. In fact the municipal system as at present constituted is an astonishing block of power, controlled by professionals who run the schools and the social services, and by the administrators and councillors who operate the machine in a bureaucratic darkness rarely pierced by public inspection' (Walker, 1983, p. 4). He challenges the notion that local government is anything more than local *administration*, whose claim to be government is merely another reflection of the high self-regard in which officials hold themselves rather than any expression of locally based decision-making. Green (1985, p. 12) argues that 'the voices most strident in their demands of the "protection of public services" are those of the middle-class government salariat' who gain directly from it in terms of income, employment and status.

This approach is influenced by a more developed analysis of bureaucracy associated with **public choice theory**. Public choice theory is an approach to the study of political decision-making using the tools of orthodox economic theory (of the type discussed in Chapter 3, section 3.2). McLean quotes Mueller's definition, according to which it is 'the economic study of non-market decision-making' (1987, p. 1). In particular, it attempts to assess how rational decision-makers will act in certain situations: 'It takes the tools of economics and applies them to the material of politics. By applying logical, deductive reasoning, economists try to work out what a rational actor . . . would do to maximize his [sic] chance of getting what he wants' (McLean, 1987, p. 1), that is, to maximize his or her 'utility'. It is a very powerful weapon in the hands of critics of bureaucracy.

Niskanen (1973) is probably the best-known proponent of public choice theory in the analysis of state bureaucracy, and a summary of his arguments, which are largely United States based, was presented to UK policy-makers through the Institute of Economic Affairs, a leading 'think-tank' devoted to spreading the message of economic liberalism and reform of the state. The key point of these arguments is the suggestion that state **bureaucracies** have certain special features which encourage them to have budgets which are significantly greater than would be 'optimal' for the provision of the services with which they deal. This is argued on the basis of assumptions about the behaviour of '**bureaucrats**' who are unable to operate by making profits from the services they provide as entrepreneurs do in the private sector. So they seek to maximize their 'utility' in other ways – Niskanen argues that they do this by maximizing budgets, because this gives them extra power, prestige and status. And he also suggests that simply policing budgets will not solve the problem either, since the basic motivation is not undermined and, in the absence of market mechanisms, financial monitors have no way of knowing when the waste has actually been eliminated.

Niskanen's approach has been modified by a number of other writers to include reference to other criteria apart from budget maximization. His analysis suggests that the spending levels of bureaux will not be 'optimal', but within the agreed budgets he concedes that management will generally be efficient, if not quite as efficient as the private sector. Others, however, have gone further, arguing that 'bureaucrats' will also be *staff* maximizers, for similar reasons to those outlined by Niskanen for budget maximization. In addition, increasing staffing levels is said to make it more likely that successful coalitions can be developed at local level to push for higher levels of spending, so that the process of expenditure growth becomes self-perpetuating (for example, Tullock, 1977, p. 285). It is therefore in the interests of bureaucrats to go for increased staffing levels as a means of constructing such coalitions, and the implications of this clearly point to increased waste and inefficiency, since, having bid for a maximum budget, within that budget, instead of adopting the most efficient form of production and delivery of services, 'bureaucrats' can be expected to choose the most labour-intensive. A survey of British local governments by Blore (1987) concludes that our local bureaucrats, too, are staff maximizers.

Underlying much of this argument is a feeling that the institutions of local democracy are very ineffective channels for the transmission of individual preferences – and, in some cases, even group preferences. The reforms which might be expected from this theoretical starting-point are moves towards market mechanisms or some surrogate for them which can be used both to influence the behaviour of bureaucrats by giving them a different set of incentives, and to increase the range of choice available to the consumers of public – in this case particularly local government – services. The extension of 'privatization' could be seen as evidence for structural change – a 'rolling back' of the state. But a number of qualifications need to be made before fully accepting such an analysis.

Two main forms of privatization can be identified at local level: first, the issuing of contracts to private agencies to undertake work for councils and, secondly, a redefinition of certain existing public services as services which should be supplied by the market. In both cases it is important not to exaggerate the extent to which it has been implemented.

As Stoker argues above, contracting out has largely been used as a threat to achieve other forms of change, often by senior bureaucrats to gain concessions from and changes in work practices by staff at lower levels of the hierarchy. Even after the introduction of legislation to increase the use of competitive tendering, it is likely that the core areas of public sector provision will be unaffected.

Privatization of this sort has less to do with increased public choice by individual consumers and more to do with the cheaper provision of a standard service. The very process of issuing a contract implies that standardization, since it also implies a checklist of activities whose perform-ance can be specified and assessed. A great deal of local government spending is already directed towards the private sector. This will merely increase it a little. It has, in any case, been argued forcibly by Dunleavy (1985, 1986a) that contracting out will not substantially undermine the position of senior bureaucrats. On the contrary he suggests that because public choice theory narrowly defines bureaucratic behaviour in terms of budget or staff maximization, it fails to grasp more important aspects of bureaucratic rationality – such as the desire to avoid conflict from trouble-some staff at lower levels and interference from councillors. Contracting out makes it possible to transfer those problems to others, who can in principle be fairly tightly controlled through contracts.

The sale of local authority assets and the shifting of activities to the private sector have been equally limited in the 1980s. Council houses were sold and buses 'deregulated' (although the housing association sector seems set to expand dramatically in the 1990s), but the bulk of existing public housing remained in council hands, and public transport has always been run on a semi-market basis, with the charging of fares coupled with separately identi-fied public subsidy. In the case of public transport Mackintosh (1987) shows very clearly for London Transport in the early 1980s that politicians from the GLC had to challenge the market-based arguments of the bureaucrats in order to increase subsidy to keep fares down and maintain services. Poli-ticians rather than bureaucrats sought to escape market pressures. The changes in public transport look more like an attack on local political autonomy than on bureaucratic power (see also Duncan and Goodwin, 1988, pp. 256–70).

The extent to which the process of privatization has involved major shifts to **market provision** at local level, then, should not be exaggerated, and public choice theory would suggest there is much more scope for the market provision of services currently handled through the state. But perhaps other changes can be understood with the help of that approach. If activities have to be organized through the state, then advocates of public choice theory would tend to favour decentralized delivery systems rather than those organized through the departments of central government. Such decentrali-zation should encourage competition between agencies.

This competition cannot come through direct market mechanisms. The 'Tiebout thesis' (Tiebout, 1956), which suggests that taxpayers will tend to move to those areas with the mix of tax levels and service provision which they prefer, has been substantially discredited (McLean, 1987, p. 91). Even the widespread belief that decisions on industrial location are (or were before the introduction of the uniform business rate) heavily influenced by the level of local taxation has been undermined by a series of research reports (including Crawford, Fothergill and Monk (1985) which was commissioned by the Department of the Environment).

So competition has to be generated through the political system, by some form of democratic decision-making. This is essentially the conclusion drawn by Salmon (1987) in his survey of **decentralization** in France in the early 1980s. He suggests that there is a strong argument for decentralization to local government (and potentially a limited hierarchy with some overlapping powers) so long as information is available which makes it possible for voters to judge between them and thus to influence the direction of their own local government through elections.

For this argument to work, however, a number of key conditions have to be met. First, of course, there really does need to be a range of choices available at local level. If local government is solely about the local administration of national services, then the possibility of comparison will be severely limited and privatization might be a more advisable option. Secondly, there needs to be a reasonably close relationship between taxation and accountability: if some voters can gain markedly greater benefits than others without making any substantial financial contribution, then the electoral system is likely to *encourage* higher levels of spending than would be justified on grounds of efficiency. (This is of course, a local variant of concerns expressed by *Johnson* (1977) regarding the welfare state as a whole, and discussed in Chapter 2, section 2.2.) Thirdly, there needs to be a reasonably clear understanding of which agencies are responsible for what activities, or else the information on which comparison is based will be highly confusing.

None of these conditions seems to be met as a consequence of the reforms of the 1980s. First, the range of choice at local level seems, if anything, to have been reduced as a consequence of a series of tighter and tighter rules, first on levels of expenditure and then on activities on which it could be spent. Every attempt by local government to evade central spending restrictions has been met by a new rule to make evasion more difficult. The possibility of expanding levels of public housing has effectively been removed. Even the possibility of using income generated by the sale of council houses has been sharply restricted. Through schemes, such as the Urban Programme and various training programmes, access to funds for local authorities has been shifted to areas in which they engage in some sort of partnership with the departments of central government. Within a declining overall level of grant, there has been a marked increase in the share targeted for particular purposes (specific and supplementary grants rose from 17.6 per cent of the total grant in 1981/82 to 23.6 per cent in 1986/87 (Douglas and Lord, 1986, p. 29)). If anything, the networks of control have become tighter and the area of independent choice has been reduced, yet public choice theory would suggest that such control was unlikely to achieve substantial cuts in spending.

Secondly, local accountability was at the centre of the arguments put forward for the community charge (or poll tax) and other reforms in local taxation. The argument was that the existing rating system made rational voting difficult. All voters tended to get more out of the system because of the levels of government grant. Hence it was important to reduce levels of grant to make it clearer to voters what services actually cost. More import-ant, *some* voters seemed to get substantially more out of the system than others, whilst paying substantially less. In particular, voters on social secur-ity receiving rate rebates could vote for increased services without having to pay for them. Large families in small flats or houses might pay less than individuals in larger ones while receiving more services. It was also argued, conversely, that, in general, middle-class families benefited more than the poor because they understood how to manipulate the non-means-tested elements of the system, such as education.

The commercial rate was felt to be a still greater source of distortion because of its rather unpredictable incidence. Councils such as Camden, Lambeth, Islington and Edinburgh, among others, were felt to be able to fund 'excessive' spending simply because of the high rateable values of commercial and office property within them. In other words local voters were able to escape the financial consequences of their (voting) decisions on spending. The flat-rate community charge coupled with a universal business rate was intended to make this far more difficult and ensure that there was some relationship between costs and local taxation levels.

The irony, however, is that in fact the new system is more likely to increase central control over, and funding of, local spending, instead of allowing for local variation, accountability and choice. The income from the business rate will appear as a grant from central government so that total grants will amount to 75 per cent of local expenditure. As a consequence, any increase in overall spending determined at local level will require a substantial increase in local taxation (assuming central grant remains the same), i.e. a 1 per cent increase will require a 4 per cent increase in locally raised funds including the community charge and specific fees and charges, thus reducing the likelihood of substantial local variation. The only choice to be made, therefore, will be between packages of services at roughly the same cost, without any direct financial accountability at local level.

Thirdly, a recurrent theme of much criticism of local government has been that the division and allocation of responsibilities have always been unclear. Social security, for example, is the responsibility of central government but housing benefit is handled through local authorities. Personal social services are the responsibility of county councils (outside metropolitan areas) and of metropolitan districts or London boroughs in England and Wales; in Scot-land personal social services are the responsibility of regional and island authorities and in Northern Ireland of Health and Social Service Boards. The probation service, many of whose clients are also involved with social services departments, is the responsibility of the Home Office and its equivalents in Wales, Scotland and Northern Ireland. Many district councils also offer welfare advice and fund community development programmes, and some voluntary agencies, including the Citizen's Advice Bureau and the National Society for the Prevention of Cruelty to Children, are involved in activities and may even have statutory powers which are similar to those of councils in this area. It is hardly surprising that there is a high degree of confusion and it is not always clear who is to blame (or can claim credit) for particular activities.

Certainly some of the reforms had as one of their *stated* intentions a reduction in confusion. In particular it was one of the arguments put forward for the abolition of the metropolitan counties and the GLC in 1986 (HMSO, 1983, paragraph 1.19). But the confusing plethora of separate joint boards on the fire service, strategic planning, waste disposal and other matters which succeeded them suggests that abolition did not achieve those ends. These boards are now under no direct electoral control, but are instead made up of nominees from often compulsorily participant councils. The bodies supervised by such boards are likely to be dominated by the bureaucrats who run them, rather than nominees who supervise them, particularly since they will be able to hide behind all the defences of professional expertise with organizations which are larger than almost all the departments within individual local governments with which councillors will be familiar. In the apparent desire to reduce levels of political controversy and so limit the powers of political opponents, it appears that the reforms have, in this area at least, helped to strengthen the position of bureaucrats, and insulate them to a great degree from scrutiny.

The contrast between what one might have expected if changes in line with public choice theory were being implemented and what has actually happened can be illustrated still more clearly by looking rather more closely at particular service areas. In the case of public housing, financial control from the centre has – as we have seen – become stronger and the opportunity for local variation has been reduced. The sale of council housing to sitting tenants is a national initiative and local authorities have been under pressure to carry it through. Council house rent levels have increasingly been influenced – if not determined – by central government order to reduce subsidies. New building has virtually been stopped. The growth of housing associations has been encouraged and subsidized from the centre, but financial rules have also made it advantageous for councils to co-operate (form partnerships) with housing associations. The financial structures of housing finance have always been confusing – with heavy subsidies hidden in mortgage tax relief – and have become more so, with, for example, tax concessions promised for investment in rented housing through business expansion schemes. Once in housing associations, few tenants have much choice of alternative landlords – and in many cases are not even eligible under the 'right to buy' legislation which has had such dramatic effects on council housing. In England and Wales, most of the major housing associations' tenants have few rights of democratic control over their landlords. New legislation at the end of the 1980s is intended to take this process further, by reducing the housing stock managed by local authorities. The attempts to shift higher numbers of tenants out of council housing do involve elements of choice. Tenants on estates are to be allowed to vote (once) on whether they wish to transfer to housing associations or private landlords, but they will have no right to transfer *back* at any future stage. In those areas which the Department of the Environment designates as Housing Action Trusts – which will operate as independent agencies for renewal – tenants are to be given no choice, and nor are the councils from whose stock the Trusts are to be extracted. In Scotland, the formation of Scottish Homes in 1989 has created a powerful agency which is intended to change the face of public housing in the country and to encourage the growth of the private rented sector. In fact development of Housing Action Trusts to deal with particularly run-down estates and Scottish Homes to break up the public sector suggests an alternative vision, based on state-sponsored restructuring and renewal from above, rather than individual choice.

Activity 4.3

The previous discussion has used the example of housing to consider whether the three conditions outlined on p.128 were met. You should now attempt a similar process in looking at reforms proposed for primary and secondary education in England and Wales at the end of the '80s. The key elements involved here seem to me to be:

(a)   the introduction of a national curriculum;

(b)   increased powers for school governors over internal budgeting and the appointment of staff and a shift in balance towards parent governors;

(c)   increased power for head-teachers (including greater responsibility for the running of the school);

(d)   the possibility for schools to 'opt out' of the local education authority (and its rules, while still receiving state funds);

(e)   the encouragement of 'city technology colleges', with substantial financial support from the private sector, separately funded from other schools and with specialist attention to teaching on science and technology;

(f)   continued limitation of finance, in most cases to be distributed through the local education authority but devolved budgetary powers to the schools and the possibility of raising additional funds from other sources.

How would you assess these changes in terms of the assumptions?

If substantial structural change is taking place, then, it does not seem to be following the lines which would be suggested by public choice theory. In part that might be explained in terms of the powers of resistance possessed by the bureaucracies under attack, so that whatever change is proposed it is soon absorbed and reinterpreted by the very groups it is intended to undermine.

Arguably the process of centralization which has taken place could be presented as a necessary precursor to the decentralization of power which is desired. Only by centralizing power in the first place, on this argument, can the all-pervasive powers of bureaucracy be challenged. Despite its initial plausibility, however, this approach has the main disadvantage that the ultimate end – if it is there at all – tends rather too easily to get lost in the detail of policy. It becomes difficult to identify signs of any significant decentralization, although an increased degree of fragmentation between different agencies is clear enough.

4.4.3   Towards local corporatism?

A second interpretation of the developments of the 1980s would set them in a longer context, dating back to the late 1960s. Within such a context it is easier to see how a series of advances, retreats and confusing divisions can be explained as part of a general shift which is of wider significance than the accumulation of a mass of detailed incidents, each of which can only be fully explained in terms of its own unique genesis. It is particularly helpful, despite the weaknesses associated with them, to think back to some of the arguments presented by Cockburn and Dearlove which were discussed in section 4.2. Cockburn looks to changes within the managerial structures of local government and relates them to changes in the methods of management adopted in the private sector. Dearlove associates local government reorganization with the need to link business and government more closely, both to undermine the basis of working-class and community power as reflected through the local government system, and to integrate more closely the infrastructural requirements of the private sector and the responses of the state. Some analysts of the eighties have in effect, developed and modified these approaches in response to some of the criticisms made earlier, and to the changing features of political life.

Paul Hoggett (1987), for example, has sought to explain changes in the organization of local government largely in terms drawn from debates within economics and the sociology of work (see, for example, Massey, 1988a; Meegan, 1988), which suggests that since the early 1970s there has been a move away from Fordist towards post-Fordist methods of production. **Fordism** is said to be characterized by high levels of mass production and work organized on standardized (Taylorist) lines, so that each element can be broken down, systematized and repeated. Alongside mass production, according to this approach, went mass consumption, so that the system could be sustained by general state-inspired (Keynesian) economic management, which encouraged a continued growth of demand for the products of the generally centralized industries with their large production units. **Post-Fordism**, on the other hand, is characterized by the growth of flexible specialization, which implies a more widely variegated and less standardized set of products, as well as the ability to change the nature of those products in response to changes in the market. Such a model also implies a change in the driving force of economic decision-making. Under Fordism mass consumption was a consequence of mass production; whilst with post-Fordism, it is changes in consumption and the identification of specialist markets which are said to determine changes in production. Post-Fordism implies that management, too, has to be decentralized and forms of work discipline changed, because they can no longer be organized through hierarchies in which standardized messages are passed from above and implemented in any very straightforward fashion. Workers are expected to be able to deal with a range of tasks and managers to be able to respond to immediate changes in demand. All of this is said to be made easier by (and possibly to have been a partial consequence of) the introduction of information technology.

Hoggett (1987) argues that the end of Fordism as a paradigm linking state and production has also undermined the basis of the old management and organizational structures of British local government. He draws an analogy between the decline of mass production (and consumption) and the pressures for an end to the standardized service delivery (and what he calls 'people processing') of the local welfare state. And he argues that changing social relations imply the need for more specialist and responsive service delivery, while changing managerial technologies (particularly information technology) make it possible to flatten managerial hierarchies by removing many of the mdidle layers and encouraging the growth of decentralized offices with less professional specialization and a greater ability to deal with individual issues across professional lines. Information can be made available more easily through computer links without the need for a significant layer of intervening administrative bureaucrats or middle managers. This would confirm the move away from the traditions of post-war local government with its large centralized service departments, towards rather more fragmented forms.

Hoggett's analysis concerns itself principally with the opportunities opened up for the left by these changes, with more direct contact between service providers and consumers through neighbourhood offices. But a similar argument could equally well explain the break-up of local governments as major employers of labour and direct providers of services. The underlying shifts which Hoggett identifies make it easier to view the local authority as a 'manager' of service delivery rather than its actual administrator. On this model the local authority would be left with a limited number of central staff concerned to monitor and regulate service delivery organized by private concerns – for example, in street cleaning and refuse disposal – or undertaken by autonomous voluntary agencies – such as housing associations or schools directly managed by elected governors. The main tasks of such an authority would be to issue contracts for the performance of particulai tasks coupled with supervisory and inspection to ensure that they were adequately performed. Bureaucrats – or potential bureaucrats – would in some cases be controlled by the need to compete for contracts, in others by the need to compete for 'clients' (or pupils).

At a theoretical level there remain some problems with this analysis. It tends to proceed by a process of *analogy*. It accepts the arguments of others that moves towards post-Fordism are taking place in economy and society, and then attempts to translate these moves into the languages of local government. So, for example, mass production becomes 'people processing'; standardized output becomes the delivery of standardized services. There are two principal problems associated with this. First, the analogy itself is rather stretched since many local government services, particularly in education and welfare, unlike those delivered by central government (for example, through social security), have always been based on discretion and variation between individuals and not on standardization in accordance with clearly identified rules. As Lipsky (1979) notes, many local government services are delivered by 'street-level bureaucrats' (such as social workers and teachers) whose decisions are the product of negotiations between client and professional. It is because they make the decisions that they are often under sharp pressure both from those above them in the hierarchy who allocate resources and from those with whom they deal who want to receive them. It also makes them difficult to control. Secondly, the analogy does not provide very much by the way of explanation. It is not clear what processes are generating these changes. At best it shows only that something similar is happening without showing why, or identifying key causal processes. Without such explanation, of course, it makes it difficult to accept that the same things really are taking place in the different spheres. And, as was argued ealier regarding Cockburn, even if similar methods have been borrowed it remains to be determined whether the implications are similar too.

Some consideration of the changing roles of corporate interests along the lines suggested by Dearlove may be more helpful here. In Chapter 2 it was argued that some of the most striking features of the post-war development of the British state, at least until the late 1970s, could be explained quite effectively in terms of 'corporate bias', that is moves away from the formal structures of democratic (electoral) representation towards the representation of major corporate interest groups (such as the trade unions and employers' organizations), as mediated through the agency of the state itself. Cawson defines **corporatism** as a process 'in which organizations representing monopolistic functional interests engage in political exchange with state agencies over public policy outputs which involves those organizations in a role that combines interest representation and policy implementation through delegated self-enforcement' (1985a, p. 8).

In the 1980s it has been acknowledged that the importance of formal (tripartite) arrangements at 'peak' levels has been reduced – indeed it is now often suggested that Britain was always less 'corporatist' in these terms than countries such as the Federal Republic of Germany, Austria and Sweden. But this does not mean that there are no longer forms of interest mediation through the state. One aspect of the changing nature of local government since the early 1970s seems to be that various local government agencies have taken on this role in one way or another, to the extent that there seems to have been a marked change in relations between those agencies and business interests at local level.

Reference has already been made to some of these changes. There has been a significant growth in non-elected local government, of local quangos. Some of this (such as the growth of joint boards and the relegation of local government in Northern Ireland in the early 1970s) has been the direct result of various local government reforms. But the process has also been a more subtle one, as new initiatives have apparently been tacked on to existing local government.

In Scotland the most obvious example of this – the Scottish Development Agency (SDA) – is not strictly a local government but a regional organization, yet in many ways it has provided a model for initiatives which have since been developed elsewhere at local level. The SDA was initially set up in 1975 'to provide a regional dimension to complement the UK-wide sectoral interventionism of the National Enterprise Board (NEB)' (Moor, 1986, p. 8). Like the NEB, it was set up to operate separately from the direct institutions of central government and the Scottish Office, although dependent on them for funds (up to £75 million in the mid-1980s) and its board included representatives of business and labour as well as government. More important perhaps, its role was to work 'with the market rather than seeking a directive role. The key to this was seen as establishing close links with the private sector' (Moore, 1986, p. 9). Although the SDA was strictly a national agency, it was also given the responsibility of managing the Glasgow Eastern Area Renewal Project (GEAR), which was then the largest inner-city project in Britain. Here it was effectively a form of non-elected local government, which had access to greater resources than Glasgow District Council.

Through GEAR (and on a smaller scale similar agencies in some other Scottish cities) the SDA pursued a policy of bargaining and negotiation designed to mobilize private sector finance, voluntary sector initiative (particularly in housing) and local authority co-operation (for example on the provision of land) (see, for example, Donnison and Middleton (1987) for a more developed discussion of GEAR). It allowed and encouraged the possibility of longer-term co-operation with business and property development, which has in the past proved more difficult to achieve with locally elected councils, through which other interests may achieve higher levels of representation.

In England and Wales these lessons were taken further through the creation of a series of urban development corporations – first set up for London's Docklands and Merseyside, and later extended to a number of other areas, including the Black Country, Trafford Park, Teesside, Salford, Tyne and Wear, Cardiff Bay and Sheffield. These, too, are dependent on central government funding and have – even more explicitly than GEAR – the role of encouraging investment through the provision of infrastructure which makes property development possible and profitable. Again, such agencies operate to allow and encourage negotiation between key groups (including developers and, in some cases, local industry) and the state in such a way that the obstacles created by a locally elected body can be bypassed. The SDA itself is now to be dismantled and replaced by a series of local agencies.

But the growth of non-elected local government is not restricted to these centrally inspired creations. Many councils have themselves encouraged their growth – sometimes to avoid the implications of centrally imposed financial constraints and sometimes explicitly to make co-operation and partnerships with the voluntary and private sectors easier and less dependent on committee cycles and bureaucratic indecision. This helps to explain the extent to which local authorities have begun to work closely with housing associations and several left-wing councils have set up enterprise boards while others are heavily involved in local enterprise agencies. Their relative independence of the councils which set them up means that deals can be negotiated and long-term arrangements achieved which do not depend on detailed discussion through council committee. It allows a relationship between professionals to develop which is unlikely to be disrupted by what are seen as more ephemeral shifts within local electoral politics.

The nature of these changes, then, can be seen as some confirmation that the trends identified by Dearlove were genuine enough, but that working them through has taken much longer to achieve and involved much more upheaval than his initial analysis would have suggested. The search for appropriate bodies through which business interests could be represented was not an easy one and has only been achieved either by completely bypassing existing councils or by involving councillors as well as officers in developing new arrangements in a context of financial pressure and legal constraints.

The extent to which it is appropriate to describe the new arrangements as local corporatism is rather more problematic. Cawson (1985b), for example, prefers the description 'corporatism at local level', since he argues that 'in most cases the local dimension is the target of intervention rather than the basis for the organization of the participating bodies' (p. 144). This certainly appears to be the case for many of the centrally inspired agencies referred to earlier, particularly the urban development corporations and development agencies. But even in these cases such an interpretation seems unnecessarily narrow. It implies the implementation of a nationally determined (and negotiated) strategy at local level, involving locally based groups (or local branches of national organizations) only with a view to ensuring a smooth process of implementation. Yet the available evidence suggests rather a different model. The various urban development corporations, for example, are recognizably different in their modes of operation and have not always followed the line favoured by central government. In some places they have negotiated with and worked together with local authorities and in some cases, at least, a local authority representative has been included on the board. In others regional representatives of the trade unions have been similarly involved. More important, perhaps, as they have begun to operate in practice, a higher degree of localized bargaining has developed, often with agencies (including unions, community groups and local authorities) which are not formally represented within the official structures. Even the London Docklands Development Corporation (arguably the least local of the boards) has been involved in negotiations with the London Borough of Newham over low-cost housing and has resisted proposals from developers to utilize land allocated for such housing for other purposes. This is still clearer with the development agencies, not only at the regional (or 'national') level where Cawson would find the corporatist label acceptable, but also at local level, particularly through agencies such as GEAR.

A stronger argument which Cawson also develops is that major interests are not directly represented at local level, because whether sectoral (for instance, professional or industrial organizations) or production (such as employers and trade unions) their main levels of organization for the purposes of representation are national or regional. It is there that key decisions are made. According to this model, local politics (see also Chapter 5, section 5.3.3, where the 'dual state' thesis is discussed) is more open to pluralist pressures, since locally based interest groups tend to be those of service consumers, rather than the various types of producer which dominate at other levels (and often play a big part in determining what is possible at local level).

Cawson's arguments are persuasive, at least insofar as he confirms that it is difficult to conceive of any independent local corporatism, based on local classes and local producer groups. Economic and political organization in the late twentieth century is more centralized than that. Certainly an analytical distinction between 'corporatism at local level' and 'local politics' is useful. But the conclusion to be drawn from this may be less acceptable to those for whom the *democratic* and *pluralist* nature of local government is one of its key defining characteristics, since local government (both elected *and* unelected) seems increasingly to be drawn into 'corporatism at local level'. This is the case across a range of local government services, including housing, where the voluntary sector is becoming accepted as a 'partner'. The language of partnership is becoming more and more important. Cawson himself acknowledges the significance of this in his discussion of 'microcorporatism', that is the detailed bargaining of the state with individual enterprises over investment and other matters, sometimes with the involvement of trade unions (see Cawson (1986, pp. 118–21) where he focuses particularly on the experiences of the GLC and the Greater London Enterprise Board). In practice micro-corporatism of this sort has only been undertaken with any consistency by local government and their agencies (such as the enterprise boards) or by the development agencies (see, for example, Greater London Council (1985) and Murray (1987)).

This implies a different role for local government – almost an echo of the Bains Report quoted earlier – with a move away from the direct delivery of services as a dominant activity, even if the bulk of the spending is still in that area, towards the management of change, in this case, economic change. Such a vision implies a wider set of partnership arrangements. In principle, of course, it also implies an independent bargaining role of government and the state, in which it is not solely responsive to the demands of particular dominant interests. The extent to which such an understanding is justified has been a matter of some debate, not only at the local level, but in terms of national politics, and even politics within the EC. Lindblom (1977), for example, argues that business interests are in a politically privileged position, to the extent that in any bargain struck between business and government, its terms will largely be dictated by business. 'In the eyes of government officials, therefore,' he says, 'businessmen do not appear simply as the representatives of a special interest, as representatives of interest groups do. They appear as functionaries performing functions that government officials regard as indispensable' (Lindblom, 1977. p. 175). Dearlove's arguments on the reform 1970s similarly stressed a shift towards business interests. So, whilst it is possible to identify some broad directions of change it remains difficult to decide the precise implications. For corporatist arrangements to survive at local level, at least according to Cawson, state agencies must be 'capable of making and delivering bargained policies, so that a potential local corporatism depends upon strong local state institutions' (1985b, p. 146). The extent to which these conditions exist at the end of the 1980s, given the extent of legal and financial changes, remains a matter of contention.

Summary of section 4.4

● There were three main elements to local government restructuring in the 1980s:

- changes in local taxation
- moves to privatization
- growth of non-elected local governments.

● These changes can be seen as elements of a programme intended to open up more aspects of public sector provision to the market and to undermine the powers of state bureaucracy, particularly as highlighted by exponents of 'public choice theory'. This approach concentrates its attention on the behaviour of bureaucrats as maximizers of budgets or staff and seeks to identify ways in which that behaviour can be modified by changing the context of their decision-making.

● But, privatization had not dramatically affected core areas of local government activity by the end of the 1980s, and in those areas where it was implemented it seemed unlikely significantly to undermine bureaucratic power.

● And, attempts to encourage greater accountability and competition between authorities have tended to flounder because it has been accompanied by a higher degree of centralization and control and a wider gap between the possibilities of locally generated finance and overall levels of spending. The distribution of responsibilities between local, national, public and voluntary sectors has also become less rather than more clear, which reduces the possibilities of accountability.

● Another interpretation of the changes would see them as part of a longer-term shift towards new relationships between government and the wider political economy.

● Like Cockburn, Hoggett stresses the links between changes in the organization of local government and those of capitalist management. But the model he develops tends to distort the past in order to exaggerate the extent of change. It remains unclear why the changes he identifies have taken place and what the implications are.

● There is some evidence that relationships between local government and business interests have become closer and more institutionalized, and this seems to support an interpretation which identifies a significant shift (or structural change) between the late 1960s and the late 1980s.

● The implications of this change, however, remain contentious. One area of contention is whether it is appropriate to describe the new arrangements as evidence of a growth of local corporatism, or even 'corporatism at local level' (Cawson, 1985b).

Further reading

There are a number of interesting academic books in this area which would repay further reading. Dearlove's analysis of local government reorganization in the early 1970s, *The Reorganization of Local Government* (Cambridge, Cambridge University Press; 1979) is particularly important because it encourages a political analysis of change and develops an impressive critique of more traditional or orthodox approaches. The way in which he mobilizes his evidence to undermine dominant arguments and to construct his own is exciting, and helps to draw local government into the mainstream of political studies. More recent academic publications include *The Local State and Uneven Development* by Duncan and Goodwin (Cambridge, Polity Press; 1988) and *Politics of Local Government* by Stoker (London, Macmillan; 1988). The former argues the case of viewing relations between central and local government in terms of tensions generated by uneven development. The latter provides a useful survey of current debates on local government.

Finally, local government is an active topic of political debate. It has generated its own publications many of which are difficult to follow if you are not actively involved in one way or another. *Democracy in Crisis: The Town Halls Respond* by Blunkett and Jackson (London, Hogarth; 1987) is a clear exception to this. It is a readable account of the conflicts and policies of the early 1980s, and puts forward a strong case for local government to be given more power.

5 The politics of locality

Mark Goodwin

Contents

5.1   Introduction

The opening chapters of this book have drawn your attention to post-war changes in the structure and position of the British state, both nationally and internationally, and Chapter 4 discussed how these changes in state structures have affected local as well as national government. This chapter will follow up this theme, and remain focused at the local level. But it will shift attention away from state structures towards a consideration of the actual politics occurring in and around these local state institutions. Hence the focus is on **local politics**, on the ways in which these have changed and developed over the post-war period and on the concepts and theories used to account for such changes. Localized variations in voting patterns may reflect changing forms of political alignment and voting behaviour (see Johnston, Pattie and Allsopp (1988) for a review), and electoral politics will be looked at in the next chapter, but here I shall consider the notion of political culture more widely. For, as we shall see, political practice and behaviour at the local level can vary widely, even with the same party in control of the council chamber.

Variations in local political practice have increased markedly since the end of the 1960s (see Curtice and Steed, 1982). This increase has been best documented with regard to voting behaviour in general elections, where a number of psephological surveys and statistical analyses support Johnston and Pattie's conclusion that 'voters in Great Britain have been increasingly influenced by their local environment when evaluating the competing claims of the political parties ... people are increasingly concerned about their local circumstances, and vote accordingly' (1988, p. 10). According to the academic orthodoxy, this local influence is a relatively recent political phenomenon. Indeed, the accepted view of post-war politics in Britain showed how diverse, localized political cultures were subsumed under, and gradually integrated into, a single homogeneous national politics. Johnson (1972) labelled this gradual ironing out of local characteristics the '**nationalization**' of local politics, and this process was reflected in the confident claim of the political pundits that 'to know the swing in Cornwall was to know, within a percentage or two, the swing in the Highlands' (Crewe, 1985, p. 103).

No analyst would make such a claim today, and the 'nationalization' thesis has had to be revised in the light of increased local variations in voting behaviour. Following the general election of 1987, media recognition of the 'two nations' of north and south fuelled such revision. But although voting behaviour in national elections has received most attention, many other forms of political activity have also become more locally differentiated. This chapter will concentrate on just one – the politics operating around and within local government – and will use this as an example to indicate how local political cultures, as well as voting behaviour, can vary geographically. This concentration is especially relevant in any consideration of a restructured Britain. For, as part of that restructuring, local government has recently emerged as a major issue, and arena, of political debate and conflict. This is not just of interest to professional politicians or academic specialists; local government has become front-page news, its leading politicians such as Ken Livingstone, David Blunkett and Derek Hatton have been catapulted to national fame and the local–central government conflict detailed in Chapter 4 has been a major issue in three successive general elections.

Borrowing the terminology used to describe national electoral politics, Gyford (1985a) has characterized this revitalization of local politics as a shift from 'nationalization' to 'reappraisal'. But if we can view 'nationalization' as the ironing out of local political characteristics during the 1950s and 1960s, 'reappraisal' has meant more than their simple re-appearance during the late 1970s and early 1980s. For the term indicates nothing less than a complete questioning of the traditional role of local government. This role, of locally providing and administering a wide range of public services, from planning and transport to housing and education, was deeply embedded in the post-war political consensus, and local government seemed to have found a safe and secure niche with the coming of a fully fledged welfare state.

However, as Chapter 4 pointed out, this niche, and the relatively stable two-party system which surrounded it, increasingly came under pressure as Britain's ever deepening economic crisis began to bite. From the mid-1970s successive governments attempted to alleviate the crisis by curbing public expenditure. Although this included controlling overall levels of local government spending, the role of local government was not in question. But when the Conservatives came to power in 1979, local government found itself at the centre of a much wider conflict regarding the role of the state as a whole, and the position of local government began to be 'reappraised'. For the new government, economic regeneration rested on more than mere control of public expenditure. It also depended on the promotion of the belief that free markets are both economically efficient and socially just – and in crucial respects local government stood in the way of such promotion. It was not only a substantial spender of public money, but also a major provider of public services, often allocated collectively, sometimes even on the criteria of social need. Moreover, in some places these services were explicitly provided, usually by Labour-controlled authorities, to offer protection against the 'purifying winds' of the market, and to mitigate the cut and thrust of commercial rationality.

Local governments are thus not just caught up in recent political conflicts as some innocent or neutral part of the political machine, but are themselves crucial in interpreting and promoting social change. The conflict between central and local government referred to in Chapter 4 has been clouded by both inter- and intra-party disputes. The institutions of local government offer a site where several alternative values and practices can be tried, tested and demonstrated to the public. The local politics of central versus local government, and Conservative versus Labour, is underlain by 'wets' versus 'drys', by 'left' versus 'right', by 'rural traditionalism' versus 'suburban

Thatcherism' and by 'working-class militants' versus 'the new urban left'. What we have witnessed over the past decade is the emergence of a whole host of competing and conflicting forms of local politics – different places have begun, in political terms, to behave very differently and British politics is now characterized by diversity rather than homogeneity.

This chapter will look at this emergence in three parts. The first will consider the nature of this new political diversity, and will also examine the historical evidence to see if, in fact, such differentiation is entirely 'new'. The second will provide an overview of the varying academic approaches towards understanding the politics of local government, and in particular will look at the concepts and wider theories that such studies draw upon in order to inform their analysis. The third will look at the actual experience of one recent, and especially contentious, form of local government activity – the development of local economic strategies. As you will see, these sections between them raise several important analytical questions. Should we conceptualize local politics as merely denoting local voting behaviour, or should we include geographical variations in a range of political activity and experience? Does this increase in variation mean that we can speak of a specifically 'local' politics, and if so is this based around local issues and is it generated through local processes? Or does it just indicate the different ways in which national political shifts are experienced locally? And if we can identify locally generated politics, are we justified in speaking of the 'local state'? Or is local government simply to be viewed as one part of the state as a whole – with no specificity of its own?

Activity 5.1

Before we go on to consider these studies of local politics, think about other major economic and social changes that have taken place within Britain since the mid-1970s – such as deindustrialization, or the large increase in home ownership. Would you expect these to be accompanied by an increasing diversity of local political activity? If so, why should this be the case? What form would you expect such local politics to take? Should they necessarily be restricted to electoral variations, or even to activity around state institutions such as local government?

5.2   The re-emergence of local politics

We have already noted how recent studies of the changing electoral geography of Britain have identified increased local variations in voting patterns. Johnston and Pattie (1988) claim that people no longer vote so much according to their class, or social, position, but rather are increasingly referrent to their spatial location. Thus, people with similar socio-economic and demographic characteristics, but living in different places, may well vote for different parties. Although the mechanisms behind this geographical variance are unclear, what is not in dispute is that spatial polarization in voting behaviour has increased steadily, especially during the three general elections of 1979, 1983 and 1987, making it difficult to disagree with the conclusion that the 'nationalization' of British politics has now been replaced by an emerging local differentiation.

Local political behaviour shows a similar path – in an appendix to the Widdicombe Report on the Conduct of Local Authority Business (1986, Cmnd 9797), Miller argues that variation in local voting can increasingly be attributed to specifically local factors, and Jones and Stewart also show how since the mid-1970s local factors have increasingly influenced the results of local elections. They note how in the local elections of 1982 local authorities in the same region showed very different results: 'In Wolverhampton, Labour made gains while in nearby Walsall Labour lost seats. Whereas in Bradford and Leeds Labour lost ground, in Barnsley they made large gains and in Sheffield they maintained their position. In Rochdale, Labour lost seats, while in Oldham Labour gained seats. In Strathclyde Labour made gains but not in Lothian' (Jones and Stewart, 1983, pp. 16–18). They point out how similar differences would be found in an analysis of Conservative and Alliance results in the 1982 local elections. Indeed, in London the Alliance made large gains in Tower Hamlets, but in neighbouring Islington it held only one seat in a council it had previously controlled. After noting how local parties differ on major issues of expenditure, financial control, privatization, transport subsidies, rents and council house sales, they conclude that 'It is not surprising that the local electorate vote in response to local circumstances' (Jones and Stewart, 1983, p. 17). But this increased local differentiation cuts across party lines, and especially within the Conservative and Labour Parties there has been an increasing ideological polarization, which, though denied expression in the tightly controlled atmosphere of Westminster, often surfaces at the local level. Thus if we widen our notion of local politics from electoral behaviour, we find increased differentiation in local political activity within as well as between the major political parties.

Indeed, local government has often been used by the right of the Conservative Party to promote the introduction of 'market forces' into, and the privatization of, certain state services, and by the left of the Labour Party to develop 'local socialism' and the extension of public sector services into areas of the community previously untouched by local government. Although radical politics of this kind remain in the minority, for both left and right, their development means that councils can experience large changes in their policies whilst remaining under the control of the same party – so increasing political variation at the local level. For instance, the London Borough of Southwark remained under Labour control after the May 1982 local elections, but two-thirds of the Labour councillors were new, following 'de-selections' and defections to the newly formed Social Democratic Party. Most of their policies were also new, and the differences between the two successive Labour Councils were probably greater than those which existed between the previous Labour Council and their Conservative opposition prior to 1982.

Indeed, the emergence of the SDP nationally, and of its alliance with the Liberal Party as the 'third force' in British politics at the beginning of the 1980s, led to increased political instability and variation across the country, as several local elections produced 'hung councils' in which no single party could claim overall control. Many other aspects of local government have also become increasingly politicized over recent years. In some councils certain key administrative officers are appointed on the basis of their political sympathies. As Derek Hatton, Deputy Leader of Liverpool City Council put it, 'We'd want to make sure that . . . those who are employed to manage and carry out the policies which we decide are those who are in general sympathy with those policies' (Gyford, 1985b, p. 58). The traditional role of the local government officer as the neutral bureaucrat has also come under stress from the growing militancy of local authority trade unions. Sometimes this is the result of the strength of left-wing groups in particular council branches, but at other times strikes have been called on a nation-wide level to protest about changes in industrial relations, cuts in local government spending and enforced job losses. Along with the rise of local voluntary and community groups, often funded by the local council, this has ensured that local authority politics have increased markedly in both their visibility and their differentiation.

Duncan and Goodwin (1988, pp. 6–9) give examples of variation in local authority service delivery. With regard to the overall provision of services they show that only 18 out of the 47 English and Welsh County Councils spent within ±5 per cent of the national average per capita expenditure in 1984/85. The variations in local government spending on single issues of some political contention are even more marked. Duncan and Goodwin examine the subsidizing of council housing, via contributions made from the rates, in London in 1984/85. In addition to finding that many Boroughs actually made a profit from council house rents, and thus subsidized ratepayers, they found that the highest transfer from rates to council housing was no less than 443 per cent above average. In all only 7 of the 32 London Boroughs are even within ±50 per cent of the average transfer. But it is one thing to document the diversity in local authority expenditure and political activity; it is another to acount for its origins and maintenance. When faced with this problem many authors have turned to the idea of '**local political cultures**', and have sought to explain political variation by reference to the existence of such 'cultures' (Butler and Stokes, 1974; Johnston, 1986a). But although this is at first appealing, on closer examination the concept is somewhat flawed. For if local political activity is the mere reflection, or embodiment, of local culture, it is difficult to see how anything changes.

Instead, as both *Mark-Lawson and Warde* (1987) and *Savage* (1989) stress, local politics are extremely dynamic, both spatially and temporally, and local cultures themselves are subject to continual change. If this is the case we need to take one conceptual step backwards. The relevant questions should not concern how local 'culture' forms local politics, but how this 'culture' itself is formed, how it is sustained or transformed, and how it affects local political activity in conjunction with a host of other structures and practices, some of which may be locally based and some of which may not.

Detailed research on local politics helps to indicate the complexity of practices and processes operating around the politics of local government, and hence points to some of the reasons underlying the recent diversity in local political activity. For instance, *Savage* (1989) examines the development of local politics in Glasgow, whilst *Mark-Lawson and Warde* (1987) look at the transformation of the **local political environment** in Lancaster. Both concentrate on the politics of local government, but both also stress how any explanation of local politics must look outside the formal political processes which operate around local political parties and the Council Chamber. They note the range of institutions and processes that contribute to the formation of local political practices. These include institutions based in the local economy, such as trade unions or Chambers of Commerce, and those based in the local community, such as tenants' groups, neighbourhood associations and women's organizations. Also important in both Glasgow and Lancaster is the existing level and type of service provision: in both cases local politics were especially affected by the nature of local housing provision. This indicates that the politics of local government do not just respond or react to the local environment, but crucially that they also help to mould this environment, and thus to a certain extent help to shape the local political agenda.

Given the range of institutions and the varying sets of social relations involved, it does not seem surprising that there should have been an increase in the diversity of local politics. However, perhaps this increase should not be seen as the emergence of local politics, but should more properly be viewed as their re-emergence. For although the 1950s and '60s may have seen the homogenization and 'nationalization' of local politics, before this period the merging of local and national political activity was the exception rather than the rule. Indeed, from the very beginning of elected local government in the first half of the nineteenth century, Britain has generally experienced a wide range of local political activity. Gyford points out that in their earliest days, the politics of local government assumed 'a somewhat kaleidoscopic form. A variety of actors in different towns – Whigs, Tories, Liberals, Conservatives, Radicals, Chartists, Improvers, Economisers, Independents, and a bevy of personal cliques and factions – argued over whether to expand, or to economise on, the provision of public services' (1985a, p. 79). This was also the case around the turn of the century, when the emerging labour movement often used local political activity in particular strongholds such as East London and Sheffield to promote its aims and objectives long before it reached the national political stage.

In the inter-war period local government had responsibility for Poor Law duties, including some hospitals, and the public utilities of gas, water, electricity and transport, in addition to its current functions of education, highways and housing. Given the diversity of these functions, their local provision was often politically contentious. Thirty councillors from the London Borough of Poplar were sent to prison in 1921 for refusing to levy rate precepts for London County Council, the Metropolitan Police and the Metropolitan Asylums Board, in a protest against the unequal nature of the rates burden as between rich and poor areas of London. In 1932 the government sent commissioners into Rotherham and Durham councils to take over their public assistance committees when they refused to operate the means test as rigorously as the centre wished. These were only the most visible of a whole series of local political challenges to the centre, built around distinct and diverse local political cultures. In Gyford's words, 'in this inter-war period, municipal and national politics were not wholly assimilated into one another . . . It is thus possible to see local politics in these years as having, in some degree, a life of its own' (1985a, pp. 82–3).

Thus political diversity at the local level, crystallizing around the politics of local government, has been widespread for one hundred and fifty years. When seen in this historical light, it seems that the 'normal' 1950s and '60s were actually quite abnormal. The nationalization of local politics arose from a specific combination of economic, social and political processes which no longer applies. This combination was expressed at the national level by 'Butskellism' – that bi-partisan approach to government relying on an expanded mixed economy, and underlain by the social-democratic compromise between capital and labour. At the local level it was expressed by a shared set of values and policies, operating within a welfare state consensus. Local government had its place within this consensus, and its role was accepted by both major political parties. The somewhat unitary, homogenized world of local politics in the '50s and '60s was thus a reflection of wider social relations, of wider values, and of a wider economic stability – all of which have now disappeared. Thus the nature of local politics has changed over the post-war period, and we will now look at the way this has been analysed, to see if the debates within the social sciences have kept pace with material change.

Summary of section 5.2

- Spatial differentiation in political activity has become increasingly marked, at both a national and a local scale.
- This is more than just a case of increased differentiation in local voting behaviour.
- Local government has seen the growth of intra- as well as inter-party

politics, and has been used by both major parties to promote 'radical' policies.

● There is a complex range of institutions and practices involved in local political activity, including economically and socially based organizations.

● The homogeneity of local politics in the 1950s and early 1960s was the exception rather than the rule.

Activity 5.2

(a) What are your local councils?

(b) What parties are in control?

(c) How has this changed since the last local elections, if at all?

(d) Are you aware of any significant changes in council policies over the past five years? If so, would you explain them more in terms of:
   – central government pressures or initiatives?
   – changes in political control locally?
   – changes within local political parties? or
   – initiatives developed by local government officers?

5.3 Analysing local politics

Before we begin this short survey of attempts to analyse local political activity, it is worth noting a dual contradiction which underpins post-war changes in British local politics. We have just noted how local politics in Britain has recently become more diversified, but, as Chapter 4 pointed out, this has happened at the same time as political power has become increasingly centralized. The politics of local government have come to the fore just as the powers of local government have declined. Of course, this is no accident, and Duncan and Goodwin (1988) in their book on the local government crisis detail how the two processes are interlinked and how each has helped to shape the other. Increasingly threatening forms of local political activity brought a response from central government, whose policies were designed to reduce the scope for local government autonomy. But these new measures from the centre, such as rate-capping and the introduction of poll tax (see Duncan and Goodwin, 1989), have resulted in new and varied forms of local politics.

This situation can be contrasted with the 1950s and 1960s when, under the boom conditions of Keynesian economic management and social-democratic political consensus, local government was largely free of detailed financial or administrative control. The result, however, and the second contradiction, was that given this freedom local authorities behaved in a very similar fashion to each other. Local political diversity was almost absent at a time when central control was at its slackest. Or this at least was the academic orthodoxy, and by examining this and subsequent debates we should have a clearer idea of the analytical tools which can be of help in understanding the changing nature of local politics in Britain.

5.3.1   The lost world of local politics

We thus have to begin our examination of local politics in a restructured Britain, at a time when there were supposedly no local politics. Indeed, according to Rhodes (1975, p. 39), 'The politics of local government was a lost world' until the late 1960s. Political scientists in the 1950s and '60s managed to maintain this position through two major lines of argument and methodology. Firstly, they mainly restricted their political analysis to the relations between local authorities and central government departments. There was a concentration, in other words, on the formal political world of intergovernmental relations. And within this relationship local authorities were seen as decentralized administrative agents, acting at the behest of the centre. Secondly, whenever local politics were looked at, they were investigated using quantitative statistical techniques, used to try to find some sort of 'link' or 'association' between local inputs (such as population density, income per capita, degree of urbanization) and policy outputs (usually levels of expenditure on particular services). Both approaches prevented any understanding of the actual processes of local politics, and thus both helped to further the orthodoxy that local politics were largely absent in the immediate post-war period.

Those studies which concentrated on local–central relations ignored local politics because they saw local authorities as mere receptacles for central policy. The opportunity for autonomous action and local diversity was limited, according to this view, because of two factors. First, it was argued that local government was financially dependent on the centre, and that 'he who pays the piper calls the tune'. Financial dependence was taken as evidence for agency status. Secondly, the imposition of centrally determined standards of provision coupled with a public demand for equality in local services was supposed to have led to an increasing uniformity in service provision. Hence, the argument runs, even without central financial control most local councils would have been providing similar levels of services. Dearlove (1973, p. 15) shows both arguments to be largely false, and concludes that such studies consisted of 'unsupported hunches based on partial research', leading to a definite exaggeration of both central control and uniformity of service provision.

However, even when research came to recognize this exaggeration and to examine the diversity of local service provision, local politics remained shrouded in mystery. Initially this local political research, following its North American counterpart, concentrated on manipulating quantifiable variables – the so-called 'output studies'. These essentially consisted of using multiple regression techniques to test the 'relationship' between local political outputs and a number of external input variables: a likely looking set of independent variables would be tested against expenditure levels to see if any of the relationships were statistically significant. There is no conceptualization here beyond statistical association. This may be able to identify some sort of 'fit' between the social and economic characteristics of a city and its public policy, but this in no sense explains that policy. Through this type of analysis we may discover that there is a relationship between certain socioeconomic inputs and political outputs, but we would not know how or why this relationship exists. Moreover, the results depend totally on what data are put in, and the methodology of necessity limits data to those which are amenable to statistical manipulation. There are obviously important facets of the local political system – such as power, patronage and personality – which cannot be quantified and so must be left out of the 'explanation'. Thus, despite its empirical sophistication, the outputs approach leaves local politics as a 'lost world'.

5.3.2   In search of the political process

Studies of intergovernmental relations, and of inputs and outputs, both failed to consider the actual political processes operating in and around local government. In reaction, the late 1960s saw the beginnings of a new type of local political analysis which consisted of intensive case studies of particular authorities. Research turned towards the policy process itself, to the people who took the decisions and to the local political institutions in which they operated. Soon a torrent of research appeared, on individual councils and on individual policies. (Jones (1975), Rhodes (1975) and Gyford (1976) provide reviews.) By their volume alone, these new studies of local politics promised to illuminate the lost world.

This new field of local political research was stimulated by an increase in local authority activity, especially in housing and urban renewal, in the 1960s and early 1970s, as well as by the responses of community groups. Indeed, the rise of 'community politics' in the late 1960s helped to focus academic interest on the North American 'community power' studies, but the new research received its most important theoretical support through the emergence of urban managerialism. This directed attention towards the activities and values of key officials – the 'urban managers' – who, through their positions in influential institutions such as local authorities, building societies, estate agents and the like, could allocate scarce urban resources and thus influence service provision locally. In Pahl's well-known expression, local political research came to be concerned with 'Who gets the scarce resources and facilities? Who decides how to distribute or allocate these resources? Who decides who decides?' (1975, p. 185).

This new flowering of empirical work on local politics usually addressed three key issues, albeit with different degrees of emphasis (see Bassett and Short, 1980, p. 132). First, the studies looked at local councillors themselves – at their attitudes and perceptions, at their organization and relationship with their political party, and at their political activity. Notions of 'political ideology', and of an 'assumptive world', were developed to account for their behaviour (see respectively Dearlove, 1973; Young and Kramer, 1978). Secondly, research looked at the relationship between these councillors and the local government officers employed to implement their decisions. Not surprisingly research on different places produced conflicting results. Davies (1972), on Newcastle, and Dennis (1972), on Sunderland, both show how council officials acted almost independently over issues of urban redevelopment, their actions being governed by a vague notion of the type of planning needed to produce 'a good society' – hence the title of Davies's book *The Evangelistic Bureaucrat*. In contrast Saunders (1979) and Newton (1976), in their studies of, respectively, Croydon and Birmingham, both trace fairly close relationships between high-level council officers and leading councillors, with each relying on the other during the policy-making process. It seems safest to conclude that this symbiotic relationship is the norm, but that it takes place to varying degrees according to policy, place and circumstance. Thus if Davies and Dennis had been studying other cities with different political and administrative structures, they would have found different results – as would Saunders and Newton! As is the norm in social science, yet one rarely acknowledged, what you find depends on where and when and – crucially – how you look.

This is borne out by the third type of managerialist study – that of the role of external 'pressure groups' in local politics. Again different results were found in different places, although there did seem to be some agreement on a broad division between those 'helpful' pressure groups that gained access to the policy-making process and those 'unhelpful', or 'unreasonable', groups whose actions were treated by the local authority with suspicion and dismissal. (See Dearlove (1973) on Kensington and Newton (1976) on Birmingham.)

Through these three strands of study, **urban managerialism** seemed to offer a convenient conceptual framework for the new case studies of local political behaviour. By its identification of, and concentration on, the 'gatekeepers' of the urban system, it gave a way of shifting research from an emphasis on empirical variables to one which stressed political processes, actual decision-making and the real exercise of political power. But the shift was actually only from one limited set of variables to another. This body of work viewed the local political sphere, and those who operated within it, as autonomous – both from local social and political pressure and from wider constraints imposed from outside agencies and institutions.

Just as the concentration on individual managers isolates them from their proper context and makes them almost personally responsible for local policy variations, so the concentration on the processes of local politics isolated these from other sets of socio-economic processes. The emphasis on councillors, officers and pressure groups proved to be a great limitation. The very studies which found the lost world of local politics, did so within a conceptual and methodological framework that ensured it would never be fully understood. For they concentrated on a very formal identification of local politics. The important objects of study were assumed, in an a priori manner, to be operating around the formal institutions of local government and its electoral process. Research stressed political and administrative factors in isolation and never succeeded in analysing the way local politics are linked to wider social and economic processes.

5.3.3   Local politics becomes urban politics: collective consumption and the dual state

Since the mid-1970s, with the recognition that urban managerialism was too narrow in its scope, the concerns of local political research have widened considerably. The almost exclusive concentration on the formal political process has been replaced by accounts that take in crucial determinants outside this sphere, and which are placed in an explanatory framework that allows links to be made with wider sets of social relations. These broadened the somewhat parochial world of local political studies in two senses, both empirically and conceptually. Local political activity came to be seen as part and parcel of changes taking place within capitalist society as a whole, especially within the capitalist state as it attempts to manage and transform a social and economic system in profound crisis. Again material changes stimulated the new thinking just as much as the perceived inadequacies of existing theory. The reorganization of local government described in Chapter 4 confirmed that local government was indeed part of a much wider state system, and the 1973 oil crisis followed by the onset of economic depression deepened the pressures on that system. As if to confirm that they had rejected the old emphasis on local political organizations, the new studies gave themselves a new title. The analysis of local politics became instead an analysis of 'urban' politics, a change given academic respectability towards the end of the 1970s, when the Political Studies Association changed the name of its Local Politics Group to the Urban Politics Group. This change of name was itself based on changes in the theories which informed the Group's work.

The biggest influence on this change came from across the Channel via the writings of the so-called 'French school' of urban sociology, whose most influential figure was undoubtedly Manuel Castells. In his early work (1977, 1978) he undertook a detailed critique of previous sociological approaches to an understanding of the urban system. His reformulation was woven around three key points. First was the argument that the urban is characterized not by any spatial or cultural boundary as had been contended by earlier theorists, but as the site of consumption processes involved in the reproduction of labour power. Castells argued that since production units were increasingly leaving the western city for rural and Third World locations, the urban unit was becoming characterized as a location for consumption. Indeed he stated that 'urban units seem to be to the process of reproduction what the companies are to the production process' (1977, p. 237). Secondly, he argued that these consumption processes are increasingly provided by the state in a collectivized form, since they become too expensive, especially at times of economic crisis, for private firms to supply. And, thirdly, he presented the notion that this increasing state intervention and action at the local urban level inevitably 'politicizes' the provision of **collective consumption** and leads to the development of political activity expressed as 'urban social movements'.

Somewhat paradoxically, however, despite this widening of enquiry, the new urban sociology managed to impose limits on its own research. These arose mainly from its reliance on a rigid theoretical framework which views the urban system as an autonomous political entity – one characterized by its position as the site of collective consumption practices. And despite detailed empirical application in France no major investigation of local politics has been carried out in Britain using these ideas. Instead their lasting legacy and major influence was the legitimacy that they gave for local politics to be reduced to urban politics, which in turn consisted solely of issues concerning collective consumption.

This double reduction was formalized by Patrick Dunleavy, who gave his book *Urban Political Analysis* (1980b) the subtitle 'The politics of collective consumption'. Dunleavy used the ideas of Castells to argue that local political analysis should not be concerned with particular communities, or specific institutions of local government, but instead should focus on the 'urban politics' of collective consumption – that is, with consumption organized on a non-commercial basis by state agencies. Dunleavy also notes the similarity of much local authority service provision in the 1950s and 1960s, and argues persuasively for an explanation of such uniform local political activity to be couched in non-local terms. He puts forward three key areas of non-local policy determination: policy formulation within the welfare state as a whole; the involvement of large private firms in urban development and service provision; and professionalism at both the local and the national level.

Although these wider influences are important to consider, Dunleavy perhaps overreacts to the limited local approach of previous analysts. For he denies the importance of local factors in accounting for local (or urban) politics, by arguing that local authorities are insulated from any electoral or public opinion influences; that local councillors are in any case only involved in decision-making in the most fragmented way; and that local policy-making is constituted by stereotyped responses with little distinctly local reference (1980b, p. 135). Dunleavy's non-local forces may well be important, but they are usually mediated by local processes, and translated into policy by local authorities sometimes in dramatically different ways. As we have already noted, the explanation for the post-war uniformity of local politics perhaps lies elsewhere than in a simple appeal to non-local forces.

An attempt to develop the idea of analysing local politics as the urban politics of collective consumption has also been made by Peter Saunders (1981, 1984, 1986), and working in conjunction with Alan Cawson (Cawson and Saunders, 1983). But, crucially, unlike Castells and Dunleavy they reject a unitary view of the state in favour of a 'dualistic' theory of politics – the **dual state thesis**. As discussed in the previous chapter, this view argues that distinct political processes operate at the national and the local level. State intervention at the central level is supposed to focus mainly on issues of production and income, and it proceeds through a policy process of corporate bargaining. On the other hand they argue that local politics have their own specific frame of reference and form of practice. Locally, they maintain, state intervention is directed towards consumption processes, and policies are developed through a plurality of political struggles. Thus those interests mobilized at the centre around the processes of production – the organized class interests of industrial and finance capital, the professions and organized labour – will differ from those organized locally, where mobilization usually cuts across class lines to be based on specific local consumption issues – council tenants, parents of under-fives and so on.

This work has been important in highlighting the specificity of the local level, and in presenting a conceptualization of local politics based primarily on their 'uniqueness' and separation from the centre. But it still presents problems for those seeking to analyse the changing nature of British local politics. A major difficulty with the thesis is that it rests on an a priori allocation of functions between national and local states, and that these functions are then assumed to produce specific and separate political processes. Local politics are assumed in advance to be of a pluralist nature, and concerned with issues of consumption. In addition to this general point about theory placing empirical practice into pre-determined boxes, there seems little historical rationale or evidence for this particular division between the types of functions and types of politics which characterize the local and the national state.

Although, for instance, British local governments are now predominantly concerned with welfare provision, before 1930 they were far more heavily involved in production issues – especially in relation to the 'utilities' of gas, electricity and water. Indeed, the historical emergence of the local state in Britain as a set of distinct institutions, was characterized by its support for production and capital accumulation, and before 1914 only a third of local authority expenditure could be classified as social consumption (Dunleavy, 1984, p. 76). Similarly, there seems little evidence to segregate types of politics by geographical scale. Corporatist politics are sometimes marked at the local level, and Cawson himself (1985b) recognizes this by distinguishing a whole category of 'local corporatism'. Likewise, pluralist and class-based politics are not at all unknown in national states. It seems that the mode of politics in any situation is governed as much by the actors and interests involved, as by the geographical scale at which it takes place. The problems of analysing real events using such a rigid divide between the national/local scale, production/consumption issues and corporatist/pluralist type of politics are only increased by Saunders' recent attempt (1985) to provide urban sociology with a distinctive disciplinary focus of study. Again he advocates research concentrating on collective consumption, and calls for urban sociology to become 'a sociology of consumption'. This only serves to confuse even further the conceptual status of the terms 'local' and 'urban'. Are local politics concerned with consumption because they are local, as the dual state thesis suggests, or because they are urban? The two distinct categories are muddled in a manner that is difficult to separate analytically.

Saunders partly deflects criticism of this sort by putting forward the dual state thesis as an 'ideal-type', claiming that it is a research strategy rather than an account of reality, and that its aim is to develop a framework which suggests research questions and which can be evaluated analytically but not empirically. Even if we accept this, it is questionable how useful an analytical framework is which has an untenable base. It may well be that the 'ideal-type', far from being ideally typical, actually represents very abnormal and atypical political conditions. As we saw in section 5.2, recent changes in the nature of local politics may well have made the ideal-type of the dual state no longer applicable.

5.3.4   The local state and social relations

One of the merits of the dual state thesis is its explicit attempt to place the understanding of local politics into a wider analytical framework. The very use of the term 'state' immediately suggests a broader focus than the often narrow concentration on the institutions and personnel of local government which had hitherto informed local political research. In 1969 Miliband's book *The State in Capitalist Society*, and the author's subsequent debate with Poulantzas, set the tone for a renewed academic debate about the nature of the state. The questions of political autonomy, of the links between the state and the ruling class, and of the ability of subordinate groups to 'take over' the state were especially prevalent in this debate. These concerns were addressed to local politics following the publication of Cockburn's book *The Local State* (1977). As the title implies, she related theoretical debates about the nature of the state to the institutions of local government. The term 'local state' gained critical acceptance and helped place on a new conceptual stage the mass of research and political activity that had gathered around local, or community, politics since the late 1960s. For those on the radical left, the state, and of course the local state, came to be seen as a site of competing political interests rather than as a neutral set of administrative institutions.

The importance of Cockburn's work was that it integrated studies of local political activity into this wider view of the capitalist state. But unfortunately the analytical use of the new concept of the local state was hampered by Cockburn's concept of the state as a whole. Essentially Cockburn updates Marx's idea that the state acts as an 'executive of the bourgeoisie', to include social reproduction as an important concern of the state and ideology as an important dimension of domination by the state. The local state plays its part in these new processes through the detailed management of people and institutions locally. But it is seen as part of a whole, differentiated from the central state only by an increased concern with social reproduction. Again, function, not process, is the major method of specifying the local state. Under this unitary model Cockburn claims that local governments 'are, and under capitalism have always been, subject to central government' (1977, p. 46).

Such a view is misleading on two counts. First, it simply projects forward Marx's descriptive generalization of the mid-nineteenth-century liberal state – without universal suffrage, parliamentary working-class parties or labour movement involvement – into a universal model. The capitalist state is viewed functionally as a given thing, a pre-existing instrument possessed by the capitalist class, rather than as a historically emerging, changing and contradictory relation. Following from this, local government as 'part of the whole' is also seen as a static instrument of capital. But if this were the case why has the local–central state system been subject to continuous conflict and occasional crisis? And why bother with all the political tension and uncertainty in the latest attempt to reduce local autonomy, which was detailed in Chapter 4? Cockburn reduces two contradictory processes of the local state – that it is simultaneously agent and obstacle for the national state – to those of a one-way agent. Not only does this ignore a whole aspect of local state activity – that which opposes the centre – but it also reduces social relations between active human agents to purely functional operations.

Elsewhere, Duncan and I have made an attempt to overcome these problems by putting forward a conceptual view of local politics which stresses the social relations involved, which highlights the importance of the locality, and which is based on the notion that local state institutions can be at once an agent of, and an obstacle to, central demands (Duncan and Goodwin, 1988). **Uneven development** is taken here as a key concept, both in explaining why there are local state institutions to begin with, and in understanding how local politics come to be differentiated from place to place. As this series stresses, the uneven social and economic development of places has been a central feature of post-war British society. But uneven development does not simply mean that types and quantities of physical and social phenomena vary from place to place. Rather, it means that socio-economic processes are themselves uneven, increasing the disparities in pre-existing social and natural systems. As the other books in the series have shown, social and physical environments are continually developed, abandoned and changed.

Duncan and Goodwin claim that state institutions are invaluable in the management and organization of the differentiated and spatially variable societies typical of capitalism, and that to be successful such state intervention should take place on a local as well as a national level. But this development of local state institutions can be a hostage to fortune. For uneven development also means that social groups are spatially constituted and differentiated, with variable local strengths and importance. In some places locally dominant groups will differ from those dominant nationally, and 'such locally constituted groups can then use these local state institutions to further their own interests, perhaps even in opposition to centrally dominant interests' (1988, p. 41).

Moreover, this lever is strengthened by electoral democracy, which legitimates the promotion of locally preferred policies, and in this way local states, and especially electoral local government, are not only used by those dominant at the centre to enable them to manage uneven development, but can also represent specifically local interests. This somewhat contradictory role is what enables us to specify the concept of a local state, as well as a national one. For the outcome of this role depends on the multiplicity of local social processes which influence the activities of the local state, but which are inaccessible to the centre. The centre will, however, often 'attempt to neutralise the influences of local interests in local states' (Duncan and Goodwin, 1988, p. 41), and we claim such an attempt has taken place from 1979 to 1988 and that it is this which lies behind the current restructuring of local–central government relations.

Duncan and Goodwin provide a conceptual framework for understanding the differential forms that these local political processes take, by claiming that particular local policies arise through the uneven development of a whole range of economic, social, cultural and political relations. We illustrate ways in which these combine with each other and with wider sets of social relations by using the examples of the development of radical forms of local politics in both the small borough of Clay Cross and in the very large Greater London Council. Despite the growth of a local political consciousness nurtured in its coal-mines, the transfer of militancy from work to council chamber could only take place in Clay Cross once the mines had been nationalized and the culturally paternalistic influence of the local coal-owners had been removed. And in London, where manufacturing industry and trade union strength have all but disappeared, the radicalism of the 'new urban left' was based on a coalition between white-collar unions and civil organizations built up outside work. (For these and other examples see Duncan and Goodwin (1988, pp. 76–89).)

Duncan and Goodwin thus claim that it is the localized heterogeneity of economic, social and cultural relations, and the plurality of influences which result, that is crucial to the distinctiveness of the local state, and to an understanding of the myriad forms of local politics which are produced. As was noted in Chapter 4, this view can be criticized for over-stressing the importance of local social relations, and for a rather restricted view of how these relations are translated into policy. More research, however, still needs to be done on the actual mechanisms involved in local political activity, to identify those causal processes which transfer the characteristics of different local socio-economic environments into diverse local political practices.

Whilst researchers will only be able to specify the ways in which large-scale social and economic restructuring has led to particular types of local political practice through empirical study, we can claim that there has been an increase in local political activity, in contrast to the relatively homogeneous picture presented in the 1950s and early '60s. Moreover, we are now in a position to examine how effectively research has analysed this change. Reviewing the arguments presented earlier, it would seem that the lack of local politics in the post-war period should not be equated with the turning of local government into mere agents of the centre; nor should it be seen as the result of non-local structural forces promoting change on a national basis. Rather, it represented one part of a very particular period in British history, and as such was 'one aspect of the mid-twentieth century rapprochement between the feudal paternalism of Tory Democracy and the Fabian centralism of Social Democracy' (Gyford, 1985a, p. 88).

As this text, and those related to it, point out, this rapprochement no longer holds. The Keynesian consensus, built on an expanding economy in which private profit could be balanced with social need, has now been destroyed by recession and economic decline. Shared assumptions and values, including those about local government, have now been replaced by competing visions of Britain's future. On the one hand, the Labour Party has turned to ideas of democratic socialism, with regard to the control and regulation of capital. On the other, the Conservatives have become committed to a free-market society, in which the market-place is seen as economically efficient and socially just. Somewhat ironically, the erstwhile consensus has been best represented by the formation of new centre parties – the Social Democratic Party and the Social and Liberal Democrats.

The starting-point for all these alternatives is the deterioration of Britain's position within the worldwide division of labour and, even more starkly, of particular places within Britain. What is the best way of stemming this decline or, even better, of regenerating the economy? And how do we rescue particular places, or should we leave them to decay? In answering these questions, local politics inevitably come to the fore again, not only because different responses have different costs and benefits for different groups of people in different places, but also because alternative policies can actually be tried out at the local level. Nowhere is this clearer than in the case of local economic policies. It is to the development of this particular type of local politics that we now turn.

Summary of section 5.3

- Several theoretical positions have been developed to analyse local politics, broadly grouped into those which highlight local autonomy, and

those which stress the role of national government and non-local determinants of change.

● Through a process of critical appraisal successive theories build on those
that go before.

● This process of appraisal is often developed through reference to empirical changes in the processes being analysed.

Activity 5.3

There are three main approaches to the analysis of local politics outlined in
this section. The first, labelled urban managerialism, focuses on the activities of councillors, officers and pressures groups; the second, labelled urban
politics, focuses on the politics of consumption and, in one version at least,
identifies a dual state in which the local state is principally concerned with
consumption issues; the third, which we can label the social relations
approach, stresses the importance of locality and uneven development as
the basis for local politics.

Looking back at these different sets of theories (outlined in sections 5.3.2,
5.3.3 and 5.3.4), consider how each of them might explain the restructuring
of local government (discussed in Chapter 4 and referred to at the start of
section 5.3) which took place in the 1980s? Which do you think would have
been most helpful as a basis for an explanation? Which provide the best
explanation for central–local conflicts?

5.4   The development of local economic strategies

Before looking at local economic strategies in more detail we should point
out that the decline of consensus politics at the national level does not
inevitably lead to an increase in local political activity. It does, however,
make it more likely to happen, and facilitates this by opening up the political
space in which local differentiation can occur. In other words it provides the
context, but the actual shape and form of local politics is the outcome of a
whole number of processes operating at both the local and the national level.
As we shall see, local economic policies are a good case in point.

5.4.1   'Traditional' policies

Until 1980 local economic strategies took their place among the many
uncontested, bipartisan policies of local government, although with the
recession and the 'de-industrialization' of Britain this was an expanding

activity for an increasing number of local authorities. But by the end of the 1970s, added impetus – and critical changes of direction – had been given to this expansion. First, several left-wing Labour councils had come to power committed to establishing more effective, and thus inevitably more contentious, local economic policies. Furthermore, their ascendancy accompanied the severest phase of the recession, which gave them the added incentive to try something different as some of their own areas were among the hardest hit. Secondly, the new Conservative national government began to introduce a whole set of nationally promoted, and equally contentious, 'local' economic strategies. Both of these developments reflected the evident failure of traditional local policies in the face of a pervasive and thorough restructuring of many local economies.

Cochrane (1983, pp. 289–92) identifies four main components of this 'traditional' approach to local economic strategies. First, publicity and advertising extols the virtues of one area over another, in an attempt to attract firms which are beginning, expanding or relocating. Secondly, assistance and information is offered to these firms, guiding them through the planning and development process, and offering advice on a range of issues from education and housing to estate agents and government grants. Thirdly, land and premises are often provided, especially for small 'nursery' or 'seed-bed' units. And fourthly, subsidies and loans help provide finance to encourage development. From these four components sprang four characteristics of 'traditional' policy. It was property-led, market- and business-related, aimed at small firms and had little emphasis on employment. There were, however, a number of serious problems with this approach and the assumptions behind it.

First of all, local authorities possess only a very limited economic power and can only exercise what powers they have in very small geographical areas. They cannot significantly alter labour or commodity markets at a scale relevant to a national, let alone an international, production system. Secondly, what they can do is further restrained by an interlocking web of assumptions, rules and regulations. Thirdly, there is no necessary or even likely reason why subsidizing capital with below-cost land, premises or advice should create more jobs or lead to local regeneration. Servicing private capital in this way is usually a matter of job redistribution rather than job creation. Moreover many firms will use relocation as an opportunity to shed jobs or introduce cheaper and less worthwhile ones. In addition, an increase in production, or even in investment, does not automatically lead to an increase in jobs – the norm is usually the exact opposite, and shedding labour is a prerequisite for a firm's expansion. Success for capital is not necessarily the same as success for labour or for a local economy. (See Massey (1988a, b) for a discussion of 'jobless growth'.) And, fourthly, because of these other limitations local authorities, especially those in the inner cities, usually end up trying to attract or influence the behaviour of a pool of small firms, which they often justify by stating that small firms are the key to local regeneration. But in reality small firms are often backwards in terms of resources, capital and innovation, as well as limited in terms of job numbers. They depend on larger companies for a market niche, and often provide low-paid and insecure jobs. Of course, some small firms do offer growth potential, but these have to be identified and given appropriate support rather than a general subsidy linked to premises or land.

The failure of these traditional local economic strategies to stimulate and sustain local economic growth in all but a minority of places has led to the development of new forms of policy. They can be grouped under two headings, those seeking to 'restructure for labour' and those seeking to 'restructure for capital'. Both assume that local intervention should be deeper and more fundamental than merely 'servicing capital', and both also accept that it is necessary to change the structure of declining local econo- mies if regeneration is to come about. They also share a rejection of the post- war consensus in both labour relations and state policy. There has been a perceived failure of old political, as well as old economic, relations. But here the similarities end and the new policies for local economic regeneration can be placed at opposite ends of the political spectrum. Indeed it is doubtful if one group can even be called local, since it is sponsored, promoted and financed by central government. We will quickly consider these, before exploring in more depth the development of those policies that are in fact locally generated.

5.4.2 'Restructuring for capital': a national approach?

Central government has always been involved in promoting local economic change, and since the 1930s has developed explicitly sub-national and spatially differentiated economic policy. By the 1980s this had come to be called 'local' economic policy, despite its national origins. Initially, how- ever, such policy was regionally based, designed to affect the growth of regions rather than localities. Regional development aid, new and expanded towns, and restrictions on metropolitan growth, especially in the south-east, were the major policy instruments. By the late 1970s, however, the emphasis had changed to inner-city regeneration: the policies were becoming more local in scale, if not in origin. The incoming Conservative government in 1979 kept this new emphasis and minimized overt regional policy. But it gave its inner-city policy a new direction by stressing the role of private enterprise in economic regeneration. Moreover local authorities, viewed by the previous Labour government as the 'natural agencies' to tackle such regeneration, were now seen as a major cause of the problem.

The government set about 'freeing private enterprise' through a number of legislative and administrative changes, the major ones seeing the intro- duction of Enterprise Zones (EZs), Urban Development Corporations (UDCs) and Freeports. Each are area-based and are concerned with encouraging economic growth in specific parts of particular cities. In this way they are 'local' – but then so is much other central government policy. By 1987 the UK had 28 EZs, 6 UDCs and 6 Freeports, with several other 'mini-UDCs' in the pipeline. All are weaker versions of earlier plans to display small Hong Kongs in run-down local areas, where laissez-faire would be 'let rip', free of government interference. Accordingly EZs give firms exemption for ten years from various taxes and duties and offer a simplified planning regime. Freeports, all near airports or docks, offer tariff and customs privileges, while UDCs go further and replace local government's powers over development control with an appointed board responsible only to the Minister.

Although marketed around the notion of freeing private enterprise, these measures in fact depend upon considerable public subsidy: the UDCs actually operate as a state development agency, buying, preparing and marketing land. They are backed by a whole host of other innovations designed to promote the private sector in certain local areas – such as Task Forces (later City Action Teams), Inner City Enterprises and Business in the Community (see Duncan and Goodwin, 1988, pp. 127–49 for details). In economic terms they seem to have had little effect: in Merseyside, for instance, which has had every new scheme, economic decline has not even been halted, let alone reversed. In general, these initiatives seem to have shifted jobs around rather than created new ones, as some firms have relocated to take advantage of the subsidies (see Roger Tym and Partners, 1981, 1982; Shutt, 1984; Erikson and Syms, 1986). Similarly, the attempt to remove barriers to investment has merely led to their redistribution, for instead of paying rates inside Enterprise Zones firms pay higher rents and property prices (Erikson and Syms, 1986). Developers and land-owners have benefited most from the subsidies, which in turn have encouraged large land-intensive concerns, such as retailing and warehousing, at the expense of labour-intensive industrial firms. And although London's Docklands has seen major development, questions are being asked about its nature. It seems that existing residents have hardly benefited at all, as most jobs created have gone to those living outside the area, and most economic gains to international finance companies, property developers and construction companies (see Goodwin, 1989, for details).

Thus neither the causes nor consequences of this type of economic strategy can be said to be specifically local. They were designed nationally, were implemented on a national basis, and have benefited interest groups of a national and an international nature. Their only claim to be local is that they are implemented in a restricted geographical area – but then so are certain aspects of defence and foreign policy! This raises the question which also runs through *The Changing Social Structure* (Hamnett, McDowell and Sarre, 1989) – what exactly do we mean by **local**? Should the term mean more than just a circumscribed spatial area? In the case of local politics, should this mean more than just the local implementation of national policy? To help tackle some of these questions we will now turn to examine the development of another recent set of local economic strategies, those designed to 'restructure for labour'.

5.4.3   'Restructuring for labour': a local approach?

In the local elections of 1981 a number of Labour Party manifestos high-lighted economic issues, and suggested ways of moving beyond the traditional approach to local economic strategies. The new approaches were designed to counter the onset of mass unemployment in the severest phase of the recession, but also reflected the shock of Labour's huge general election defeat of 1979, and the realization that Labour's national industrial policy of the 1970s had failed. Significantly the policies stressed the importance of local initiatives, and were offered as a decentralized alternative to the centralized bureaucratic planning of national government. These Labour local authorities were developing conscious efforts to alter local economies so as to bring about long-term economic development, through job creation and job enrichment, for the benefit of local workers and the local community. The emphasis was thus on using firms for the development of a local area and for its people – rather than with using people for the development of private firms in an area. Hence the strategy was given the name 'restructuring for labour'.

There are four major components to this strategy:

(a)   identifying strategic plants, firms and sectors where intervention should be directed. Support for firms is not just a matter of marginal servicing, nor should it be property-led or based on the notion of any jobs at any price. Rather intervention will mean changing how workplaces operate and is defined as much socially as economically in terms of developing local skills, satisfying local needs and enriching the working life of local people;

(b)   strengthening the position of workers through planning agreements, stressing, in return for help to the firm, improvements in conditions, pay, unionization, equal opportunities etc.;

(c)   encouraging alternative forms of management and production, and encouraging the development of 'socially useful' products;

(d)   improving the influence of local communities on their own economic management and development, through democratic planning initiatives known as 'popular planning'.

Although elements from each of these components are usually found in the new initiatives, they vary in their emphases from place to place. Some authorities support strategic manufacturing businesses in difficulty, others help small businesses and co-operatives. Some concentrate on local authority employment, others stress the council's planning role. Some conduct strategic research, others help develop new products and new markets. To implement these strategies new institutions have been set up, but these are also diverse. Some councils set up new industry or employment committees, staffed by their own departments. Others concentrated on setting up enterprise boards, outside the council itself. Yet more have restructured their planning or personnel departments, or established economic development units in a central co-ordinating role. As Blunkett and Jackson (1987, p. 113) put it, such differences 'reflect the responsibilities of different types of authority, their local economic structure and their political traditions'.

This is a clear indication that these initiatives have developed locally, have taken account of local conditions, have started from different political positions and bases, and have had their roots in very different local experiences. In opposition to centrally imposed 'local economic strategies', these initiatives of the left explicitly recognize that what is appropriate in one place, may not be of much use in another. The London Industrial Strategy (*Greater London Council*, 1985) details the strategy developed for London, and outlines the social, economic and political reasons which led to this particular form of local policy being adopted for London. It would seem sensible that strategies to help Sheffield, with the recent and very sudden collapse of its steel industry, may not be able to assist Liverpool or Newcastle, where steel has never been an important industry and where decline has been long-term. A short look at one of these initiatives, that developed by Sheffield City Council, will help to tease out the local roots and separate the influence of local politics and local processes from those operating on a wider scale. It will also help us to assess the extent to which these local policies are, in fact, local and whether they can be viewed as autonomous from national and international forces.

5.4.4 Local politics in practice: economic policy in Sheffield

In May 1981 Sheffield City Council set up the country's first Employment Committee, serviced directly by a new council department. This section will analyse the development of this initiative over its first few years, in order to give a particular example of local political activity at a particular time in a particular place. It should be emphasized that this policy initiative was part of much broader policy changes in the city, set in motion by a new Labour leadership elected in May 1980. Many of the leading figures were young left-wing councillors with professional jobs, part of a new breed of local politician promoted to take the place of older, more right-wing politicians who had close links with the city's steel and engineering trade unions. Although this kind of shift was common to many local Labour Parties, and has been characterized as the rise of the 'new urban left' (Gyford, 1985b), in Sheffield it was given a particular twist by the nature of the local economy and society.

The Labour Party in the city had developed a political structure which closely linked representatives of the labour movement to its borough politics. Delegates from the workplace-based Trades and Labour Council were sent to meetings of Sheffield's Labour councillors, which in return sent delegates to the executive of the Trades and Labour Council. In addition several other Labour councillors would be present as delegates from other constituent organizations. This tightly knit framework of liaison between the three sections of Sheffield's labour movement – Labour Council, Labour Party and trades unions – helped unite its political and industrial wings. When local government reorganization in 1974 led to Sheffield being ordered by the national Labour Party to disband these structures, the city's labour movement set up other channels of influence, and the trade union delegates were elected directly to the new District Labour Party, which in turn monitored the activities of the new District Council.

These lines of influence were felt particularly in industrial and economic policy. The early 1980s witnessed dramatic changes in Sheffield's economy. Severe unemployment followed redundancy and closure in the city's manual workforce. Councillors, who had grown up and learnt their politics in a labour movement founded on the dominance of Sheffield's skilled workers in the steel and engineering industries, now had to formulate a response as this dominance quite literally crumbled to the ground. Committees and forums were set up inside the local authority, the local Trades Council and the local Labour Party, and together they formulated the idea of a new Employment Department to co-ordinate all the council's efforts to tackle the economic crisis in the city. *Blunkett and Jackson* (1987) explore some of its policies in more depth, and indicate how the new strategy departed from traditional policies of supporting private sector employment in a number of ways. Crucially, the close lines of influence and power drawn between the political and industrial wings of the city's labour movement meant that in Sheffield the task of the new committee was one of political as well as economic regeneration. In the words of the council leader, the new department was set up to 'act in a political manner' with a function of 'political mobilization' and, according to its first co-ordinator, 'part of the challenge for us in the local authority is to try to reintroduce some political perspective' (quoted in Duncan and Goodwin, 1988, p. 85). However, reconciling these dual political and economic functions proved difficult.

In its initial year the new department spent a great deal of time and energy intervening in the private sector to try to save jobs, especially in the cutlery and engineering sectors. This was partly as a result of inherited policies, but was also because of the council's desire 'to be seen to be doing something' to support its traditional political base of the skilled manual working class. The most obvious place for this was in the private sector, where these jobs, and skills, were being lost. The 'imagined community' of a vibrant, important and expanding city, controlled by the organized, skilled, male working class and built on the strength of its steel and cutlery industries long outlived its real dissolution. The council was responding as much to this as to real economic circumstance. For this strategy, founded as much on local politics as on economics, was ultimately based on investing considerable time and money in rescuing firms on the brink of collapse.

A crucial breaking-point came in 1983, when the Labour councillors first took a decision to support a small steel firm and save around sixty jobs, but later withdrew their support leaving the firm to collapse. The local labour movement was split between those who wanted to intervene politically to support members of the skilled manual working class and those who wanted to act on financial grounds and not intervene in a declining enterprise. As one council officer said of the firm, 'It was crazy to support in economic terms, but the councillors felt a political need to deliver' (quoted in Duncan and Goodwin, 1988, p. 88).

It is indicative of the particular local society in Sheffield that this gesture had to be made. It is perhaps more significant that the political gesture was overturned in favour of more pragmatic financial reasoning – but this itself is indicative of broader changes in Sheffield's local politics. The former political coalition which directed support towards the skilled working class in the private sector had begun to dissolve. In its place the councillors now found an amalgam of interest groups, some class-based, some not, some based on workplace issues, others concerned with matters of production. The older organic links between the council, the Labour Party and the trade unions have been replaced by a much wider constituency and coalition. As a result local government policies have changed, and employment strategy has entered a phase of negotiation. At first, from around 1984–85, policy concentrated on saving and creating jobs within the council's own workforce. To a certain extent this made economic and political sense: in economic terms it is where the council had most leverage and control, and in political terms it represented a move to a new base, one built on the strength of the white-collar and public sector unions in the changing economy and society of Sheffield.

This new coalition may not, however, be strong enough to last in the face of increasing economic decline and continued cut-backs in local authority expenditure. The emphasis could well be changed once again, and may be switched back to the private sector, but in a new and different form – especially given the fact that an Urban Development Corporation was designated in Sheffield in March 1988. This UDC, imposed by central government, straddles the Lower Don valley, once the site of massive steel and engineering firms. New economic strategy may well have to be based around this UDC, and could thus become one of partnership and co-operation between the city council and private firms. Should this scenario happen, crucial to its success would be changing the image of the area, and a key part in this is being played by the city's successful bid for the World Student Games in 1990. Where steel-workers once laboured in their thousands, the facilities built for student athletes from around the world are hoped to provide the backbone for a different kind of economic prosperity – one which acknowledges the changing economy and society of both Sheffield and the nation.

5.4.5 Evaluating local economic strategies

As the example of Sheffield makes clear, local economic policies of the left are heavily influenced in their development by changes in local economic, social and political structures and practices. It also shows how a combination of these can easily result in a local economic strategy which has clear political as well as economic goals. Many other Labour councils recognize this explicit political role. Geoff Edge, the chair of West Midlands County Council Economic Development Committee, sees their purpose as 'advocates and missionaries of new Socialist ideas', while Michael Ward, his counterpart in the Greater London Council, has written that 'local initiatives can demonstrate that the alternative works; that greater democratic control and the planned use of resources can be used to create jobs. Local initiatives can lay out the line of policy that a future Labour government can follow' (quoted in Duncan and Goodwin, 1988, p. 128).

This political role has perhaps become more important as the economic and employment claims originally made for these new strategies fail to be met. For recognizing the restraints and limitations of the old policies is not at all the same as removing them. The new initiatives suffer from all the financial, administrative and geographical problems which affect the traditional approaches. The limited resources available to individual local authorities prevent them solving employment problems caused by national deflationary policies and world recession. The Greater London Enterprise Board (renamed Greater London Enterprises in 1986) can claim some considerable success in saving or creating up to 4000 jobs between 1982 and 1985, but London had lost over 250 000 jobs between 1978 and 1982 alone (Duncan and Goodwin, 1985, p. 81). This shows the difficulty that local intervention faces. Local strategies are, not surprisingly, unable to cope with major sets of problems generated outside the area. The new initiatives of the left made a start by identifying strategic sectors of the economy in which to intervene, rather than adopting a blanket approach to all firms in their area – but the problem was that the local authorities were still geographically limited. The London Industrial Strategy (Greater London Council, 1985) highlights some of these problems, and although it argues for a positive role for local authorities, in the end it concludes that national help and assistance will be necessary in order to have any major impact.

Discussions of these problems are similar to those raised in *The Economy in Question* (Allen and Massey, 1988) concerning the nature of 'an economy'. Labour-controlled local authorities have faced very real questions about the nature of a 'local economy'. They have been forced to confront two important facts. First, no economy is spatially bounded, and the economic relations and processes occurring in their districts are connected through a myriad of links to the wider world. It is therefore not adequate to speak of a local economy. We should rather refer to economic processes which are constituted in a particular place, which of course does not make them local. Some firms, or companies, may recruit workers locally, and sell their products locally – but this does not constitute a 'local economy'. It only means that certain sets of economic processes are more referrent to a local area than others. And, secondly, local economic strategies have shown that the economy cannot be abstracted from other sets of relationships within society. Economic policies are actually about social relations and social values, which is why they are as much political as they are economic. The term economic hides the fundamental point that economic change is at the same time social change.

Activity 5.4

What is it about local economic policies that make them 'local'?

Summary of section 5.4

• Traditional local economic policies developed during the 1970s have been replaced by two new forms of economic strategy, labelled by observers 'restructuring for capital' and 'restructuring for labour'.

• That which restructures for capital cannot, however, be called local, as neither its causes nor consequences are locally based.

• That which restructures for labour is local, in that it arises from a desire to tackle local problems with locally based solutions to benefit local people.

• These local strategies are subject to change, as local political activity changes in response to different social and economic circumstances.

5.5 Conclusions

Having read this chapter so far, you should now be in a position to answer some of the questions posed at its beginning. The works cited by Savage, Mark-Lawson and Warde, Blunkett and Jackson and the Greater London Council (see the associated Reader, Anderson and Cochrane, 1989) illustrate some of the more general points made in the chapter. First, it seems as though we can identify a locally based form of politics, arising from local social relations and social processes. The rise in local politics over recent years is not just the passive outcome of national forces working themselves out at the local level. Instead, factors such as local political parties, local trade unions, local community groups, local economic structures and local culture will all combine to influence and shape these wider forces in different ways in different places. Thus the activities of successive Conservative governments since 1979 may have made the re-emergence of local political activity more likely, but the form that this activity takes, how it varies from place to place and how it develops will be shaped by the interaction of local and national processes.

The examples given have also indicated that local government is much more than just an agent of the centre. Its actions and policies are formed by local as well as national events, and it must be seen as both an agent of, and an obstacle to, central government. The economic policies developed by Sheffield City Council and the Greater London Council, amongst many others, are testimony to this fact. They are locally based, and have been formulated in direct opposition to those policies preferred by the centre. But just as these new politics have been developing at the local level, so too we need new theories and new concepts to take account of them. So far political science has been unsuccessful in doing this. Some of its theories stress the role of local processes, whilst others analyse national structures. Some concentrate on formal political institutions, others look at economic and social factors. Some specify the collection of quantifiable data, others use more subjective qualitative forms of analysis. As this indicates, most are somewhat one-sided and limited in scope, and we need to move towards a synthesis which can enable us to grasp the most significant relationships and processes involved in the local politics of an increasingly diversified, and 'restructured', Britain.

Further reading

On the restructuring of relations between central and local government see M. Loughlin, M. Gelfand and K. Young (eds) *Half a Century of Municipal Decline, 1935–1985* (London, George Allen and Unwin; 1985), S. Duncan and M. Goodwin's *The Local State and Uneven Development* (Cambridge, Polity Press; 1988) and N. Flynn, S. Leach and C. Vielba's *Abolition or Reform?* (London, George Allen and Unwin; 1985).

On the rise of locally based political activity see P. Dickens' *One Nation? Social Change and the Politics of Locality* (London, Pluto Press; 1988), and those with a special interest in the 'new urban left' should look at *The Politics of Local Socialism* by J. Gyford (London, George Allen and Unwin; 1985), *Local Socialism* by M. Boddy and C. Fudge (London and Basingstoke, Macmillan; 1984) or *Democracy in Crisis: The Town Halls Respond* by D. Blunkett and K. Jackson (London, Hogarth Press; 1987).

For those interested in the historical development of particular types of local political activity, the following provide good examples of different places in Britain: *Poplarism* by N. Branson (London, Lawrence and Wishart; 1979); *Little Moscows* by S. Macintyre (London, Croom Helm; 1980); *Class Struggle and the Industrial Revolution* by J. Foster (London, Methuen; 1974); 'Gender and local politics: struggles over welfare, 1918–34' by J. Mark-Lawson, M. Savage and A. Warde in L. Murgatroyd, M. Savage, D. Shapiro, J. Urry, S. Walby and A. Warde (eds) *Localities, Class and Gender* (London, Pion; 1985); and *Housing, Social Policy and the State* edited by J. Melling (London, Croom Helm; 1980). 'Region, class and gender: a European comparison' by P. Cooke (in *Progress and Planning*, Vol. 22, pp. 85–146) provides comparative information for Europe.

For those wishing to follow up the more theoretical points, surveys of the political science/urban politics literature are contained in S. Duncan and M. Goodwin's *The Local State and Uneven Development* (op. cit.), P. Dunleavy's *Urban Political Analysis* (London and Basingstoke, Macmillan; 1980) and P. Saunders' *Urban Politics: A Sociological Interpretation* (London, Hutchinson; 1979).

A. Cochrane's 'Local economic policies: trying to drain an ocean with a teaspoon' in J. Anderson, S. Duncan and R. Hudson (eds) *Redundant Spaces in Cities and Regions? Studies in Industrial Decline and Social Change* (London, Academic Press; 1983) and M. Boddy's 'Local economic and employment strategies' in M. Boddy and C. Fudge's *Local Socialism* (op. cit.) both give good general accounts of the transition from 'traditional' to 'radical' local economic policies. *Developing Local Economic Strategies* edited by Allan Cochrane (Milton Keynes, The Open University Press; 1987), *Democracy in Crisis* by D. Blunkett and K. Jackson (op. cit.) and *London Industrial Strategy* (London, GLC; 1985) explore particular examples in more depth.

6 The end of class politics?

Patrick Dunleavy

Contents

6.1   Introduction

In many ways the political restructuring of contemporary Britain is the central nub, the key to all the other shifts documented in this series, especially for the 1980s when political changes have been dramatic. In that decade the Conservative Party won three successive general elections, with 43 per cent of the vote but steadily increasing Parliamentary majorities. Labour's electoral fortunes reached a low point in 1983, unprecedented since the party first competed nationwide in the 1918 election, a nadir from which it has only slowly and partially recovered. Simultaneously, third party voting for the Liberal and Social Democratic Parties in alliance swelled almost to parity with Labour's vote in 1983 before receding somewhat after a disappointing campaign in 1987. A post-election split within the SDP over attempts to merge it with the Liberals precipitated a slump in opinion poll support for the new party, the Social and Liberal Democrats, and for the rump of the unmerged SDP.

In academic electoral studies these sweeping alterations in party fortunes have shattered the 1960s orthodoxy, according to which Britain functioned under a stable two-party system based on a fundamental cleavage between non-manual people, voting overwhelmingly for the Conservatives, and manual workers, voting preponderently for Labour (Butler and Stokes, 1969). Table 6.1 shows that the proportion of the non-manual group voting Conservative declined sharply from the 1950s to the 1970s, stabilizing thereafter. The Labour vote amongst non-manual people was static until the 1980s when it fell somewhat, but Liberal or Liberal/SDP support in this group grew rapidly across all four decades, almost quadrupling over the period as a whole. Amongst manual voters the Labour vote was solid through the 1960s, but in the next two decades fell sharply to well below majority support. Conservative support amongst manual voters fell a bit in the 1960s and '70s, but has grown back strongly in the 1980s. Liberal/SDP voting amongst manual workers has trebled over the period as a whole, but has tended to be lower than their support amongst the non-manual.

Table 6.1   Voting by occupational classes, averaged across three election groupings, 1950–87

Average vote for	Non-manual				Manual			
	1950s	1960s	1970s	1980s	1950s	1960s	1970s	1980s
Conservative	71	63	56	58	33	28	27	34
Labour	23	23	24	20	61	63	57	43
Liberal/Lib–SDP	6	14	20	23	6	9	16	23

1950s elections are 1950, 1951 and 1955; *1960s* elections are 1959, 1964 and 1966; *1970s* elections are 1970, February 1974 and October 1974; *1980s* elections are 1979, 1983 and 1987.

Table 6.2   The comparative performance of the three major parties or party groupings, 1950–88

		1950s	1960s	1970s	1980s
Average % of vote	Conservative	47	45	40	43
	Labour	47	45	40	32
	Lib/Lib–SDP	5	9	15	21
Average % of Commons seats	Conservative	51	49	48	58
	Labour	47	50	48	37
	Lib/Lib–SDP	1.1	1.4	1.7	2.9
% of time in government	Conservative	74	47	42	100
	Labour	26	53	58	0
	Lib/Lib–SDP	0	0	0	0

The periods here are: *1950s* – February 1950 to October 1959; *1960s* – October 1959 to June 1970; *1970s* – June 1970 to April 1979; *1980s* – May 1979 to present (= September 1988). The votes and seats figures averaged here are those for general election results only.

The consequences of these new patterns of linkages between social classes and political parties can be charted in their comparative records over these decades in terms of shares of the national vote, seats in the Commons, and control of government; these are shown in Table 6.2. The major long-run change in the parties' share of the vote is the steady increase in Liberal/Liberal–SDP support. But the slump in Labour's average total vote in the 1980s has had the most implications for the parties' share of seats and of government power. Because the UK's electoral system discriminates so consistently against third parties like the Liberals and SDP with less support nationally and no major concentrations of votes into 'heartland' areas, they receive derisory levels of seats and have played no part in government since 1950. Up to the 1970s the two major parties split the Commons seats between them relatively evenly. In the 1980s Labour's share fell sharply in response to its badly reduced share of the vote. Control of government was also shared relatively evenly between the parties in the 1960s and '70s, and although the Conservatives dominated government in the 1950s, Labour was always a viable contender. The key difference in the 1980s is that as the Labour vote has lagged behind Conservative support, so its share of the seats has dropped, and its access to government power has been eliminated – prompting speculation that Britain is becoming a '**dominant party system**' (Drucker and Gamble, 1986). In these systems, such as post-war Japan, multi-party electoral competition remains vigorous but the leading party repeatedly wins elections with little or no realistic prospect of defeat. Clearly whether or not such predictions are borne out, the changing balance of support for political parties across classes charted in Table 6.1 can be associated with a major alteration in the British political system and in the climate for public policy-making.

Much of the popular and mass media discussion of political restructuring has tended to characterize trends in British society from the evidence of rising or falling levels of party support. Thus, changing social structures are read backwards through the lens of political change, a style of analysis which John Goldthorpe (1987, p. 347) terms 'reverse sociologism'. Because political changes have been so dramatic the approach can easily lead to exaggerated accounts of the alterations in other aspects of society in order to fit with the scale of political changes. In practice, however, most social change is slower moving and less dramatic than political shifts. My concern in the next three sections of this chapter is to analyse the (inherently partial) extent to which class-linked changes can account for political developments. I begin by looking at changes in the class structure itself, and then examine the vexed question of whether the political polarization of classes has shifted in a clear-cut way. Various ways of extending the concept of class influences on politics are surveyed in section 6.4. Sections 6.5–6.7 turn to considering what other social and political changes (apart from class) may underlie political restructuring: I examine sectoral accounts in section 6.5, and studies of ideological change amongst voters in section 6.6; finally, section 6.7 considers some 'unconventional' sources of political change not fully integrated into the competition between the major parties.

6.2   Class structure and politics

Where class differences matter politically, the most basic way in which social change might influence political alignments is via increases or decreases in the sizes of the different classes. The phrase **class structure** simply refers to the relative size and number of classes. There is no theoretical agreement about the ways in which **class** itself should be defined (Sarre, 1989a). Weberian accounts root the concept of 'class' in people's work tasks and skills, their occupation. Different occupations are rated by a society as a whole as of varying levels of 'status', and these ratings can be uncovered by survey research and various other measures. Once a hierarchy of diverse occupational rankings has been constructed, similarly ranked occupations can be progressively collapsed into smaller numbers of categories. Thus *occupational classes* are just categories boiled down by analysts from the myriads of relative rankings of occupations in the society as a whole. An alternative Marxist-influenced approach is that classes are defined by fundamental aspects of where people stand in a system of production. Modern Marxist schemas classify people by whether they control the means of production or not, whether they control other people's labour or not, and whether they dispose of substantial amounts of 'educational capital' which can form the basis for social closure practices. In this approach analysts move fairly directly to distinguish a smallish number of *social classes* on theoretical grounds. Both approaches argue in terms of the theoretical significance of their schemas, but also seek to show empirically that class differences structure other aspects of social relations in fundamental ways.

Happily, there has been a considerable practical convergence of modern Weberian and Marxist work in distinguishing similar numbers of classes. Both approaches agree that workplace/occupational/production positions must form the core of any reputable 'class' conception. They also concur that recent occupational and social class schemas are much better than older categorizations previously employed in electoral studies – such as the now discredited opinion poll 'social grades', originally defined by measures of the 'buying power' of different groups. The best synoptic picture of the changing social structure of Britain uses a Weberian five-class schema divided between a narrowly defined working class, a large and inclusive upper middle-class group known as 'the salariat', a routine non-manual group (composed almost four-fifths by women), a small group of foremen and technicians (composed almost 90 per cent by men), and a petit bourgeois/own account workers group (Heath, Curtice and Jowell, 1985a, pp. 13–16). The schema's chief difference from alternative approaches is that it assigns people wherever possible *away from* the working-class category, a limitation which I remind readers of by labelling their category the 'small working class'. Figure 6.1 shows the pattern of changes in class sizes in the electorate since the mid-1960s. The small working-class share has apparently declined dramatically, with all the change being absorbed by increases in the proportion of voters in the salariat and the routine non-manual group. The foreman/technician group has also declined, and the petit bourgeoisie has varied.

Changes of this magnitude in class sizes would in and of themselves imply major alterations in the fortunes of the political parties which can be estimated in a simple way. Suppose that the people in different occupational classes had gone on voting in all subsequent elections exactly as they did in 1964 (when the Conservatives narrowly lost to Labour) or as they did in 1966 (when Labour won handsomely) – what would have happened to the major parties' levels of support? If the *1964* pattern had continued, then with changes in the class structure Labour's vote should have dropped gradually by 5 per cent by 1974 but then held steady up to 1983 (Figure 6.2a). In fact the party almost conformed to expectations in 1974, but collapsed dramatically especially in 1983 to fully 12 per cent below their projected level. If people had gone on voting as they did *in 1966*, then Labour was already performing below its projected levels by 1974, and was some 18 per cent below its projected level by 1983. By contrast, the Conservatives performed well below their projected vote in 1974, but almost completely recovered to conform with the projection by 1983 (Figure 6.2b). On 1966 projections, however, the Conservatives' underperformance was small in the mid-1970s, and by 1983 the party was overperforming against its expected vote. The Liberal projected vote on a 1964 basis is a virtually flat curve, well below their actual vote by 1974, and less than half their actual 1983 total (Figure 6.2c). The growth of Liberal and SDP support is even less well explained by projecting forward 1966 voting patterns.

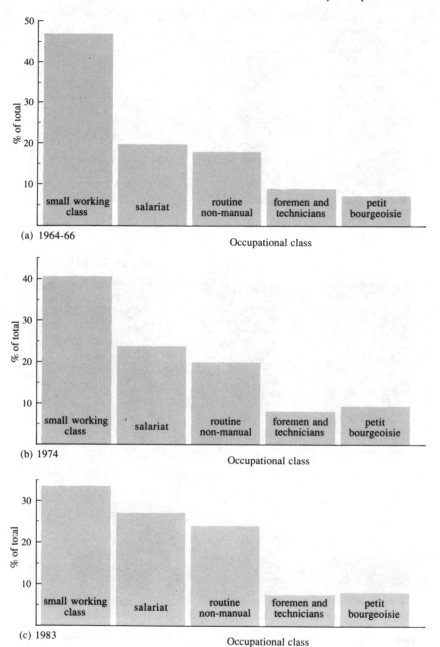

Figure 6.1   The changing occupational class structure of Great Britain, 1964–83

Note: To control for sampling errors in earlier studies I have taken the median of the 1964 and 1966 voting studies' figures, and the median of the figures from the two voting studies in February and October 1974.

Source: Dunleavy, 1987, p. 418, note 10

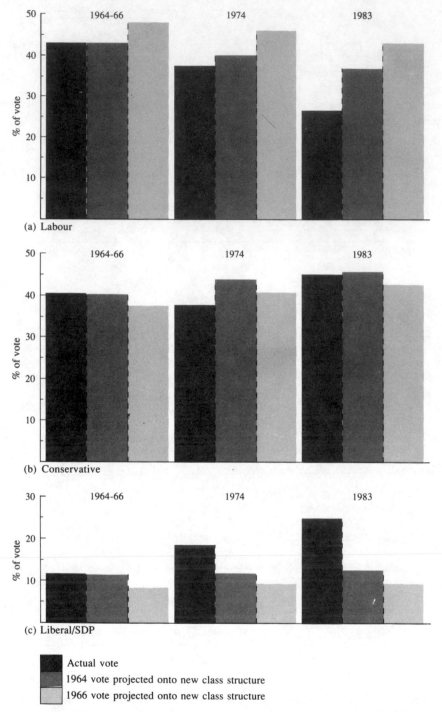

Figure 6.2   Differences between the actual votes of the major parties and projections of their mid-1960s vote patterns

Note: The vote projections show how the party would have fared if occupational classes had continued voting as in 1964 or 1966, but class sizes changed as in Figure 6.1.

The precise size of these estimates of the impact of changing class sizes is not especially important, but their overall pattern is. Clearly the growth of Liberal and later Liberal/SDP voting in the mid-1970s and mid-'80s cannot be explained by social change (Heath *et al.*, 1985a, pp. 36–7). Nor can Labour's slump in support in the 1980s be attributed just to the decline of the working class and expansion of the salariat and routine non-manual group. By contrast, Conservative support levels across occupational classes may have stayed relatively constant from the mid-1960s, but with the party reaping the benefits of large and favourable shifts in the class structure. Trends in the late 1980s have included the growth in self-employment in the UK from 7.6 per cent of the labour force in 1979 to 11.2 per cent by 1986 (after previously fluctuating in a range from 6.5 to 8.1 per cent) (see Allen, 1988a). Since the petit bourgeoisie are especially strong Conservative supporters, this recent shift may strengthen Tory voting over and above the estimates given here.

Important questions arise about the origins of these class-structure changes, for which purely British explanations may not be very useful. Wright and Martin (1987) studied the change in the US class structure from 1960 to 1980, using a different social class schema with a 'large working class' including most routine non-manual people. Their data therefore show only a small decline in the size of the US 'working class' from 54.3 to 50.5 per cent over two decades. But the US managers and experts group shows the same substantial expansion as the British data, with an additional small growth in the supervisors category. These changes confounded Wright's previously published work, which predicted a slowing down of the growth of non-worker categories, and a continued 'proletarianization' of non-employer groups in American society. Detailed analysis shows that the decline of workers and growth of managers/experts cannot be attributed simply to the changing balance of industries in the US economy, such as the closure of heavy industry and the growth of public employment and business services. Instead the US workforce became more managerial and less worker-based, in both the 1960s and the '70s, after controlling for (that is, statistically allowing for) the changing sizes and sectoral composition of industries.

Post-industrial theory interprets the British and US trends as evidence that shifts in technology and knowledge are accomplishing irreversible changes in capitalist societies, away from the class structures and economic activities characteristic of the industrial/manufacturing era (Allen, 1988b). The post-industrial thesis carries very pessimistic implications for parties of the left in class-based party systems like Britain. The new non-manual groups may have become more socially and politically mixed, a so-called 'service class' whose rapid numerical expansion and more meritocratic composition in the post-war period have pulled in people from more diverse social backgrounds. But with the passage of time service class positions are likely to be increasingly filled by children from the same social backgrounds, so that this key social group is likely to revert to a more homogeneous conservatism (Goldthorpe, 1987).

An alternative interpretation is advanced by Marxists who argue that metropolitan countries like the USA and UK are becoming more non-manual and managerial, and less working class, because of changes in the international division of labour (Wallerstein, 1981; Warren, 1980). The working class proletarianized by a globally organized capitalism is increasingly located in the countries of the Third World. The countries of the First World are becoming less class-divided and more homogeneous, with all their social groups participating in the exploitation of developing countries. Again the implications of this analysis for parties of the left in metropolitan countries with class-based party systems are unremittingly pessimistic. The western working class in advanced democracies is increasingly implicated in patterns of worldwide class conflict on the side of the 'exploiters'. Manual workers' declining numerical significance goes along with their dwindling incentive to contest the internal political control of advanced capitalist societies.

Summary of section 6.2

● There has been a major change in the UK class structure, with manual workers falling in numbers and non-manual groups expanding. This pattern seems to be reflected also in the United States.

● Even if occupational classes had carried on voting as they did in the 1960s this change would have implied a falling Labour vote. In fact, Labour's decline has been steeper, and the growth of third party voting much more marked, than class structure changes would predict.

6.3   Class alignments: decay or trendless fluctuation?

Most non-academic observers have concluded that Labour's decline and increased third party voting reflect a manifest weakening of the political loyalties which previously attached manual workers to voting Labour and (to a lesser degree) non-manual people to the Conservative Party. There are long-standing grounds for expecting class-party linkages to decay and hence for a process of '**class dealignment**' to occur. In the late 1950s and early '60s the so-called 'embourgeoisement' thesis predicted the break-up of allegedly 'solidary' working-class loyalties to Labour, under the pressure of increasing affluence, wider dissemination of consumer durables, lifestyle changes, and increased geographical and social mobility (Goldthorpe, Lockwood, Bechhofer and Platt, 1968). Much disputed in the mid-1960s following two Labour victories, the thesis survives as one of the most common mass media explanations of recent political changes.

Yet Labour's decline in the late 1970s and early '80s coincided not with a period of generalized affluence but with sharply increasing social inequality. Rising affluence has certainly occurred in some regions and classes, but alongside greatly increased unemployment and evidence of increasing closure in occupational and geographical mobility elsewhere. Perhaps surprisingly, the key modern academic debate is not about the origins of 'class dealignment' – the alleged trend towards weakening non-manual/Conservative and manual/Labour linkages. Instead it focuses on how class dealignment should be measured and (arising from divergent definitions) whether it has occurred at all.

For some analysts third party voting is the resultant or *symptom* of weakening class loyalties to the Conservative and Labour Parties respectively. From this viewpoint, for example, it matters that the absolute level of Conservative voting amongst non-manual people in the 1980s is below what it was in the 1950s or '60s. It is also significant that the proportion of all voters who were non-manual Conservatives or manual Labour voters behaving in a supposedly 'class typical' manner has fallen from two-thirds in 1966 to less than half in the 1980s (Crewe, 1986).

Other observers argue that the level of class voting should be assessed not by reference to absolute levels of Conservative or Labour support in their supposedly 'natural' classes, but in relative terms. For example, although manual support for Labour fell in the 1980s, so did the party's support amongst non-manual people – suggesting that what has happened is chiefly an across-the-board loss of Labour popularity. A change only counts as 'class dealignment' in this view if it can be shown that the non-manual and manual groups have become more similar after discounting for the growth of third party voting. Liberal/SDP voting is here treated as an exogenous change quite separate from questions about declining class loyalties (Heath *et al.*, 1985a, Ch. 3).

The impetus behind the sceptical view of 'class dealignment' comes mainly from social mobility studies analysing whether the post-war growth of non-manual jobs has made British society a more equal one. Large numbers of children from manual families moved into non-manual jobs (a high level of absolute upward social mobility). But compared with the upward mobility of children from non-manual families, children from the working class still fared worse in life-chance terms (Goldthorpe, 1987). Thus their *relative* mobility remained little changed. Anthony Heath carried the same argument into the analysis of voting behaviour arguing that what matters is the **odds ratio** for Conservative/Labour voting across occupational classes. This measure is computed by the following formula:

$$\frac{\% \text{ non-manual Conservative}}{\% \text{ non-manual Labour}} \text{ divided by } \frac{\% \text{ manual Conservative}}{\% \text{ manual Labour}}$$

For example, suppose that 60 per cent of non-manual people vote Conservative while 25 per cent support Labour, and in the manual group 30 per cent support the Conservatives and 55 per cent Labour. Then we can compute the odds ratios as:

$\frac{60}{25}$ divided by $\frac{30}{55}$, which equals $\frac{2.4}{0.54}$ which equals 4.4.

The odds ratio provides a single number score which summarizes the difference in the odds of someone voting Conservative rather than Labour across two classes. However, it is a very eccentrically behaved statistic. In some circumstances odds ratios may remain static where voting patterns change radically, but in other circumstances the ratios respond dramatically to very small vote shifts (Dunleavy, 1987).

Nonetheless applying the formula above to the twelve elections since 1950 yields the following odds ratios:

1950	1951	1955	1959	1964	1966	1970	1974F	1974O	1979	1983	1987
5.5	6.3	5.9	6.1	6.4	6.4	4.5	5.7	4.8	3.7	3.9	3.6

Heath *et al.* (1985a, p. 34) claim that there is no trend detectable in this series up to 1974, while they argue that the later results for the 1980s probably reflect only the inadequacy of the non-manual/manual dichotomy in capturing changes in the occupational class structure (see section 6.2). However, an alternative and simpler interpretation is possible, namely that there was a clear shift downwards in the non-manual/manual odds ratio from an average of 6.1 in the period 1950–66 to an average of under 4.4 thereafter. The sole exception to this pattern was the election of February 1974 held in crisis conditions caused by a confrontation between Heath's Conservative government and the coal-miners. So it is not very surprising 'that there should be an isolated reaffirmation of older occupational class allegiances among two-party loyalists in such a conjuncture, a blip which subsequently faded considerably within six months' (Dunleavy, 1987, p. 409).

Activity 6.1

(a)   The figures below show the votes for the two major parties in the non-manual (NM) class and manual (Man) class, averaged across three elections, for the 1950s, 1960s, 1970s and 1980s respectively. Thus this table just rearranges the information already presented in Table 6.1. Using the formula for calculating the odds ratio above, try to work out the Conservative vs Labour odds ratios across the two classes for these four decades. You will need a calculator.

Average vote for:	1950, 1951 and 1955		1959, 1964 and 1966		1970 and both 1974		1979, 1983 and 1987	
	NM	Man	NM	Man	NM	Man	NM	Man
Conservative	71	33	63	28	56	27	58	34
Labour	23	61	23	63	24	57	20	43

(b)   Do your results help you to decide between the conflicting interpretations offered by Heath *et al*. and Dunleavy of the odds ratios for all twelve elections since 1950 in the paragraph directly above this activity?

(I give the correct odds ratios for the data above at the end of this chapter. Try not to look them up till you have tried to work them out yourself!)

Using fine-grain occupational class measures, however, the apparent reduction of overall non-manual/manual differences in relative class voting looks less certain. Cross-class voting (by people in the small working class for the Conservatives, and by the salariat for Labour) undoubtedly increased sharply in 1970, and to a lesser degree in 1979. It is also somewhat higher throughout the 1970s and '80s than it was in the 1960s (Heath *et al*., 1985a, pp. 32–3). But the pattern of voting across all five of Heath *et al*.'s occupational classes is interpreted by these authors as one of 'trendless fluctuation' rather than any regular decline in the distinctiveness of class voting patterns over time, after allowance is made for increased Liberal/SDP support. A technique known as log linear analysis has also been used to test whether the changing voting patterns across the five classes can be modelled successfully on the assumption that relative class voting has remained stable, or whether it is necessary to introduce the hypothesis that relative class voting patterns have changed (Heath *et al*., 1985a, pp. 41–2; Marshall, Newby and Rose, 1988, pp. 236–9). These tests suggest that it is not *essential* to assume a change in relative class voting to model the patterns across successive elections once general cross-class increases or decreases in party support have been allowed for. However, the tests are limited by analysing the influence of class without other social variables (Dunleavy, 1987, pp. 412–13). Assuming constant relative class voting seems to be more acceptable in modelling voters' so-called 'party identifications' (general attachments to parties) than in modelling actual votes.

A simpler and intuitively understandable way to picture trends in relative class voting is to look at the proportion of the combined Conservative and Labour vote taken by the Conservatives across different occupational classes over time (Figure 6.3). Because the two-party vote excludes from attention the rising levels of Liberal and Liberal/SDP support in this period, it provides an index of relative class voting. If class dealignment is to occur in the sense used by Heath, then the lines for each occupational class in Figure 6.3 should move closer together, whereas if relative class voting has stayed constant they should remain roughly the same distance apart, irrespective of whether the trend of Conservative voting is up or down. In fact the figure shows that the small working class behaves differently from all the other occupational classes. While all other classes moved closer together in the 1980s, the small working class remained apart, as it did in February 1974, when bunching of the other classes also occurred. In addition the 1970 election saw a sharp increase in small working-class conservatism at a time

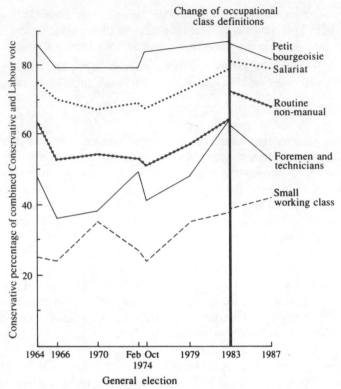

Figure 6.3   The Conservative share of the two-party vote across occupational classes, 1964–87

Note: The occupational class categories changed in 1983, so that figures are not comparable before and after this date. However, 1983 figures are given using both older and newer occupational class categories.

Sources: Computed from Heath et al., 1985, pp. 32–3; except October 1974 figures supplied by John Curtice; and 1983 and 1987 new occupational class basis figures supplied by Anthony Heath

when the other four classes' alignments hardly changed. Does any of this add up to a consistent change in relative class voting patterns? The answer will rather depend on where you look. Heath *et al.* focused mostly on a contrast between the salariat and the small working class (the two biggest classes), and these groupings do indeed remain almost equally far apart (except for 1970) in Figure 6.3. One might add to this the fact that the routine non-manual curve tracks the salariat at a fairly constant rate. On the other hand, the small working class does behave in a pattern rather different from the other classes, which do seem to be bunching together over time.

Perhaps the most important criticism of the relative class voting argument is not statistical but theoretical, however. Why should we see class dealignment only when cross-voting increases (i.e. when more manual workers vote Conservative or more of the salariat vote Labour), while discounting the impact of third party voting in making different classes voting patterns more similar? Why should only class-specific changes of party fortunes matter, rather than a decline in party support across both classes? This point is crucial because Labour has always depended heavily on manual workers. In 1964, 70 per cent of its vote came from the small working class, and by 1983 that proportion still stood at 55 per cent. The Conservatives and the Liberal/ SDP have never drawn more than a third of their vote from a single class, so Labour's support is far more class-dependent than the other parties. What happens, then, if evidence emerges in advance of a general election, suggesting that manual workers are no longer going to support Labour? Because the party is known to be so dependent on working-class support, evidence of slippage here will produce demoralization amongst Labour's potential non-manual voters. Reasoning that the party stands no chance of winning if it loses working-class support, they might well be tempted to switch their own votes to an alternative, such as the Liberals/SDP. The result would then be a general decline in Labour voting across all classes, which Heath *et al.* would regard as evidence that no 'class dealignment' has occurred. Yet the root and whole motor of that decline would be Labour's weakening grip on working-class support (Dunleavy, 1987, pp. 414–17).

Nor is the scenario sketched above a hypothetical one. At successive general elections voters have confronted evidence of weakening manual worker support for Labour. The 1970 election followed within two years of sweeping Labour local election defeats in its inner-city heartland areas. The February 1974 election came after disastrous Labour by-election losses in supposedly safe working-class seats such as the mining constituency of Ashfield. In 1979 the minority Callaghan government lost a Parliamentary vote on devolution and was forced to go to the country at a time not of its own choosing. Public dissatisfaction with the 'winter of discontent' was still fresh, much of it reflecting working-class disaffection from militant trades unionism. In 1983 at Southwark and in 1987 at Greenwich Labour spectacularly lost by-elections in inner-city heartland seats just weeks before voters went to the polls in the ensuing general election. Once we get away from looking at class dealignment as something to be deduced from abstract sets of numbers in tables, and instead situate these numbers within their historical context, it seems perfectly consistent for a process of class dealignment to go ahead over many years *without* any particular change in relative class voting. Voters will react and modify their behaviour to take account of what other people are doing. And unlike social mobility (where changes occur very slowly), voting is a context where people can rapidly and quickly change their behaviour in response to popularly perceived realities.

Summary of section 6.3

• There is considerable academic debate about whether a process of 'class dealignment' has occurred in the UK. Advocates of this shift point to trends for non-manual and manual classes to vote more similarly since the 1960s.

- Critics argue that class dealignment should be measured in terms of 'relative class voting', and that within modern occupational class schemas odds ratios measuring relative class voting have been subject only to 'trendless fluctuation'.

- But this restrictive focus seems to ignore voters' capacity to respond to developments between elections, which may produce even changes in especially Labour support across classes.

6.4   Extended class effects and political alignments

However class is defined, however class dealignment is detected or impugned, a more fundamental problem remains – namely that class now determines relatively little voting behaviour. The proportion of the variation between people which can be explained in terms of class effects is small, always under 20 per cent of the total in regression equations. In the three elections from 1979, the proportion of all voters who are 'correctly' aligned in terms of class determination has bobbed around just above the 50 per cent level even on the Heath *et al.* class schema (Rose and McAllister, 1986, Ch. 3). In 1983 just 49 per cent of voters polled in line with the main party supported by their (production-based) social class (Dunleavy and Husbands, 1985a, p. 124).

Some analysts responded by broadening out 'class' from an occupational/production-based concept to include various other ways in which people's social situation is influenced by what work they do or what income they get paid. Thus Rose (1976) saw 'class' effects as being mediated by trade union membership, housing tenure, car ownership, and even by access to a telephone. The 'class typical' working-class voter must be a union member, live in a council house, depend on public transport, and not have a telephone. Apparently:

> having a telephone indicates that an individual relates easily to others at a distance, he is not confined in a network of face-to-face relationships . . . [And] increasing independence of face-to-face ties would be expected to weaken class influences upon voting, especially in the working class where a substantial degree of face-to-face communal solidarity is often considered a precondition for strong Labour support. (Rose, 1974, p. 504)

This kind of approach always contained a danger that any social variable apparently associated with class in survey data would be incorporated into the *definition* of class, with highly misleading effects in some cases. For example, Dunleavy (1980a) demonstrated that there is in fact no occupational class influence upon union membership whatsoever, once the production sector that people are working in has been controlled for. This result contradicted twenty years of confident misanalysis of union influence as a class-related variable by all previous election studies. More recently *Webb* (1987) has shown that by 1983 unionization made no difference at all to whether people described themselves as being 'middle class' or 'working class' (the so-called 'subjective class' measure), nor to whether they voted in line with their actual occupational class. However, there are four legitimate versions of an **extended class model**, focusing on: family socialization; social mobility effects; education; and so-called 'class environmental' influences.

The **socialization model** remains the core theoretical position of liberal political science. It views alignments as learned primarily in personal inter-actions, and is most plausible in explaining why the family is an important context in which people first become aware of politics. Children are exposed to the ideological views of their parents at an impressionable age, learning political attitudes and party loyalties informally (Franklin and Page, 1984). This effect is likely to partially insulate the major parties' levels of support, smoothing out changes over time and producing a continuous stream of new voters to replace older supporters who die. However, over a long period this influence seems to have fallen considerably. In the mid-1960s 70 per cent of voters who claimed to recall at least one parent's alignment, voted in line with it, whereas by 1983 the proportion was only just over half (54 per cent). But because not all voters know their parents' political views, the share of all voters aligned consistently with their parents dropped from 51 per cent in the mid-1960s to just 43 per cent by 1983 (Rose and McAllister, 1986, p. 105). These figures need to be interpreted cautiously, since there is a well-known tendency for people to 'recall' their parents' vote to fit with their own current alignment. But they do seem to suggest a continuing reduction in family background influences on current voting.

A second important socialization effect arises from social mobility, where children from one occupational class move into a different class. Most analysts have expected people with a current occupation diverging from their class of origin to be 'cross-pressured' or tugged in opposing directions by the pull of their interests and their upbringing. In fact, there is only limited evidence of this phenomenon, as Table 6.3 shows. The table uses a simplified version of the five class Heath *et al.* categories in which an 'intermediate' category is created to hold all those people who are neither in the salariat nor the small working class. The combination of current class with class of origin reveals only three distinct groups of voters. The most Conservative group (39 per cent of voters) is constituted by people in the salariat or intermediate class who also come from backgrounds in these two classes. A clearly non-Conservative group (32 per cent of voters) are those currently in the small working class who also come from a similar back-ground or one in the intermediate class. The cross-pressured groups are people who are upwardly mobile from the working class to either of the non-manual categories (27 per cent of voters), plus the 2 per cent of voters

Table 6.3   The Conservative share of two-party (Con/Lab) voting intentions in 1984

	Current occupational class		
Class of origin	Salariat	Intermediate	Small working class
Salariat	58	59	45
Intermediate	57	59	24
Small working class	42	41	22

___ most Conservative   . . . least Conservative

Source: Recomputed from Marshall *et al.*, 1988, p. 241

downwardly mobile from a service class background into the small working class. Recent changes in class voting patterns have also been mirrored by a decreasing influence from parental class positions on their children's current voting behaviour. From 1964 to 1974 the statistical influence of parents' class positions on voting behaviour fell by more than half (Franklin, 1985, p. 119).

Socialization accounts also argue that schooling and higher education can affect political alignments, since these experiences are key parts of the context in which people first become aware of politics. In fact the impact of education on the Conservative/Labour split is small (Heath *et al.*, 1985a, pp. 67–8). A large group of people in the small working class with less than 'O' level education are the most pro-Labour group, and a small group of manual workers with more educational qualifications are evenly cross-pressured between the Conservatives and Labour. All other types of voters show Conservative preponderance over Labour. However, Liberal/SDP voting is clearly much higher than average amongst the salariat with degrees (4 per cent of the electorate), and a bit higher amongst the salariat with 'O' level or better qualifications. Heath *et al.* suggest on this slender basis that education is a causal influence behind Alliance voting. But even this weak effect is complicated by public/private sector influences (see section 6.5): people with post-school qualifications form a proportion of the public sector work-force which is three and a half times greater than the same group in the private sector (Parry, 1985, p. 85).

Class influences on alignments have so far been discussed in terms of *individual level* effects, of the kind detectable by survey research. However, political scientists and political geographers especially have devoted much attention also to class influences on voting observable at the constituency level. While knowing someone's occupational class has been decreasingly useful in predicting how they will vote in the 1970s and '80s, *the class composition of an area* continues to provide a very reasonable guide as to how that constituency's aggregate vote will split up between the parties. In the mid-1960s 69 per cent of the variation in the Conservative share of the two-party vote could be accounted for in a simple regression analysis by the proportion of employers and managers in each constituency. By 1987 the variance explained by this two-variable relationship at the area level was 68 per cent, with a *strengthening* of the class coefficient (Heath, 1988, p. 10).

Exponents of the socialization model have interpreted these results as demonstrating the existence of **'class environmental' influences**, in which people vote in line with both their own class position and the class character of their neighbourhood. The cues given in lots of small interactions alert voters to what their neighbours believe about politics and will influence their views over time. Thus manual workers in non-manual areas are more Conservative than manual workers in working-class neighbourhoods. And similar effects apply to non-manual people in areas where they are in the majority or minority. People in the 'wrong' class neighbourhoods or in socially mixed areas make more personal contacts with people from other classes compared with those voters living in areas consistent with their personal class position. People in other words tend to conform to the political colouration of their area, across all occupational classes: 'those who speak together, vote together' (Miller, 1978; Johnston, 1986b; Johnston, Pattie and Allsopp, 1988; Heath *et al.*, 1985a, pp. 74–82).

The problem here is that the statistical evidence of 'class environmental' influences has not been matched by any evidence that the alleged causes of the effect actually exist. The socialization model seems to be accepted for blind faith reasons (Dunleavy, 1979). Very few voters ever admit to being influenced by the behaviour of other people in their locality. In 1983 one survey showed that only 2 per cent of voters mentioned 'how people around you are intending to vote' as an important influence upon their choice of party. Only 3 per cent mentioned personal contacts as their most important source of information in deciding how to vote, with a further 8 per cent putting personal contacts as their second most important information source (Dunleavy and Husbands, 1985a, pp. 99, 111).

In addition the alleged influences on people's alignments in single-class neighbourhoods may be explicable in terms of other variables. Regression analyses of area data with multiple explanatory variables show that although a manual/non-manual class dichotomy explains a good deal of the variance in voting figures there are other important influences (Dunleavy and Husbands, 1985a, pp. 193–5). In 1983 these included the level of unemployment, share of agricultural occupations in the workforce, the extent of council housing, levels of car non-ownership, and the proportion of residents from the New Commonwealth (which is the closest thing the UK Census has to a race/ethnic background question). Taken together with class these influences explained about 81 per cent of the variation across constituencies of the 1983 Labour vote, but only 67 per cent of the Tory vote. Including dummy variables for region adds another 16 per cent to the variation explained for the Conservatives, suggesting that their support is more regionally patterned than any other party. The Liberal/SDP vote varies much less across areas than the other parties' support. Analysts sceptical of class environmental influences conclude that it is not necessary to posit neighbourhood interactions to explain so-called 'class environmental' influences:

> Manual workers in working-class and non-manual areas vote differently because their interests vary substantially. For example, a manual worker in an inner-city area is much more likely to own a run-down house or live in council housing, use public transport and other public services, be unemployed, or belong to an ethnic minority: while a manual worker in an affluent suburb is more likely to own a decent house, drive a car, have a reasonably paid job, and be white. (Harrop, 1986, p. 58)

Studies of individual-level survey data which feed in controls for these other aspects of people's social situation show that the alleged 'class environmental' effects attenuate dramatically or disappear completely (McAllister, 1986; Kelly and McAllister, 1985).

Two final aspects of extended class explanations are at present poorly analysed but may turn out to be interesting effects in future work. The first concerns the handling of **gender**. Electoral analysis in the 1960s suggested that women were more Conservative-inclined than men. However, these results were problematic because womens' class positions were normally coded by their husband's occupation. Comparing all women with all men is also misleading since women live longer than men, and people get more Conservative with age. In the 1980s most analysts have concluded that gender effects have diminished or vanished altogether. However, in a deeper way, gender causally determines people's class positions. Women fare worse than men in the competition for better paid and higher status occupations (and also for educational qualifications) because of sexist attitudes and the impacts of child-bearing and child-caring in breaking up their career paths. One British study argued that when women are coded by their own occupation, women manual workers in 1983 were noticeably more Labour-orientated than equivalent men, creating a small gender/class interaction effect (Dunleavy and Husbands, 1985a, pp. 124–9). Other authors have begun to examine in depth the impact of mixed-class households in influencing political attitudes (Duke and Edgell, 1987b). If there are gender or household composition effects, they are likely to be subtle ones; in the meantime these results remain isolated findings.

A second perennial problem has been whether people's income or wealth levels affect political alignments inside classes. Attempts to assess incomes using such proxy variables as home ownership or car ownership seem inadequate, because these consumption patterns are also influenced by life-cycle and age effects, plus whether people live in inner-city, suburban or rural areas (see next section). Asking people directly about their income is also problematic, since people may not know their income accurately or may misrepresent it to an interviewer more commonly than with other variables. However, Charlot (1988) suggests that the more people possess financial assets – such as unit trusts, shareholdings, national savings or building society accounts – the greater their support for the Conservatives. There seems to be a small extra strengthening of Conservative support amongst those people who acquired shares during the 1980s (a period which, as Mohun notes in Chapter 3, was marked by public corporation asset sales as part of the Conservative's privatization policies).

Summary of section 6.4

• Because class influences explain a relatively low proportion of individual voting behaviour, some analysts have developed 'extended' class explanations mediated through other variables.

• Four legitimate influences can be identified. Family socialization effects are fairly strong, but have appreciably declined in recent decades.

• Social mobility effects are still present but are not very strong. Education influences have been detected by some analysts but seem weak.

• Controversy continues to surround patterns of 'class environmental' influences detected in constituency-level voting patterns. Some analysts interpret such effects as evidence of socialization effects, others as reflecting other differences in people's interests.

• The influence of gender and household composition, and of wealth/income, on political alignments remain to be adequately analysed.

The second half of this chapter turns from the analysis of class-based explanations of political change in contemporary Britain to consider three different non-class accounts: sectoral explanations; the hollowing out of older political ideologies and the growth of issue voting; and the impact of social movements and 'unconventional' politics.

6.5   Public/private sector cleavages

Marx, Weber and Durkheim virtually defined modern social theory around themes of class, conflict and social integration. If there are only dim shadows of their work in much current electoral analysis, class-based explanations can nonetheless demonstrate an impressive intellectual pedigree. No similar lengthy process of theoretical debate underpins the analysis of very modern social changes, of which the growth and stabilization of the extended state is a primary instance. The small state of the late nineteenth century hardly featured in Marx's or Weber's work as an influence upon the social structure, let alone a potent source of change in political alignments. Contemporary political scientists too have virtually ignored state growth before 1979, and subsequent privatization, as elements to be considered in assessing electoral change. Thus Crewe (1976, p. 76) identifies only 'glacially slow

Table 6.4 The growth and stabilization of state employment, collective consumption and state dependency in Britain, 1961–86

	Public employment		State dependent population		Council housing	
	Number (million)	% of employees	Number (million)	% of all incomes	Dwellings (million)	% of households
1961	5.86	26	8.00	25	4.40	27
1966	6.06	26	9.05	26	5.06	29
1971	6.63	29	10.64	30	5.98	31
1976	7.30	32	11.75	32	6.56	31
1981	7.19	33	13.85	36	6.76	31
1986	6.52	30	–	–	5.89	27

The figures are for the United Kingdom, except council housing which relates to Great Britain.

Sources: *Economic Trends*, 1987, p. 201; Parry, 1985, p. 88; *Annual Abstract of Statistics*, 1988, p. 47

changes in the British social structure' – the changing class structure (see section 6.2), the process of ex-urbanization in which the countryside is taken over by commuters and the retired rich, and the emergence of ethnic minorities. But he declares confidently of such changes: 'in all these cases, shifts in party support have been small, often only temporary, and always localized; no shift in the social structure has produced an enduring, nation-wide realignment of party support since 1945'.

Conspicuously missing from Crewe's list of modern shifts in the social structure is any reference to the expansion of the welfare state up to the mid-1970s, with its major implications for public employment, collective consumption of services and dependency upon the state for welfare benefits or pensions (Table 6.4). Equally neglected in more recent liberal electoral studies is the impact of the Thatcher government in the 1980s in privatizing public corporations, selling off council houses to tenants, pushing ahead private sector or quasi-private options in education, health care and social housing, enforcing mandatory competitive tendering in a wide range of public services (Ascher, 1987), and proclaiming the long-term decline of the public share of GDP and employment. This pattern of analytic neglect is not just a coincidental series of empirical oversights. Rather it represents a deeply embedded intellectual blind spot in pluralist thinking, a conviction that the liberal democratic state is 'neutral' in its impacts upon the social structure and electoral politics (Dunleavy and O'Leary, 1987, Ch. 2).

By contrast, **sectoral theory** insists that the chief underlying cause for the weakening or fragmentation of a class-based party system in Britain must be sought in the multiple impacts on the social structure, electoral politics and party competition of the growth and stabilization of the welfare state. In its most ambitious form, sectoral theory claims that welfare state growth is a politically self-stabilizing process. The initial expansion of government intervention in most countries was founded upon a working-class political movement or some form of class-based political coalition. But this social base thereafter tended to be broken up by the process of public service expansion which welfarist polices set in train (Dunleavy, 1986b), creating a long-run public policy cycle of a kind also analysed in recent neo-pluralist writing (Hirschman, 1982; Hogwood and Peters, 1983). The growth of the welfare state in the UK seems to have had three main effects in restructuring the social bases of party support: production sector effects; consumption sector effects; and state dependency effects.

6.5.1   Production sector effects

Public employment expansion has been concentrated mainly in non-manual groups, contributing to the expansion of intermediate classes between capital and labour. In the UK public sector workers are three-quarters unionized, compared with just 40 per cent for private sector employees, so the new public sector, non-manual groupings are partially radicalized, or at least markedly non-Conservative. Public sector unionism was also boosted by public corporations, although their labour force was stable or shrinking for most of the period, before falling decisively with privatization in the 1980s. Over the 1960 to 1980 period, the balance of TUC membership shifted decisively to a public sector majority. Even more noticeably members recruited from the public sector began to predominate in the Labour Party's constituency parties, and amongst Labour MPs. At the same time, there was a substantial growth of taxation, especially the extension of income tax coverage from less than one third of manual workers in the early 1950s to virtually universal coverage of all those on non-poverty wages by the mid-1970s (Turner and Wilkinson, 1972). The connections between public sector wages and taxation levels were highlighted by a series of industrial actions over restrictive government incomes policies stretching from 1968 to the 1978–79 'winter of discontent'. Public sector strikes receive twice the proportion of mass media coverage of industrial disputes that would be warranted by their percentage of working days lost (Dunleavy, 1980a, pp. 535–6).

These developments acquired political significance because throughout this period the two major parties progressively changed the bases of their appeal to the electorate to run on sectoral rather than class lines. Labour's change of appeal was accomplished by the mid-1950s, especially in the adoption of a revisionist form of socialism focusing upon the extension of the public services and piecemeal additional nationalizations as its key components – neither of which has very much to do with 'class politics' *per se* (Crosland, 1956). But throughout the 1950s and '60s the Conservatives essentially competed with Labour to run the welfare state and mixed economy more efficiently. Their change of heart towards a more aggressive anti-public sector appeal was first signalled in 1968 by the Selsdon declaration, but then subdued in government under Heath. It re-emerged with full force under Thatcher's leadership from 1975, and it has since been decisive in maintaining and extending the party's appeal to manual voters. By the late 1980s most of the key dimensions of domestic policy conflict between the Conservatives and Labour seem to be straightforward sectoral issues – with only the shifting of tax burdens away from the very rich standing out as an overtly class-based Tory policy. The consequences of restructuring Conservative/Labour conflicts around private/public issues has been very unfavourable for Labour, since only 30 per cent of the employed workforce are state employees. And even within this total some substantial sections (such as the police, military and law and order branches) are traditionally Tory and have been consistently privileged by Conservative governments in pay terms.

Sectoral effects on voting show up clearly in survey data after controlling for occupational class (Table 6.5). The Conservative share of the two-party vote is markedly lower in the two non-manual classes in the public sector than in equivalent private sector groups, and a slight effect is visible also amongst other classes. The level of Liberal/SDP support is also noticeably higher in two public sector classes – the salariat and foremen/technicians. Finally, if we look at the odds ratios within sectors (identified by Heath *et al.* (1985a) as key guides to relative class voting), two apparently separate patterns emerge. In the private sector the petit bourgeoisie and salariat are over eight times more likely to vote Conservative rather than Labour compared with private sector manual workers, and the routine non-manual group are five times more likely. By contrast amongst state employees the salariat are only three and a half times more likely to vote Conservative rather than Labour compared with manual workers, and the routine non-manual group only twice as likely. Public/private employment effects are

Table 6.5 Production sector effects on voting intention, 1984, after controlling for occupational class

Occupational class	Conservative share of two party vote (%)		Liberal/SDP support (%)		Con/Lab odds ratio against workers	
	Private	Public	Private	Public	Private	Public
Petit bourgeoisie	80	–	22	–	8.5	–
Salariat	79	54	21	31	8.1	3.4
Routine non-manual	71	42	22	24	5.2	2.1
Foremen/technicians	55	49	16	28	2.6	2.8
Small working class	32	21	16	17	–	–
All classes	53	40	18	24		

Source: Computed from Marshall *et al.*, 1988, p. 251

closely related to the effect of union membership, itself chiefly determined by production sector and gender, with women being markedly less unionized in all classes (Dunleavy and Husbands, 1985a, pp. 129–36).

6.5.2 Consumption sector effects

Governmental provision of services also has electoral implications where the political parties adopt polarized stances about private or public consumption. The sectoral model argues that people's access to a wide range of services and goods – such as housing, transport, health care, education and care for dependent elderly people – is determined as much by government intervention as it is by occupational or social class (see Hamnett, 1989). Although class clearly influences these consumption positions, there are also strong life-cycle, family type, lifestyle choice, locational, and public policy influences which determine people's access to different forms of consumption.

In the post-war period the two main instances of party polarization over consumption have been in housing (with Labour promoting low-rent council renting and the Conservatives defending income tax subsidies for homeowners) and transport (where Labour from the late 1970s has generally prioritized public transport and the Conservatives have assigned it lesser weight against road schemes favouring private car users). From the late 1960s to the early '80s conflict over housing was especially intense, with the Conservatives pressing for 'economic' council house rents, an end to municipalization of housing and, later, council house sales, and Labour resisting these initiatives. There is little room for doubt that throughout this period voting became progressively more associated with people's housing tenure positions, even while the influence of class on individual voting was declining. For example, the data in Table 6.6 use a technique known as a 'logit analysis' to analyse survey data from 1964 and 1983 and to calculate the log odds of someone voting Conservative in terms of the class position of their household head and their type of housing (Heath, 1988, p. 10). [If this description leaves you none the wiser, don't worry! Simply look at the relative sizes of the class and tenure coefficients at the two dates. The larger the number the more important the variable is in predicting voting, while the smaller it becomes the less important it is.] Over the period the influence of

Table 6.6 The relative importance of occupational class and housing tenure as influences predicting people's votes, 1964–83

	1964	1983
Class coefficient	0.41	0.20
Tenure coefficient	0.26	0.33

Table 6.7 Voting in 1983 by social class and consumption sector

	Conservative share of the two-party vote (%)				Liberal/SDP vote (%)			
	None	One	Two	Three or more	None	One	Two	Three or more
Manual workers	27	34	49	63	21	29	26	37
Non-manual workers	56	70	71	84	16	29	37	39
Controllers of labour	56		76	92	25		30	24
Employers etc.	–	–	79	100	–	–	25	12

Source: Dunleavy and Husbands, 1985, p. 142

occupational class fell by almost half, whereas the tenure coefficient clearly strengthened over time. More detailed analysis of class and tenure effects shows that the changes in Table 6.6 are not due just to the changing class structure.

However, there are grounds for believing that housing and transport effects need not continue to be the main sectoral influences in future. By the mid-1970s owner-occupation was clearly the dominant tenure form, and within a decade Labour had accepted a residual role for council housing. During the late 1980s housing and transport have decreasingly polarized the parties: for example, the Conservatives share of the home-owner vote has slightly shrunk from 53 per cent in 1979 to 47 per cent in 1987. At the same time there has been an increasingly obvious sectoral polarization of the parties around two new areas of consumption. In health care the Conservatives in the 1980s have restricted funding to the NHS to increase efficiency and promoted private health insurance, most of which is provided by companies as fringe benefits to managers, while Labour defends an NHS 'free at the point of need' and funded more generously. And in education, the Conservatives' 1988 legislation to allow schools to opt out of local authority control will create a new 'grant-maintained' sector controlled by quasi-autonomous school-governing bodies funded directly by central government, and hence intermediate between local authority schools and the private sector. With some estimates suggesting a third of schools will opt out (Davies, 1988), a considerable growth in private schools in the 1980s, and the Conservative government also promoting special business-funded 'magnet schools', policy differences on sectoral lines in eduation are now pronounced between the Conservatives and Labour at a party leadership and activist level, and may emerge also at the voter level.

Exponents of sectoral theories claim that there is already evidence of multiple **consumption cleavages** affecting voter attitudes (Table 6.7). (The class schema used in Table 6.7 distinguishes four production-based social classes: a large manual worker group; a large non-manual worker group composed of all non-supervisory employees; a 'controllers of labour' group whose work tasks involve them in regulating other people's work; and an employer/petit bourgeois category.) Five consumption processes are analysed, where the 'private' options are: ownership of a house; family access to a car; family use of private medical care; family use of a private old people's home; and past or prospective use of private schooling by family members. The patterning of the Conservative/Labour vote fits closely with the sectoral model's expectation. Conservative support relative to Labour increases across classes moving down the table, and also goes up markedly *within* classes as the level of private consumption rises. Among non-manual workers there is a fairly constant level of Conservative support, but with more private consumption Labour voting goes down and there is a marked increase in the level of Liberal/SDP support. Amongst manual workers both Conservative and Liberal/SDP voting increase with greater private consumption, as the Labour vote falls steeply. These multiple consumption sector effects have now been charted in several studies (Duke and Edgell, 1984; Edgell and Duke, 1986) and are matched by significant consumption sector patterning of political attitudes towards privatization and other issues (Duke and Edgell, 1987a).

6.5.3   State dependency effects

The number of people whose source of income derives from state benefits of various types has increased greatly. In 1951 around a fifth of all income recipients in the UK were pensioners, unemployed, receiving supplementary benefits, widows or disabled and students on full grant (Parry, 1985, p. 88). Thirty years later the absolute numbers of people in these categories had more than doubled, and they accounted for 36 per cent of all income recipients in British society (Parry, 1986). Yet the state-dependent population remained largely invisible to most electoral analysts as an electoral influence.

The differentiation of party attitudes towards the state-dependent population has been episodic and rather selective. Old age pensions and help for the disabled have benefited from more consensual political support. But unemployment pay and supplementary benefits have not been similarly insulated from controversy, and seem to have become increasingly involved in party competition in the 1980s. Especially since its social security reforms of the late 1960s (Banting, 1979), and its index-linking of pensions to wages in the late 1970s, Labour has become progressively more identified with the state-dependent population (Taylor Gooby, 1985). By contrast, the Conservatives have moved steadily towards a 'tougher' anti-welfarist line, both in terms of exploiting a populist anti-'scrounging' rhetoric (Golding and Middleton, 1978 and 1982) and in terms of actual policies. One recent study has documented thirty significant Conservative changes to unemploy-

Table 6.8 Voting intentions in 1984 by number of state benefits received in household and by low/high state dependency

% support for	State benefits received				Proportion of household income from state	
	None	One	Two	Three or more	Under 5%	Over 5%
Conservative	44	41	32	23	46	27
Labour	34	38	54	69	33	60
Liberal/SDP	23	22	13	7	21	17
Total %	100	100	100	100	100	100
Con % of two-party vote	56	52	37	25	58	31
% of voters	31	48	14	7	67	33

Source: Marshall *et al.*, 1988, p. 233

ment benefit legislation and regulations since 1979, of which all but three had the effect of reducing or restricting entitlements (Atkinson, 1988).

At present there is only fragmented evidence that party differentiation over state dependency has begun to affect voters. However, Marshall *et al.* (1988) found that there is a clear differentiation in the major parties' support groups in relation to high state dependency, which they define as more than 5 per cent of household income deriving from state benefits. Three-quarters of both Conservative and Liberal/SDP support in 1984 came from people in low dependency households, and only a quarter from people in high dependency households. By contrast, only just over half of Labour voters were in low dependency households, and fully 45 per cent received more than 5 per cent of household income from state benefits. Labour support predominated in the third of households classed as high dependency, while the Conservatives were clearly the leading party in the two-thirds of households less dependent on benefits (Table 6.8). A simple count of benefits received also showed Labour support increasing with state dependency. Other research suggests some polarization between the most and the least state-dependent groups. In 1983 unemployed people with low private consumption were strongly pro-Labour. More than counteracting this effect, however, was a much larger group of retired people with relatively high private consumption (almost certainly in occupational pension schemes) who were markedly Conservative (Dunleavy and Husbands, 1985a, p. 145). Other unemployed and retired people voted in line with working people in their consumption sector.

Sectoral explanations remain very controversial (Franklin and Page, 1984; Rose and McAllister, 1986, pp. 47–9, 64–6; Harrop, 1988, pp. 41–6). Critics argue that the evidence for sectoral effects remains inconclusive since many of the individual effects (such as housing or state dependency influences) can also be fitted into class-based explanations. Little evidence has yet been produced showing that cleavages which can only be sectoral (such as public/private employment differences) structure the views of voters as a whole – as opposed to specific groups such as non-manual state employees. Nor have the causal mechanism supporting alleged sectoral effects been well described in terms of influences upon voters' issue attitudes or beliefs. And the influence of sectoral changes in shaping the decline of class politics over time is difficult to chart because data on most aspects of voters' sectoral locations only began to be collected in the late 1970s.

However, few serious commentators now deny that the domestic political issues which divide the Conservative and Labour Parties can fit more easily and immediately into a public/private sector cleavage system, rather than trying to force them into a 'class politics' framework. Equally, the social bases of the political parties and of the trade unions have clearly shifted dramatically away from the class-structured patterns of the early post-war period. Conservative and Labour leaders, MPs and activists can be distinguished more easily in terms of their sectoral backgrounds than their class positions. The basic idea of *multiple* different public/private cleavages eroding class-based patterns of alignment in different ways but nonetheless responding consistently to a basic redefinition of the major parties' electoral appeals along pro- and anti-state intervention lines has neither been fully established nor yet effectively criticized.

Summary of section 6.5

• Sectoral explanations argue that a main cause of class dealignment and the growth of third party voting has been the impact of the extended welfare state in restructuring the conflicts between the major parties on sectoral lines, triggering the emergence of a complex of sectoral effects in mass voting behaviour.

• Sectoral effects can be detected in employment terms, some significant consumption processes where the state intervenes, and in the politicization of state dependency.

• Critics argue that the evidence for these effects is slender, and their causal role (if any) in class dealignment remains to be established.

Activity 6.2

Here are two contrasting views of the possibility that sectoral effects will develop in health care and education. First, two exponents of the sectoral model writing in 1984:

> A really potent new issue may emerge over privatization of health care provision . . . If a 'two tier' health care system emerges more explicitly than at present and if more people begin to confront a costly 'coerced exchange' forced on them by service deterioration in the public sector, then it is possible to foresee a period when health care issues could assume the electoral significance hitherto reserved for housing tenure questions . . . [And] as the

> Conservative Party in the 1980s presses ahead with plans to encourage private provision in education, so patterns of sectoral differentiation in voting might come into existence in this area as well. (Dunleavy and Husbands, 1985a, p. 144 and p. 24)

Second, some strong critics of the sectoral approach writing two years later:

> A division of the electorate into two competing consumption classes [sic] – public and private – is a non-starter. Two important examples of public versus private consumption cleavages – education and health – cannot sustain electoral competition, because they tend to unite the electorate. More than 90 per cent depend upon state education and upon the national health service; private health care and fee-paying education are consumed by only a minority of the middle class [sic]. Mrs Thatcher has given implicit recognition to the cross-class importance of the welfare state services by *not* scheduling them for privatization, a step that would risk electoral suicide. (Rose and McAllister, 1986, p. 64)

Thinking about political developments since 1987, how would you evaluate these competing predictions? Have health and education issues become more politically polarized on private vs public sector lines between the Conservatives and Labour recently? Or have the Conservatives carefully held off from attempts to privatize the NHS or aspects of state education?

6.6   Political issues and ideological change

Analysts who claim that relative class voting patterns have not changed, and also dispute the importance of sectoral effects, are left arguing that the key reasons for the growth of third party voting and decline of Labour are *political* ones related to changes in voters' values and attitudes (*Heath* et al., 1985b). Those analysts who accept that class dealignment has occurred also look for political changes, especially in terms of voters' longer-term attachments to the major parties, and their shorter-term responses to governmental performance, immediate issues and leadership performance (Rose and McAllister, 1986). An influential view formulated by 1970s election studies linked class dealignment with the notion of '**partisan dealignment**' in which the strength of voters' loyalties to the party they usually support has progressively declined over time (Särlvik and Crewe, 1983; Crewe, 1976; Crewe, Särlvik and Alt, 1977). In the mid-1960s only one in twelve voters had no 'party identification' or general attachment to voting for one party or another. By the 1980s between one in seven and one in five voters had no party identification. Although the proportion of people identifying with the Conservatives stayed stable, the share of Labour identifiers decreased by about a quarter. Furthermore the proportion of Conservative and Labour 'identifiers' combined who described their allegiance as 'very strong' declined from just under half to a third across these two decades.

However, opinion is divided about the reasons why, and the mechanisms by which, these changes have come about. A long-term study of the decline of class voting by Franklin (1985) suggests that party identifications have remained fairly consistent influences upon voting behaviour, reflecting in turn the importance of family socialization influences. Nor has there been a *continuous* decline of occupational class influences, but rather a set of apparent shocks to previous voting patterns. The 1970 election was marked both by a sharp decline in class voting and by a distinct shift upwards in the importance of issue voting – where people choose whom to support on the basis of the party stances on issues that are important to them. On this account, then, **issue voting** remained at very similar enhanced levels throughout the rest of the 1970s and '80s, reinforced by the growth of third party support and the expansion of voters' options which this change implied.

Franklin's account makes a partial effort to address a fundamental problem in analysing the interrelationship between voting, party identification and issue attitudes. The difficulty is that these three variables are interrelated so that causal influences run in both directions. People may vote for a party because of its stance on key issues, or they may adjust their issue attitudes to bring them into line with their decision to support a particular party. Some American accounts have developed sophisticated statistical techniques for handling these problems (Page and Jones, 1979; Markus and Converse, 1979), but similar techniques have not been applied in Britain. Most authors have simply assumed that the primary direction runs from attitudes to vote. However, Franklin (1985) does show that even allowing for two-way causal flows the increasing links between votes and issue attitudes since 1970 indicate a strengthening of the influence of shorter-term political stimuli. The extent to which attitudes changed during election campaigns themselves also increased from 1974 to 1983 although the 1987 campaign reverted to a very static pattern of opinion.

Problems caused by people adjusting their issues attitudes (and even their responses to party identification questions) also vitiate the style of electoral analysis which simply throws attitudes, party identifications and sociological variables into a large pot, then stirs them up and gets the computer to extract estimates of the relative importance of the variables (see, for instance, Whiteley, 1983, pp. 94–106; Franklin and Page, 1984, pp. 531–4). For example, Rose and McAllister (1986) compare socialization variables, current sociological variables, a set of alleged political 'principles', and voters' evaluations of the government and party leaders. They argue that the United Kingdom has moved decisively away from 'closed' elections where most voters responded in predictable ways to fixed class and socialization influences. Instead, the current system of party competition is described as 'open' elections, with far more voters choosing how to vote in relation to political principles and short-term issues or performance assessments. The problems here are that only one of four 'principles' turns out to have any importance at all for voting, and this seems to consist just of pro- or anti-attitudes to prominent Labour policies (of the 1960s)! Clearly the two-way causal linkages between party choice and these kind of variables is likely to be substantial. So if the combined effect of ideology/attitude variables is only as strong as sociological/socialization variables even with this probable overestimation, then the 'openness' of electoral competition remains to be established.

However, if voters possess a consistent ordering of their views, and if they act in line with this ordering, then the notion of ideologically-based voting becomes more plausible. Early British surveys, echoing the scepticism of American studies in the 1950s, argued that only a quarter of British voters in the mid-1960s could give any coherent account of what the terms 'left' and 'right' mean in politics (Butler and Stokes, 1969, pp. 200–14). More recent studies have argued that because most voters do not devote large amounts of time to analysing electoral politics this kind of test is unrealistic. Looking instead at whether people take a consistent stance across a large number of attitude questions might reveal greater coherence in their views. And in addition people's means of political orientation might have become more consistent over time, with rising levels of education and the expansion of broadcast media coverage.

There seem to be two fundamental dimensions in the ways that British voters organize their attitudes (see *Heath* et al., 1985b; Robertson, 1984). The first is a basically left/right economic one, measuring people's attitude to nationalization, state intervention in the economy and egalitarianism. The second indicates where people stand between more 'authoritarian' or 'tough-minded' responses and more liberal or 'tender' responses on a range of diverse social issues – such as capital punishment, abortion, race relations and, increasingly, defence policy. Different authors offer slightly varying dimensions, depending on the survey questions asked and type of analysis employed. But Harrop and Miller (1987, p. 123) argue that something like a left/right economic dimension and a vertical authoritarian/liberal dimension appear in most of them (Scarborough, 1984; Särlvik and Crewe, 1983; Alt, 1979).

Many of the studies trying to tap changes in ideology have been limited by focusing on a few 'standard' questions asked across a run of elections. In survey research the ways in which voters respond to interviewers can vary dramatically depending on the precise phrasing of the questions asked, so data are only comparable if the questions maintain exactly the same wording over time. However, there is a key drawback here as well. Someone replying that they favour 'further nationalization' in 1964 might well mean something completely different from someone giving the same response in 1974 or 1984. Supposing they favour the nationalization of the steel industry but draw the line at the state taking over one of the clearing banks. Then they would be 'pro-nationalization' in 1964 and 1966 (before steel was national-ized), but thereafter opposed to it. Without their views having changed they would be counted as part of the 'haemorrhaging of support' for Labour's 'core' principles detected by some analysts (Crewe, Särlvik and Alt, 1977). In addition, of course, party positions on issues as diverse as incomes policy, nationalization and nuclear deterrence have varied strongly over time. Hence there is fundamental Catch 22 in analysing **ideological change** over time via survey research: use varying wording and responses are non-comparable; but keep the same wording and the *meaning* of 'standard' responses changes radically anyway.

A final sceptical note about ideological influences on voting has been struck by some studies. Scarborough (1984, pp. 190–94) argues for the importance of ideology, but her own results from a small exploratory study seem to show that only two out of five voters (39 per cent) have well-ordered views associated with a consistent choice of party. A further one in six voters (16 per cent) have consistent views which *prevent* them voting for a disliked party, but are not determinate enough to fix their votes between the remaining parties. The rest of the electorate have consistent sets of views but vote erratically (10 per cent), or have consistent views but vote irrationally for a party they are opposed to (6 per cent), or have no consistently ordered views (29 per cent). Some studies have also examined the extent to which people give directly inconsistent responses about their views (Dunleavy and Husbands, 1985a, pp. 178–80), suggesting that between a quarter and a half of voters show some degree of inconsistency in their responses to attitude questions.

Radical analysts argue that studies of ideological change have ignored the external influences acting upon voters to shape their views. Most liberal analysts take it as axiomatic that voters make up their own minds. Yet people do not decide how to vote in isolation except for reading a set of party manifestoes. The chief external influences in addition to political parties themselves are, first, the mass media and, second, the incumbent government manipulating state power for partisan advantage. Liberal orthodoxy blanked out much discussion of media influences on electoral politics in the early 1960s by concluding that television, radio and even newspapers mainly reinforce pre-existing views, rather than constituting an agency capable of effecting changes in views (Blumler and McQuail, 1968). In addition, British studies argued that although the UK press is intensely partisan most voters rely more on the impartial broadcast media news for political information. Some recent research queries both viewpoints, on theoretical grounds and by demonstrating the very close relationship between partisan newspaper readership and voting behaviour (*Dunleavy and Husbands*, 1985b). More orthodox writers now acknowledge a need to reappraise previous neglect of media influences (Harrop, 1988, pp. 44–6). Problems of two-way causation again recur here. Do people read particular newspapers because of their political views, or do newspapers shape what they think? At the least, the debate remains open. If it could be resolved, then changes in the mass media system from the early 1970s to the late '80s – such as the growth of a massive Conservative bias in the newspaper industry (Harrop, 1986) and the return of newspaper ownership to a few powerful media barons – again hardly fit the picture of 'glacially slow social change' painted by Crewe and other pluralist writers.

The extent to which an incumbent government (with a secure majority) can reshape public opinion has also been stressed by radical accounts, especially to explain the consolidation of Conservative support in the 1980s and the apparent advent of a 'dominant party system' (Dunleavy and Ward, 1981; Dunleavy and Husbands, 1985a, Ch. 2). Programmes such as the sale of council housing, the privatization of public corporations, the hiving off of three-quarters of the civil service to independent agencies, the introduction of restrictive anti-trade union laws and so on are very unlikely to be neutral in their political implications. Instead they seem certain to confer on the Conservatives real partisan advantages which are small in their individual effects (since new council house owners or newly private sector workers will not alter their value or votes overnight), but cumulatively impressive in shifting millions of marginal votes away from Labour.

Summary of section 6.6

● Many observers have sought to explain swings of party fortunes in terms of political/ideological change in the electorate, despite the difficulties of measuring ideological shifts.

● 'Issue voting' probably increased noticeably from 1970 to a new higher level.

● British voters' beliefs seem to be organized in terms of two underlying ideological dimensions, one a left/right spectrum of economic positions and the other an authoritarian/liberal range on social issues. But estimating the degree to which attitudes and values influence voting behaviour or are influenced by it is fraught with problems.

● Radical models argue that mass media changes plus partisan uses of state power could also explain shifts in the electorate's views, rather than autonomous changes of mind by voters.

6.7   'Unconventional' politics and social movements

The final dimension of political restructuring in contemporary Britain is the least well analysed by existing electoral studies because it concerns 'unconventional', minority or apparently marginalized forms of politics. The attitudinal shifts and social movements involved are almost impossible to study via survey research, because minority groups rarely show up in enough numbers in most surveys. Yet despite long series of seeming defeats and disappointments, and notwithstanding their apparent exclusion from mass appeal, it is often these same groups and issues which achieve significant influence in innovating and pushing new issues onto the agenda of conventional party politics. I discuss first racism, ethnicity and nationalism – three forces that are still formally unintegrated into major party competition but which seem to be influences of continuing importance in shaping mass opinion. Secondly, I analyse a clutch of social movements which have achieved political influence within the labour movement if not yet mass electoral appeal, hailed by some writers as a potential 'rainbow coalition' of the left. Finally, I briefly examine the relative strengths of 'materialist' and 'post-materialist' politics in contemporary Britain.

6.7.1   Racism, ethnicity and nationalism

Racism emerged as an issue in electoral politics cross-cutting class lines during the early and middle 1960s, after some conspicuous defeats for Labour by-election candidates over delays in introducing immigration controls, and following Enoch Powell's speech forecasting 'rivers of blood' in the inner cities if more Afro-Caribbean and Asian people were not excluded from entry into the UK. Ever since the Notting Hill race riots of 1959, the Conservative and Labour Party leaderships have mistrusted the strength of populist feeling of a semi-racist kind which periodically surfaces in various ways, such as public opinion reactions and some popular press coverage. The parties have pursued an effective joint strategy to contain and exclude the growth of any mass racist political movement or party (unlike France where their National Front Party achieved 14 per cent of the vote in some national elections in the mid-1980s). The strategy has two tracks. The first involves progressive tightening of immigration entry rules to remove or control the most emotive source of racist feeling. The second places relatively strict barriers on the expression of racist sentiments in public life or the practice of overt discrimination in employment and housing, slightly extended by some not very effective legislation to counter racial disadvantage and latent forms of discrimination.

The twin-track strategy has been partially successful in that no racist party or movement has emerged to challenge the established parties in anything more than a marginal manner. The British National Front and its multiple splinter groups have never polled more than one in twenty votes in local elections, although they have at times drawn support from a wide range of urban wards many of which show long-term histories of racist sentiment (Husbands, 1986). But the strategy has also implied the partial incorporation of latent racism into the Conservative Party, where around thirty MPs in the 1980s Parliaments have adopted more or less overt anti-black attitudes and pressurized the government to further toughen up immigration rules. Conservative leaders have never explicitly sought to exploit racist sentiment, and only 1 per cent of voters mentioned immigration as an influence on their vote by the time of the 1983 elections. The major parties have mostly tried to keep race issues out of electoral competition. There have been occasional lapses (such as Thatcher's 1978 remark about people fearing being 'swamped' by coloured immigrants) and relatively thinly veiled domestic campaigns (such as Tory attacks on 'loony Left' councils with black leaders and ministerial harassment of Labour education authorities with proactive anti-racist policies) (see Sarre, 1989b). These incidents have kept alive the popular image of the Conservative party as 'tougher' on blacks than Labour or the Liberals/SDP. If the twin-track strategy has not prevented the politicization of racism issues neither has it effectively combated racial disadvantage or prevented the emergence of distinct inner-city ghetto areas. Together with an unprecedented decay in police relations with the black community in inner-city areas, this neglect has produced a serious social malaise punctuated by widespread and severe urban riots involving predominantly black communities in both 1981 and 1985.

These developments have reinforced and reflected other pressures for **ethnicity** to play an increasingly important role in Labour politics. At least 65 per cent of black voters supported Labour in the 1980s elections, making them far and away the party's most reliable social base, despite some propensity to turn out less (Husbands, 1986, p. 301). And the growing importance of black populations in London (where one in five voters could be black by the early 1990s) and other inner cities has made ethnicity an important variable structuring overall Labour support. By 1983 the proportion of an area's residents from the New Commonwealth was the fourth best social variable for explaining the size of the Labour vote across constituencies (Dunleavy and Husbands, 1985a, pp. 193–8). At the same time, Labour has probably suffered a net loss of votes at successive elections in terms of the defection of some white semi-racist voters to other parties, an effect which may have been particularly enmeshed with the apparent reaction against the 'loony Left' in London during the 1987 election. The difficulties Labour has experienced in recruiting black candidates to the ranks of its MPs, accommodating demands for 'black sections' and responding to the divergent interests of its Asian and Afro-Caribbean supporters in some areas reflect the problems of managing an urban coalition destabilized by the growth of black voters and their increasing political muscle.

Nationalism resembles ethnicity in being a spatially concentrated influence, but one which has become an enduring and relatively strong source of distinctiveness in Scottish and to a lesser extent Welsh voting since the late 1960s. This difference takes two main forms. In the 1970s and '80s support for separatist parties has varied from 12 to 30 per cent for the SNP in Scotland, peaking in 1974, while in Wales Plaid Cymru support has been a more stable 8–10 per cent of the national vote. Second, the Labour vote has been consistently around 12 per cent higher in both countries than in England, with the Conservative vote correspondingly depressed. Indeed Labour came to occupy almost a 'dominant party' position within Scotland by the late 1980s, with a pronounced marginalization of Conservative influence in local government. Again the major parties have so far managed to contain the expression of more overt nationalist sentiment by deferring to minority demands at a symbolic politics level (as with Welsh dual language road signs and forms and the Welsh language television channel, or the maintenance of separate Scottish legal forms), and by pursuing significantly more generous regional policies in both areas than in depressed regions of England.

6.7.2   The rainbow coalition

There has been a growth of a 'new urban left' in many liberal democracies since the early 1970s, which is as strongly marked in countries like the USA and Canada which lack any distinctive socialist parties as in the UK where Labour has provided the main channel of political integration (Magnussen, 1988). There are three distinctive elements of the new urban left **social movements**. The first is a strong commitment to the anti-nuclear peace movement – itself a worldwide phenomenon of the new cold war from 1978 to 1986 – with the British Campaign for Nuclear Disarmament following the international pattern closely. Second, there has been a strong growth of opposition to civilian nuclear power, often closely linked to the peace movement but also extending more widely in terms of mass electoral appeal. Labour conferences moved to reject nuclear power in the late 1980s despite major trade union opposition. Opposition to nuclear energy has spilled over also into a more general environmental/ecological concern, although there is an increasing divergence in environmentalist movements generally between socialist and green/ecological strands (Ward, 1983). Third are some strong culturalist developments, especially the evolution of the liberal-radical wing of the women's movement (Byrne and Lovenduski, 1983) and the growth of gay/lesbian movements (at least before the Aids period of the later 1980s). These 'sexual politics' elements have been added into the previous concerns of urban social movements with collective consumption issues (Lowe, 1986). There has been no equivalent in Britain of the rise to political influence of the San Francisco gay movement (Castells, 1983), but there was an enhanced openness to gay/lesbian demands in some inner-city councils for a few years in the mid-1980s. Womens' issues have been more slowly but more widely integrated into the Labour Party and have been more accepted by the other major parties.

Some analysts of the left have suggested that these developments together with the growth of ethnic politics are cumulatively enough to justify a decisive shift in Labour's appeal away from a class-based/labour movement one. Instead Labour would become a 'rainbow coalition' in which different minorities on the left which felt strongly about their own key issue could co-operate in a log-rolling fashion to build majority support. In practice, the strength of Labour's class-based support, even given the decline of working-class numbers and allegiances, continues to dwarf the electoral significance of these alternative bases. The rainbow coalition idea is itself rendered less distinctive by recognizing the extent to which Labour's class-based appeals are already playing a secondary role to sectoral issues and cleavages. The different components of the rainbow coalition have probably tapped some new sources of support for Labour (especially perhaps among young voters otherwise socialized politically in an atmosphere of increasing conservatism). But in opening up new dimensions of cleavage to politicization, some elements of the rainbow coalition (such as gay/lesbian influences) have also lost Labour other votes, almost certainly far more numerous than those the party has gained.

6.7.3   Materialist and post-materialist politics

Many of the developments in the rainbow coalition argument fit into but form only a part of a wider pattern of post-materialist politics which Inglehart (1971) claimed to detect in Western Europe. His thesis was that class-based and scarcity-based economic issues are being displaced as the sole or the primary influences on political parties' electoral performance. Inglehart claimed to detect a growing trend for a significant minority of voters (7 to 14 per cent) in different countries to ascribe primary importance instead to non-material issues. This change reflected the transition to a period of relative affluence in the 1960s and the broadening out of people's concerns to embrace previous 'luxury' issues, such as environmentalism, the extension of civil liberties, overseas aid and other policies, and some kinds of moral issues. The post-materialist hypothesis fared less well in the 1970s and '80s, as the world recession re-prioritized economic concerns and inaugurated a rightward shift in many European countries for a time (Inglehart, 1981). But there has been a wide shift of public attitudes towards greater concern for the environment in the 1980s (in addition to the rainbow coalition movements), suggesting several countervailing strands reasserting the importance of non-material issues even in this later period.

Many of the issues associated with the growth of third party voting, such as nationalism in Scotland and Wales, and the role of a few distinctively progressive issues such as civil liberties concerns in boosting Liberal/SDP support, also seem to fit the 'post-materialist' model fairly well. Of course, the mass appeal of these issues may normally be fairly restricted. However, it may expand considerably in appropriate circumstances. For example, the Westland crisis of early 1986 not only came near to toppling Mrs Thatcher's premiership, it also produced a drastic if temporary slump in Conservative opinion poll support.

Summary of section 6.7

●   A clutch of 'unconventional' movements continue to influence electoral politics. Racism remains a live force in British society, lightly tapped in a latent way by the Conservatives despite a general effort by the major parties to exclude populist racism from achieving overt political expression.

• Ethnic influences on politics are increasing with the importance of the black vote to Labour. Nationalist sentiment has at times helped Labour in Scotland and Wales, and at others boosted the SNP and Plaid Cymru.

• A series of left social movements over peace issues, opposition to nuclear power and sexual political issues have added some important new elements to Labour support, but have probably antagonized other supporters of the party.

• Although expectations of a growth of 'post-material' politics have not been borne out, neither have these issues disappeared.

6.8 Conclusions

At the end of the 1980s there is still vigorous debate amongst political scientists about the character of the political restructuring which has taken place in contemporary Britain. Some authors stress that class differentials in relative class voting remain, even though third party voting has increased. Others argue that the era of 'closed' class-based party competition has given way to a much more issue- and ideology-based competition. Radical approaches see class influences as declining because of the growth of sectoral issues, and account for ideological change in terms of mass media influences and party exploitation of state power for political purposes.

Whatever interpretation you find most convincing, the importance of these electoral shifts can be charted in the impact of the Conservatives' successes on the climate of public policy throughout the 1980s. Not all political change becomes manifest in electoral politics. But that which does carries implications far beyond the political sphere as party control of state power magnifies and re-presents electoral change across a wide canvass of social and economic restructuring.

Activity 6.3

The future development of electoral politics and party competition will almost certainly see substantial changes from the patterns of the last twenty years. What cleavages or issues do you feel will most divide Britain's political parties ten years from the time of writing, in 1998?

Here's my list of possible changes. I would expect a slow decline of class influences on voting behaviour. Public/private employment influences may begin to decline in the early 1990s, as the number of state employees shrinks with various forms of privatization, but consumption sector cleavages will continue to grow in health and education. Racism and ethnicity are unlikely to die out as influences upon social behaviour. As moves towards a United

Europe continue, a revival of controversy about the EC is possible. Environmental issues will probably increase in political importance, but may not divide the parties very clearly. Cultural movements and developments such as the spread of Aids may also become more involved in party competition.

Try jotting down *three* expectations of your own. Can you cite reasons in support of them?

Answer to Activity 6.1

	1950s	1960s	1970s	1980s
Odds ratios for Con/Lab voting across non-manual and manual classes	5.72	6.17	4.93	3.67

Further reading

In A. Heath, R. Jowell and J. Curtice's *How Britain Votes* (Oxford, Pergamon; 1985) an important but very compressed statement of the case that class voting has not declined is given in the first four chapters, but it is difficult reading. An updated edition is promised for 1989.

P. Dunleavy and C.T. Husbands' *British Democracy at the Crossroads: Voting and Party Competition in the 1980s* (London, Allen and Unwin; 1985) provides a broader theoretical and empirical survey, and sets out a radical model of voting, focusing on sectoral and mass media influences. Based on 1983 election data, but given very small net changes in 1987 the analysis remains applicable.

G. Marshall, H. Newby and D. Rose's *Social Class in Modern Britain* (London, Hutchinson; 1988, Chapter 9 only) provides a detailed sociological style of electoral analysis, focusing on occupational class influences using data from a 1984 survey.

References

ADDISON, P. (1975) *The Road to 1945: British Politics and the Second World War*, London, Jonathan Cape.

AGLIETTA, M. (1979) *A Theory of Capitalist Regulation*, London, New Left Books.

AGNEW, J. (1987) *The United States in the World Economy: A Regional Geography*, Cambridge, Cambridge University Press.

ALLEN, J. (1988a) 'Towards a post-industrial economy?', Ch. 3 in Allen J. and Massey, D. (eds).

ALLEN, J. (1988b) 'Fragmented firms, disorganized labour?', Ch. 5 in Allen, J. and Massey, D. (eds).

ALLEN, J. and MASSEY, D. (eds) (1988) *The Economy in Question* (Restructuring Britain), London, Sage/The Open University.

ALT, J. (1979) *The Politics of Economic Decline*, Cambridge, Cambridge University Press.

ANDERSON, J. AND COCHRANE, A. (eds) (1989) *A State of Crisis: The Changing Face of British Politics* (Restructuring Britain Reader), London, Hodder and Stoughton/The Open University (associated Reader).

ANDERSON, P. (1965) 'Origins of the present crisis', in Anderson, P. and Blackburn, R. (eds).

ANDERSON, P. (1982) 'Themes', *New Left Review*, No. 134, pp. 1–4.

ANDERSON, P. (1987) 'The figures of descent', *New Left Review*, No. 161, pp. 20–77.

ANDERSON, P. and BLACKBURN, R. (eds) (1965) *Towards Socialism*, London, Fontana.

ARTHUR, P., and JEFFREY, K. (1988) *Northern Ireland since 1968*, Oxford, Basil Blackwell.

ARTIS, M.J. (ed.) (1986) *Prest and Coppock's The UK Economy: A Manual of Applied Economics* (11th edition), London, Weidenfeld and Nicolson.

ASCHER, K. (1987) *The Politics of Privatization: Contracting Out in the Public Services*, London and Basingstoke, Macmillan.

ATKINSON, A. (1988) 'Income maintenance for unemployed Britons and the response to high unemployment', paper to 'Philosophy and the Welfare State' Conference, London, Suntory-Toyota International Centre for Economics and Related Disciplines, LSE, 8–10 June.

ATKINSON, A., HILLS, J., and LE GRAND, J. (1987) 'The welfare state', Ch. 7 in Dornbusch, R. and Layard, R. (eds).

AUDIT COMMISSION (1984) *The Impact on Local Authorities' Economy, Efficiency and Effectiveness of the Block Grant Distribution System*, London, HMSO.

BACON, R. and ELTIS, W. (1976) *Britain's Economic Problem: Too Few Producers*, London and Basingstoke, Macmillan.

BANTING, K. (1979) *Poverty, Politics and Policy: Britain in the 1960s*, London and Basingstoke, Macmillan.

BARNETT, A. (1982) 'Iron Britannia', *New Left Review*, No. 134, pp. 5–96.

BARNETT, C. (1984) *The Collapse of British Power*, London, Alan Sutton.

BARNETT, C. (1986) *The Audit of War: The Illusion and Reality of Britain as a Great Nation*, London and Basingstoke, Macmillan.

BARRY, N. (1987) 'Understanding the market', in Loney, M. *et al.* (eds).

BASSETT, K. and SHORT, J. (1980) *Housing and Residential Structure*, London, Routledge and Kegan Paul.

BENINGTON, J. (1976) *Local Government Becomes Big Business*, London, Community Development Project.

BENN, A.W.G. (1965) *The Regeneration of Britain*, London, Victor Gollancz.

BLACKABY, F.T. (ed.) (1978) *British Economic Policy 1960–74*, Cambridge, Cambridge University Press.

BLANK, S. (1977) 'Britain: the politics of foreign economic policy, the domestic economy, and the problem of pluralistic stagnation', *International Organization*, Vol. 31, No. 4, pp. 673–721.

BLORE., I. (1987) 'Are local bureaucrats budget or staff maximisers?', *Local Government Studies*, Vol. 13, No. 3.

BLUMLER, D. and McQUAIL, D. (1969) *Television and Politics*, London, Faber.

BLUNKETT, D. and JACKSON, K. (1987) *Democracy in Crisis: The Town Halls Respond*, London, Hogarth. Ch. 6 reprinted as 'Local politics and the economy: the case of Sheffield' in Anderson, J. and Cochrane, A. (eds) (1989) (associated Reader).

BOYD, L.V. (1976) *Britain's Search for a Role*, Farnborough, Saxon House.

BRETT, E.A. (1986) 'Britain's international decline', Ch. 6 in *The World Economy Since the War: The Politics of Uneven Development*, London and Basingstoke, Macmillan. Reprinted as 'Britain in the post-war world' in Anderson, J. and Cochrane, A. (eds) (1989) (associated Reader).

BRITTAN, S.C. (1971) *Steering the Economy: The Role of the Treasury*, Harmondsworth, Penguin Books.

BRITTAN, S.C. (1975) *Second Thoughts on Full Employment Policy*, London, Centre for Policy Studies.

BUTLER, D. and STOKES, D. (1969) *Political Change in Britain: Forces Shaping Electoral Choice*, London and Basingstoke, Macmillan.

BUTLER, D. and STOKES, D. (1974) *Political Change in Britain*, London and Basingstoke, Macmillan (second edition).

BYRNE, D. and LOVENDUSKI, J. (1983) 'Two new protest groups: the peace and women's movements', in Drucker, H., Dunleavy, P., Gamble, A. and Peele, G. (eds) *Developments in British Politics*, London and Basingstoke, Macmillan, pp. 222–37.

CASTELLS, M. (1977) *The Urban Question*, London, Edward Arnold.

CASTELLS, M. (1978) *City, Class and Power*, London and Basingstoke, Macmillan.

CASTELLS, M. (1983) *The City and the Grassroots*, London, Edward Arnold.

CAVES, R.E. and KRAUSE, L.B. (eds) (1980) *Britain's Economic Performance*, Washington DC, Brookings Institution.

CAWSON, A. (1985a) 'Varieties of corporatism: the importance of the meso-level of interest mediation', in Cawson, A. (ed.) *Organized Interests and the State: Studies in Meso-Corporatism*, London, Sage.

CAWSON, A. (1985b) 'Corporatism and local politics', in Grant, W. (ed.).

CAWSON, A. (1986) *Corporatism and Political Theory*, Oxford, Basil Blackwell.

CAWSON, A. and SAUNDERS, P. (1983) 'Corporatism, competitive politics and class struggle', in King, R. (ed.) *Capital and Politics*, London, Routledge and Kegan Paul.

CENTRAL STATISTICAL OFFICE (1987) *Blue Book 1987 Edition (United Kingdom National Accounts)*, London, CSO.

CHARLOT, M. (1988) 'Un effet patrimoine?', unpublished paper: mimeo.

CLARKE, A. and COCHRANE, A. (1987) 'Investing in the private sector: the enterprise board experience', in Cochrane, A. (ed.).

COCHRANE, A. (1983) 'Local economic policies: trying to drain an ocean with a teaspoon', in Anderson, J., Duncan, S. and Hudson, R. (eds) *Redundant Spaces in Cities and Regions? Studies in Industrial Decline and Social Change*, London, Academic Press.

COCHRANE, A. (ed.) (1987) *Developing Local Economic Strategies*, Milton Keynes, Open University Press.

COCKBURN, C. (1977) *The Local State: Management of Cities and People*, London Pluto.

CRAWFORD, P., FOTHERGILL, S. and MONK, S. (1985) *The Effect of Rates on the Location of Employment*, Final Report, Department of Land Economy, University of Cambridge.

CREWE, I. (1976) 'Party identification theory and political change in Britain', in Budge, I., Crewe, I. and Farlie, D. (eds) *Party Identification and Beyond: Representations of Voting and Party Competition*, London, John Wiley, pp. 33–61.

CREWE, I. (1985) 'Great Britain', in Crewe, I. and Denver, D. (eds) *Electoral Change in Western Democracies*, London, Croom Helm.

CREWE, I. (1986) 'On the death and resurrection of class voting: some comments on *How Britain Votes*', *Political Studies*, Vol. 34, No. 4, pp. 620–38.

CREWE, I., SÄRLVIK, B. and ALT, J. (1977) 'Partisan dealignment in Britain, 1964–74', *British Journal of Political Science*, Vol. 7, pp. 129–90.

CROSLAND, A. (1956) *The Future of Socialism*, London, Jonathan Cape.

CROSLAND, S. (1983) *Tony Crosland*, London, Coronet.

CURTICE, J. and STEED, M. (1982) 'Electoral choice and the production of government: the changing operations of the electoral system in the UK since 1965', *British Journal of Political Science*, Vol. 12, pp. 249–98.

DAVIES, H.J. (1988) 'Local government under siege', *Public Administration*, Vol. 66, No. 1, pp. 91–101.

DAVIES, J. (1972) *The Evangelistic Bureaucrat*, London, Tavistock.

DEARLOVE, J. (1973) *The Politics of Policy in Local Government*, Cambridge, Cambridge University Press.

DEARLOVE, J. (1979) *The Reorganization of Local Government: Old Orthodoxies and a Political Perspective*, Cambridge, Cambridge University Press.

DENNIS, W. (1972) *Public Participation and Planners' Blight*, London, Faber and Faber.

DICKENS, P. (1988) *One Nation? Social Change and the Politics of Location*, London, Pluto.

DONNISON, D. and MIDDLETON, A. (eds) (1987) *Regenerating the Inner City: Glasgow's Experience*, London, Routledge and Kegan Paul.

DORNBUSCH, R. and LAYARD, R. (eds) (1987) *The Performance of the British Economy*, Oxford, Clarendon Press.

DOUGLAS, I. and LORD, S. (1986) *Local Government Finance: A Practical Guide*, London, Local Government Information Unit.

DRUCKER, H. and BROWN, G. (1980) *The Politics of Nationalism and Devolution*, London, Longman.

DRUCKER, H. and GAMBLE, A. (1986) 'The party system', in Drucker, H., Dunleavy, P., Gamble, A. and Peele, G. (eds).

DRUCKER, H., DUNLEAVY, P. GAMBLE, A. and PEELE, G. (eds) (1986) *Developments in British Politics 2*, London and Basingstoke, Macmillan (revised edition, 1988).

DUKE, V. and EDGELL, S. (1984) 'Public expenditure cuts in Britain and consumption sectoral cleavages', *International Journal of Urban and Regional Research*, Vol. 8, pp. 177–201.

DUKE, V. and EDGELL, S. (1987a) 'Attitudes to privatization: the influence of class, sector and partisanship', *Quarterly Journal of Social Affairs*, Vol. 3, No. 4, pp. 253–84.

DUKE, V. and EDGELL, S. (1987b) 'The operationalization of class in British sociology', *British Journal of Sociology*, Vol. 38, No. 4, pp. 445–63.

DUNCAN, S. and GOODWIN, M. (1985) 'Local economic policies: local regeneration or political mobilisation?', *Local Government Studies*, Vol. 11, pp. 75–96.

DUNCAN, S. and GOODWIN, M. (1988) *The Local State and Uneven Development: The Local Government Crisis in Britain*, Cambridge, Polity Press.

DUNCAN, S. and GOODWIN, M. (1989) 'The crisis of local government', in Mohan, J. (ed.) *The Political Geography of Contemporary Britain*, London and Basingstoke, Macmillan.

DUNLEAVY, P. (1979) 'The urban basis of political alignment: social class, domestic property ownership and state intervention in consumption processes', *British Journal of Political Science*, Vol. 9, No. 4, pp. 409–43.

DUNLEAVY, P. (1980a) 'The political implications of sectoral cleavages and the growth of state employment: Part 1, The analysis of production cleavages' and 'Part 2, Cleavages structures and political alignments', *Political Studies*, Vol. 28, No. 3, pp. 364–83, and No. 4, pp. 527–49.

DUNLEAVY, P. (1980b) *Urban Political Analysis: The Politics of Collective Consumption*, London and Basingstoke, Macmillan.

DUNLEAVY, P. (1981) *The Politics of Mass Housing in Britain: A Study of Corporate Power and Professional Influence in the Welfare State*, London, Oxford University Press.

DUNLEAVY, P. (1984) 'The limits to local government', in Boddy, M. and Fudge, C. (eds) *Local Socialism*, London and Basingstoke, Macmillan.

DUNLEAVY, P. (1985) 'Bureaucrats, budgets and the growth of the state', *British Journal of Political Science*, Vol. 15, pp. 299–328.

DUNLEAVY, P. (1986a) 'Explaining the privatisation boom', *Public Administration*, Vol. 64, No. 1.

DUNLEAVY, P. (1986b) 'The growth of sectoral cleavages and the stabilization of state expenditures', *Environment and Planning D: Society and Space*, Vol. 4, pp. 129–44.

DUNLEAVY, P. (1987) 'Class dealignment in Britain revisited', *West European Politics*, Vol. 10, No. 3. pp. 400–19.

DUNLEAVY, P. and HUSBANDS, C.T., (1985a) *British Democracy at the Cross-roads: Voting and Party Competition in the 1980s*, London, George Allen and Unwin.

DUNLEAVY, P. and HUSBANDS, C.T. (1985b) 'Media influences on voting in 1983', in Dunleavy, P. and Husbands, C.T. (1985), pp. 110–17. Reprinted in Anderson, J. and Cochrane, A. (eds) (1989) (associated Reader).

DUNLEAVY, P. and O'LEARY, B. (1987) *Theories of the State: The Politics of Liberal Democracy*, London and Basingstoke, Macmillan.

DUNLEAVY, P. and WARD, H. (1981) 'Exogenous voter preferences and parties with state power: some internal problems of economic theories of party competition', *British Journal of Political Science*, Vol. 11, No. 3, pp. 351–80.

EDGELL, S. and DUKE, V. (1986) 'Radicalism, radicalization and recession: Britain in the 1980s', *British Journal of Sociology*, Vol. 37, pp. 479–512.

ERIKSON, R. and SYMS, P. (1986) 'The effects of enterprise zones on property prices', *Regional Studies*, Vol. 20, pp. 1–14.

FLYNN, R. (1983) 'Co-optation and strategic planning in the local state', in King, R. (ed.) *Capital and Politics*, London, Routledge and Kegan Paul.

FRANKLIN, M. (1985) *The Decline of Class Voting in Britain: Changes in the Basis of Electoral Change, 1964–83*, Oxford, Clarendon Press.

FRANKLIN, M. and PAGE, E. (1984) 'A critique of the consumption cleavage approach in British politics', *Political Studies*, Vol. 32, No. 4, pp. 521–36.

GAMBLE, A. (1985) *Britain in Decline: Economic Policy, Political Strategy and the British State*, London and Basingstoke, Macmillan (second edition).

GOLDING, P. and MIDDLETON, S. (1978) 'Why is the press so obsessed with welfare scroungers?', *New Society*, 26 October.

GOLDING, P. and MIDDLETON, S. (1982) *Images of Welfare*, Oxford, Basil Blackwell.

GOLDSMITH, M. (1986) 'Managing the periphery in a period of fiscal stress', in Goldsmith, M. (ed.) *New Research in Central–Local Relations*, Aldershot, Gower.

GOLDTHORPE, J., LOCKWOOD, D., BECHHOFER, F. and PLATT, J. (1968) *The Affluent Worker: Political Attitudes and Behaviour*, Cambridge, Cambridge University Press.

GOLDTHORPE, J. *et al.* (1987) *Social Mobility and Class Structure in Modern Britain*, Oxford, Clarendon Press (second edition).

GOODWIN, M. (1989) 'Housing and employment policies in London's Docklands', in Allen, J. and Hamnett, C. (eds) *Labour Markets and Housing Markets*, London, Hutchinson.

GOULDNER, A. (1979) *The Future of Intellectuals and the Rise of a New Class*, New York, Seabury.

GRANT, W. (ed.) (1985) *The Political Economy of Corporatism*, London and Basingstoke, Macmillan.

GREATER LONDON COUNCIL (1985) *London Industrial Strategy*, London, Greater London Council. Sections 1.15b–1.197 reprinted as 'Alternative forms of state intervention: the London Industrial Strategy' in Anderson, J. and Cochrane, A. (eds) (1989) (associated Reader).

GREEN, D. (1985) 'From socialism to the new liberalism', in Selsdon, A. (ed.) *The 'New Right' Enlightenment*, London, Economic and Literary Books.

GYFORD, J. (1976) *Local Politics in Britain*, London, Croom Helm.

GYFORD, J. (1985a) 'The politicisation of local government', in Loughlin, M., Gelfand, M. and Young, K. (eds) *Half a Century of Municipal Decline, 1935–1985*, London, George Allen and Unwin.

GYFORD, J. (1985b) *The Politics of Local Socialism*, London, George Allen and Unwin.

HABERMAS, J. (1976) *Legitimation Crisis*, London, Heinemann.

HALL, S. (1988) 'Brave new world', *Marxism Today*, October pp. 24–9.

HAMNETT, C. (1989) 'Consumption and class in contemporary Britain', Ch. 6 in Hamnett, C., McDowell, L. and Sarre, P. (eds).

HAMNETT, C., McDOWELL, L. and SARRE, P. (eds) (1989) *The Changing Social Structure* (Restructuring Britain), London, Sage/The Open University.

HARRIS, L. (1988) 'The UK economy at a crossroads', Ch. 1 in Allen, J. and Massey, D. (eds).

HARROP, M. (1986) 'The press and post-war elections', in Crewe, I. and Harrop, M. (eds) *Political Communications: The General Election Campaign of 1983*, Cambridge, Cambridge University Press, pp. 137–49.

HARROP, M. (1988) 'Voting and the electorate', in Drucker, H., Dunleavy, P., Gamble, A. and Peele, G. (eds).

HARROP, M. and MILLER, W. (1987) *Elections and Voters: A Comparative Introduction*, London and Basingstoke, Macmillan.

HEATH, A. (1988) 'Social stratification in political attitudes', in *Social and Community Planning Research*, *Survey Methods Newsletter*, summer issue, pp. 10–12.

HEATH, A., CURTICE. J. and JOWELL, R. (1985a) *How Britain Votes*, Oxford, Pergamon.

HEATH, A., JOWELL, R. and CURTICE, J. (1985b) 'Ideological change in the electorate', Ch. 9 in Heath, A. *et al.* (eds) (1985a). Reprinted in Anderson, J. and Cochrane, A. (eds) (1989) (associated Reader).

HELM, D.R. (1986) 'The economic borders of the state', *Oxford Review of Economic Policy*, Vol. 2, No. 2, pp. i-xxiv. Reprinted in Anderson, J. and Cochrane, A. (eds) (1989) (associated Reader).

HEPWORTH, N. (1984) *The Finance of Local Government*, London, George Allen and Unwin (seventh edition).

HIRSCHMAN, A., (1982) *Shifting Involvements: Private Interests and Public Action*, Princeton, NJ, Princeton University Press.

HMSO (1970) *Reform of Local Government in England*, Cmnd 4276, London, HMSO.

HMSO (1983) *Streamlining the Cities*, Cmnd 9063, London, HMSO.

HOGGETT, P. (1987) 'A farewell to mass production? Decentralisation as an emergent private and public sector paradigm', in Hoggett, P. and Hamilton, R. (eds) *Decentralisation and Democracy: Localising Public Services*, Occasional Paper No. 2, School for Advanced Urban Studies.

HOGWOOD, B. and PETERS, B. Guy (1983) *Policy Dynamics*, Brighton, Wheatsheaf.

HUDSON, R. and WILLIAMS, A. (1986) *The United Kingdom*, London, Harper and Row.

HUSBANDS, C.T. (1986) 'Race and gender', in Drucker, H., Dunleavy, P., Gamble, A. and Peele, G. (eds).

INGLEHART, R. (1971) 'The silent revolution in Europe', *American Political Science Review*, Vol. 65, pp. 991–1017.

INGLEHART, R. (1981) 'Post-materialism in an environment of insecurity', *American Political Science Review*, Vol. 75, pp. 880–99.

JACKSON, P. (1982) 'The impact of economic theories on local government finance', *Local Government Studies*, Vol. 8, No. 1, pp. 21–34.

JOHNSON, N. (1977a) *In Search of the Constitution: Reflections on State and Society in Britain*, Oxford, Pergamon.

JOHNSON, N. (1977b) 'The failure of the post-war political order', in Johnson, N. (1977a), Chs 1 and 2, reprinted in Anderson, J. and Cochrane, A. (eds) (1989) (associated Reader).

JOHNSON, N. (1987) 'The break-up of consensus: competitive politics in a declining economy', in Loney, M. *et al.* (eds).

JOHNSON, N. and COCHRANE, A. (1981) *Economic Policy-making by Local Authorities in Britain and West Germany*, London, George Allen and Unwin.

JOHNSON, R.W. (1972) 'The "nationalization" of English rural politics: southwest Norfolk, 1945–70', *Parliamentary Affairs*, Vol. 26, No. 1.

JOHNSTON, R.J. (1986a) 'The neighbourhood effect revisited: spatial science or political regionalism', *Environment and Planning D: Society and Space*, Vol. 4, No. 1, pp. 41–55.

JOHNSTON, R.J. (1986b) 'Research policy and review 9 – A space for place (or a place for space) in British psephology: a review of recent writings with a special reference to the General Election of 1983', *Environment and Planning A*, Vol. 18, pp. 573–98.

JOHNSTON, R.J. and PATTIE, C. (1988) 'The geography of general elections', paper given at IBG Conference, University of Loughborough, January.

JOHNSTON, R.J., PATTIE, C. and ALLSOPP, G., (1988) *A Dividing Nation: The Electoral Map of Great Britain, 1979–87*, London, Longman.

JONES, G. (1975) 'Varieties of local politics', *Local Government Studies*, Vol. 1, No. 2, pp. 1–16.

JONES, G. (ed.) (1980) *New Approaches to the Study of Central–Local Government Relations*, London, Gower/ESRC.

JONES, G. and STEWART, J. (1983) *The Case for Local Government*, London, George Allen and Unwin.

KAY, I. and THOMPSON, D. (1987) 'Policy for industry', Ch. 6 in Dornbusch, R. and Layard, R. (eds).

KEEGAN, W. (1984) *Mrs Thatcher's Economic Experiment*, Harmondsworth, Penguin Books.

KELLY, J. and McALLISTER, I. (1985) 'Social context and electoral behaviour in Britain', *American Journal of Political Science*, Vol. 29, pp. 564–86.

KING, R. (1985) 'Corporatism and the local economy', in Grant, W. (ed.).

LASH, S. and URRY, J. (1987) *The End of Organized Capitalism*, Cambridge, Polity Press.

LEYS, D. (1983) *Politics in Britain*, London, Heinemann (second edition). Chapters 5 and 6 reprinted as 'From the paralysis of social democracy to the crisis of the 1970s' in Anderson, J. and Cochrane, A. (eds) (1989) (associated Reader).

LINDBLOM, C. (1977) *Politics and Markets: The World's Political–Economic Systems*, New York, Basic Books.

LIPSKY, M. (1979) 'The assault on human services: street-level bureaucrats, accountability and the fiscal crisis', in Greer, S., Hedlund, R.D. and Gibson, J.L. (eds) *Accountability in Urban Society: Public Agencies under Fire*, Urban Affairs Annual Review, Vol. 15, London, Sage.

LONEY, M. *et al.* (eds) *The State or the Market: Politics and Welfare in Contemporary Britain*, London, Sage/The Open University.

LOVERING, J. and BODDY, M. (1988) 'The geography of the military industry in Britain', *Area*, Vol. 20, No. 1, pp. 41–51. Reprinted in Anderson, J. and Cochrane, A. (eds) (1989) (associated Reader).

LOWE, S. (1986) *Urban Social Movements: The City after Castells*, London and Basingstoke, Macmillan.

MACKINTOSH, M. (1987) 'Planning the public sector: an argument from the case of transport in London', in Cochrane, A. (ed.).

MAGNUSSEN, W. (1988) 'Radical cities: a cross-national analysis of the new urban left', unpublished paper: mimeo.

MARK-LAWSON, J. and WARDE, A. (1987) 'Industrial restructuring and the transformation of a local political environment: a case study of Lancaster', Working paper 33, Lancaster Regionalism Group, University Lancaster; pp. 6–25, 31–3. Reprinted as 'The changing political environment of Lancaster' in Anderson, J. and Cochrane, A. (eds) (1989) (associated Reader).

MARKUS, G. and CONVERSE, P. (1979) 'A dynamic simultaneous equation model of electoral choice', *American Political Science Review*, Vol. 73, pp. 1055–70.

MARSHALL, G., NEWBY, H. and ROSE, D. (1988) *Social Class in Modern Britain*, London, Hutchinson.

MARTIN, R. (1988) 'Industrial capitalism in transition: the contemporary organization of the British space-economy', Ch. 10 in Massey, D. and Allen, J. (eds).

MASSEY, D. (1984) *Spatial Divisions of Labour: Social Structures and the Geography of Production*, London and Basingstoke, Macmillan.

MASSEY, D. (1986) 'The legacy lingers on: the impact of Britain's international role on its internal geography', in Martin, R. and Rowthorn, B. (eds) *The Geography of De-Industrialisation*, London and Basingstoke, Macmillan.

MASSEY, D. (1988a) 'What's happening to UK manufacturing?', Ch. 2 in Allen, J. and Massey, D. (eds).

MASSEY, D. (1988b) 'What is an economy anyway?', Ch. 6 in Allen, J. and Massey, D. (eds).

MASSEY, D. and ALLEN, J. (eds) (1988) *Uneven Re-Development: Cities and Regions in Transition* (Restructuring Britain Reader), London, Hodder and Stoughton/The Open University.

MAYHEW, K. (1985) 'Reforming the labour market', *Oxford Review of Economic Policy*, Vol. 1, No. 2, pp. 60–79.

McALLISTER, I. (1986) 'Social context, turnout and vote', *Political Geography Quarterly*, Vol. 5.

McDOWELL, L., SARRE, P. and HAMNETT, C. (eds) (1989) *Divided Nation: Social and Cultural Change in Britain* (Restructuring Britain Reader), London, Hodder and Stoughton/The Open University.

McGREW, T. (1988) 'Security and order: the military dimension', in Smith, S.,

Smith, M. and White, B. (eds) *British Foreign Policy: Tradition, Change and Transformation*, London, Unwin Hyman.

McLEAN, I, (1987) *Public Choice: An Introduction*, Oxford, Basil Blackwell.

MEEGAN, R. (1988) 'A crisis of mass production?', Ch. 4 in Allen, J. and Massey, D. (eds).

METCALF, D. and RICHARDSON, R. (1986) 'Labour', Ch. 5 in Artis, M.J. (ed.).

MIDDLEMAS, K. (1979) *Politics in Industrial Society: The Experience of the British System since 1911*, London, André Deutsch.

MIDDLEMAS, K. (1986) *Power, Competition and the State*, Volume 1: *Britain in Search of Balance, 1940–61*, London and Basingstoke, Macmillan.

MIDWINTER, A., KEATING, M. and TAYLOR, P. (1983) ' "Excessive and unreasonable": the politics of the Scottish hit list', *Political Studies*, Vol. 21, No. 3.

MILLER, W. (1978) 'Social class and party choice: a new analysis', *British Journal of Political Science*, Vol. 8, No. 3, pp. 257–84.

MILLER, W. (1981) *The End of British Politics? Scots and English Political Behaviour in the Seventies*, Oxford, Clarendon Press.

MISHRA, R. (1984) *The Welfare State in Crisis: Social Thought and Social Change*, Brighton, Wheatsheaf.

MOORE, C. (1986) 'Scottish Development Agency: market consensus, public planning and local enterprise', *Local Economy*, Vol. 3.

MORAN, M. (1985) *Politics and Society in Britain*, London and Basingstoke, Macmillan.

MORRISON, H. (1933) *Socialisation of Transport*, London, Constable.

MOTTERSHEAD, P. (1978) 'Industrial policy', Ch. 10 in Blackaby, F. (ed.).

MURRAY, R. (1987) *Breaking with Bureaucracy: Ownership, Control and Nationalisation*, London, Centre for Local Economic Strategies.

NAIRN, T. (1977a) *The Break-up of Britain: Crisis and Neo-Nationalism*, London, New Left Books.

NAIRN, T. (1977b) 'The twilight of the British state', *New Left Review*, No. 101–2, pp. 3–61.

NEWTON, K. (1976) *Second City Politics*, London, Oxford University Press.

NEWTON, K. and KARRAN, T. (1985) *The Politics of Local Expenditure*, London and Basingstoke, Macmillan.

NISKANEN, W. (1973) *Bureaucracy: Servant or Master? Lessons from America*, London, Institute of Economic Affairs.

NORTHEDGE, F.S. (1974) *Descent from Power: British Foreign Policy 1945–1973*, London, George Allen and Unwin.

NOSSISTER, B. (1978) *Britain: A Future that Works*, London, André Deutsch.

O'CONNOR, J. (1973) *The Fiscal Crisis of the State*, London, St Martin's Press/St James' Press.

O'CONNOR, J. (1987) *The Meaning of Crisis: A Theoretical Introduction*, Oxford, Basil Blackwell.

O'DOWD, L. (1985) 'The crisis of regional strategy: ideology and the state in Northern Ireland', in Rees, G., Bujra, J., Littlewood, P. and Newby, N. (eds) *Political Action and Social Identity*, London and Basingstoke, Macmillan.

O'DOWD, L. (1987) 'Trends and potential of the service sectors in Northern Ireland', in Teague, P. (ed.) (1987b).

O'DOWD, L. (1989) 'Devolution without consensus: the experience of Northern Ireland', in Anderson, J. and Cochrane, A. (eds) (associated Reader).

O'DOWD, L., ROLSTON, B. and TOMLINSON, M. (1980) *Northern Ireland: Between Civil Rights and Civil War*, London, Zed Press.

O'LEARY, B. (1987) 'Why was the GLC abolished?', *International Journal of Urban and Regional Research*, Vol. 11, No. 2.

PAGE, B. and JONES, C. (1979) 'Reciprocal effects of policy preferences, party loyalties and the vote', *American Political Science Review*, Vol. 73, No. 4, pp. 1071–89.

PAHL, R. (1975) *Whose City?*, Harmondsworth, Penguin (second edition).

PARRY, R. (1985) 'Britain: stable aggregates, changing composition', in Rose, R., Page, E., Guy Peters, B., Cendall Pignatelli, A. and Schmidt, K-D. (eds) *Public Employment in Western Nations*, Cambridge, Cambridge University Press.

PARRY, R. (1986) 'The United Kingdom', in Flora, P. (ed.) *Growth to Limits: The West European Welfare States since World War II*. Volume 2: *Germany, United Kingdom, Ireland, Italy*, Berlin, de Gruyter, pp. 155–240.

POLLARD, S. (1982) *The Wasting of the British Economy*, London, Croom Helm.

POLLITT, C., HARRISON, S., HUNTER, I. and MARNOCH, G. (1988) 'The reluctant managers: clinicians and budgets in the NHS', *Financial Accountability and Management*, Vol. 4, No. 3.

REES, G. and LAMBERT, J. (1979) 'Urban development in a "peripheral" region: some issues from south Wales', mimeo. cited in Massey, D. 1984.

RHODES, R.A.W. (1975) 'The lost world of British local politics', *Local Government Studies*, Vol. 1, pp. 39–60.

RHODES, R.A.W. (1981) *Control and Power in Central–Local Government Relations*, Aldershot, SSRC/Gower.

RHODES, R.A.W. (1985) ' "A squalid and politically corrupt process?" Intergovernmental relations in the post-war period', *Local Government Studies*, Vol. 11, No. 6. Reprinted in Anderson, J. and Cochrane, A. (eds) (1989) (associated Reader).

RHODES, R.A.W. (1986) 'Corporate bias in central–local relations: a case study of the Consultative Council on Local Government Finance', *Policy and Politics*, Vol. 14, No. 2.

ROBERTSON, D. (1984) *Class and the British Electorate*, Oxford, Basil Blackwell.

RODNEY, W. (1972) *How Europe Underdeveloped Africa*, London, Bogle L'Ouverture.

ROGER TYM and PARTNERS (1981) *Monitoring the Enterprise Zones: Year 1 Report*, London, Roger Tym and Partners.

ROGER TYM and PARTNERS (1982) *Monitoring the Enterprise Zones: Year 2 Report*, London, Roger Tym and Partners.

ROSE, R. (1974) 'Britain: simple abstractions and complex realities', in Rose, R. (ed.) *Electoral Behaviour: A Comparative Handbook*, New York, Free Press, pp. 481–541.

ROSE, R. (1976) *The Problem of Party Government*, Harmondsworth, Penguin Books.

ROSE, R. and McALLISTER, I. (1986) *Voters Begin to Choose: From Closed-Class to Open Elections*, London, Sage.

ROWTHORN, B. (1987) 'Northern Ireland: an economy in crisis', in Teague, P. (ed.).

SALMON, P. (1987) 'Decentralisation as an incentive scheme', *Oxford Review of Economic Policy*, Vol. 3, No. 2.

SÄRLVIK, B. and CREWE, I. (1983) *Decade of Dealignment: The Conservative Victory of 1979 and Electoral Trends in the 1970s*, Cambridge, Cambridge University Press.

SARRE, P. (1989a) 'Recomposition of the class structure', Ch. 3 in Hamnett, C., McDowell, L. and Sarre, P. (eds).

SARRE, P. (1989b) 'Race and the class structure', Ch. 4 in Hamnett, C., McDowell, L. and Sarre, P. (eds).

SAUNDERS, P. (1979) *Urban Politics: A Sociological Interpretation*, London, Hutchinson.

SAUNDERS, P. (1981a) *Social Theory and the Urban Question*, London, Hutchinson.

SAUNDERS, P. (1984) 'Rethinking local politics', in Boddy, M. and Fudge, C. (eds) *Local Socialism*, London and Basingstoke, Macmillan.

SAUNDERS, P. (1985) 'Space, the city and urban sociology', in Gregory, D. and Urry, J. (eds) *Social Relations and Spatial Structures*, London and Basingstoke, Macmillan.

SAUNDERS, P. (1986) 'Reflections on the dual politics thesis', in Goldsmith, M. (ed.) *Urban Political Theory and the Management of Fiscal Stress*, Aldershot, Gower.

SAVAGE, M. (1989) 'Whatever happened to red Clydeside?', in Anderson, J. and Cochrane, A. (eds) (associated Reader).

SCARBOROUGH, E. (1984) *Political Ideology and Voting: An Exploratory Study*, Oxford, Clarendon Press.

SCHOOL FOR ADVANCED URBAN STUDIES (1983) *The Future of Local Democracy*, SAUS, University of Bristol.

SCHWARZ, B. (1987) 'Conservatives and corporatism', *New Left Review*, No. 166, pp. 107–28.

SHANKS, M. (1961) *The Stagnant Society: A Warning*, Harmondsworth, Penguin Books.

SHARPE, L.J. and NEWTON, K. (1984) *Does Politics Matter? Determinants of Public Policy*, London, Oxford University Press.

SHRAPNEL, N. (1986) *The Seventies: Britain's Inward March*, London, Constable.

SHUTT, J. (1984) 'Tory enterprise zones and the labour movement', *Capital and Class*, No. 23, pp. 19–44.

SKED, A. (1987) *Britain's Decline: Problems and Perspectives*, Oxford, Basil Blackwell.

SMITH, A. (1970) *The Wealth of Nations* (edited by Andrew Skinner), Harmondsworth, Penguin Books. (Originally published in 1776.)

STOKER, G. (1988) *Politics of Local Government*, London and Basingstoke, Macmillan.

STRANGE, S. (1971) *Sterling and British Policy*, Cambridge, Cambridge University Press.

TAYLOR, P. (1989) 'Britain's century of decline: a world-systems interpretation', in Anderson, J. and Cochrane, A. (eds) (associated Reader).

TAYLOR GOOBY, P. (1985) *Public Opinion, Ideology and State Welfare*, London, Routledge and Kegan Paul.

TEAGUE, P. (1987a) 'Multinational companies in the Northern Ireland economy: an outmoded model of industrial development?', in Teague, P. (ed.) (1987b).

TEAGUE, P. (ed.) (1987b) *Beyond the Rhetoric: Politics, the Economy and Social Policy in Northern Ireland*, London, Lawrence and Wishart.

THOMAS, H. (ed.) (1959) *The Establishment*, London, Anthony Blond.

THRIFT, N. (1989) 'Images of social change', Ch. 1 in Hamnett, C., McDowell, L. and Sarre, P. (eds).

TIEBOUT, C. (1956) 'A pure theory of local government expenditure' *Journal of Political Economy*, Vol. 64.

TITTERTON, M. and WADE, E. (1984) 'Local government', in NUPE, *Scottish Public Services under Attack*.

TOMLINSON, M. (1980) 'Relegating local government', in O'Dowd, L., Rolston, B. and Tomlinson, M. (eds).

TULLOCK, G. (1977) 'What is to be done?', in Borcherding, T. (ed.) *Budgets and Bureaucrats: The Sources of Government Growth*, Durham, NC, Duke University Press.

TURNER, H. and WILKINSON, F. (1972) 'The wage–tax spiral and labour militancy', in Jackson, D., Turner, H. and Wilkinson, F. (eds) *Do Trade Unions Cause Inflation?*, Cambridge, Cambridge University Press.

VADNEY, T.E. (1987) *The World since 1945*, Harmondsworth, Pelican.

WALKER, D. (1983) *Municipal Empire: The Town Halls and their Beneficiaries*, London, Temple Smith.

WALLERSTEIN, I. (1974) *The Modern World System*, New York, Academic Press.

WALLERSTEIN, I. (1981) *Historical Capitalism*, London, Verso.

WARD, H. (1983) 'The anti-nuclear lobby', in Marsh, D. (ed.) *Pressure Politics: Interest Groups in Britain*, London, Junction Books, pp. 182–211.

WARDE, A. (1982) *Consensus and Beyond: The Development of Labour Party Strategy Since the Second World War*, Manchester, Manchester University Press.

WARREN, W. (1980) *Imperialism: Pioneer of Capitalism*, London, New Left Books.

WARWICK, P. (1985) 'Did Britain change? An inquiry into the causes of national decline', *Journal of Contemporary History*, Vol. 20, No. 1, pp. 99–133.

WEBB, P. (1987) 'Union, party and class in Britain: the changing electoral relationship, 1964–83', *Politics*, Vol. 7, No. 2, pp. 15–21. Reprinted in Anderson, J. and Cochrane, A. (eds) (1989) (associated Reader).

WHITELEY, P. (1983) *The Labour Party in Crisis*, London, Methuen.

WIDDICOMBE, D. (Chair) (1986) *Report of the Committee of Inquiry into the Conduct of Local Authority Business*, Cmnd 9797, London, HMSO.

WIENER, M.J. (1981) *English Culture and the Decline of the Industrial Spirit 1850– 1980*, Cambridge, Cambridge University Press.

WRIGHT, E. and MARTIN, B. (1987) 'The transformation of the American class structure, 1960–80', *American Journal of Sociology*, Vol. 93, No. 1, pp. 1–29.

YARROW, G. (1986) 'Privatization', *Economic Policy*, April 1986, pp. 323–77.

YOUNG, K. and KRAMER, J. (1978) *Strategy and Conflict in Metropolitan Housing*, London, Heinemann.

Acknowledgements

Grateful acknowledgement is made to the following sources for permission to use material in this text:

Text

O'Dowd, L. (1985) 'Ideology and the state in Northern Ireland', from Rees, G. *et al.* (eds) *Political Action and Social Identity*, reproduced with the permission of Macmillan, London and Basingstoke.

Figures

Figure 3.1: Central Statistical Office, *Economic Trends*, October 1987, reproduced with the permission of the Controller of Her Majesty's Stationery Office.

Tables

Table 3.2: Department of Trade and Industry, *British Business*, September 1988, reproduced with the permission of the Controller of Her Majesty's Stationery Office; *Table 4.3*: Chartered Institute of Public Finance and Accountancy, *Local Government Trends*, CIPFA, 1987.

Author index

Subject index

Key concepts are printed in bold and the page number in bold indicates where this concept is defined.